INTIMATE PARTNER VIOLENCE

Clinical Interventions with Partners and Their Children

Samuel R. Aymer

Silberman School of Social Work at Hunter College

ROWMAN & LITTLEFIELD
Lanham • Boulder • New York • London

Acquisitions Editor: Mark Kerr
Acquisitions Assistant: Courtney Packard
Sales and Marketing Inquiries: textbooks@rowman.com

Credits and acknowledgments for material borrowed from other sources, and reproduced with permission, appear on the appropriate pages within the text.

Published by Rowman & Littlefield
An imprint of The Rowman & Littlefield Publishing Group, Inc.
4501 Forbes Boulevard, Suite 200, Lanham, Maryland 20706
www.rowman.com

6 Tinworth Street, London SE11 5AL, United Kingdom

Copyright © 2022 by Rowman & Littlefield Publishing Group, Inc.

All rights reserved. No part of this book may be reproduced in any form or by any electronic or mechanical means, including information storage and retrieval systems, without written permission from the publisher, except by a reviewer who may quote passages in a review.

British Library Cataloguing in Publication Information Available

Library of Congress Cataloging-in-Publication Data

Names: Aymer, Samuel R., 1957– author.
Title: Intimate partner violence : clinical interventions with partners and their children / by Samuel R. Aymer, Hunter College.
Description: Lanham : Rowman & Littlefield, [2022] | Includes bibliographical references and index.
Identifiers: LCCN 2021029551 (print) | LCCN 2021029552 (ebook) | ISBN 9781538124949 (cloth) | ISBN 9781538124956 (paperback) | ISBN 9781538124963 (epub)
Subjects: LCSH: Intimate partner violence. | Family violence.
Classification: LCC HV6626 .A96 2022 (print) | LCC HV6626 (ebook) | DDC 362.82/92—dc23
LC record available at https://lccn.loc.gov/2021029551
LC ebook record available at https://lccn.loc.gov/2021029552

∞™ The paper used in this publication meets the minimum requirements of American National Standard for Information Sciences—Permanence of Paper for Printed Library Materials, ANSI/NISO Z39.48-1992.

Brief Contents

Acknowledgments   ix
Preface   xi

1   The Traditional Framing of Intimate Partner Violence   1

2   Sociocultural and Intersectional Factors Underlying IPV: Centering Black and Brown Women   15

3   Women's Formative Experiences and Exposure to IPV in the Family: An Object Relations Framework   33

4   Adolescent Males' Exposure to IPV: Practice Issues   49

5   Mothering and Motherhood in the Context of IPV   63

6   Toxic Masculinity and Men Who Batter   81

7   A Self-Psychological Frame for Working with an Abused Woman   97

8   Men's Work: A Call to Action Concerning Violence against Women and Girls   113

9   Shared Vulnerability: Countertransferential Reactions, Supervision, and Self-Care   129

Appendix 1: Key IPV Terms   151
Appendix 2: A Biopsychosocial Assessment Framework for IPV Cases Involving Cisgender Women   153
Appendix 3: A Biopsychosocial Assessment Framework for IPV Cases Involving Cisgender Men   157
References   161
Index   169

Contents

Acknowledgments ix
Preface xi

1 The Traditional Framing of Intimate Partner Violence 1
Person-in-Environment Perspective 2
  The Relevance of PIE to IPV 2
A Historical Overview of Marital Relationships 3
Social Movements and Feminism 4
Features of the Battered Women's Movement 6
The Power-and-Control Model of IPV 7
  The Power-and-Control Wheel 8
  The Cycle of Violence 10
Conclusion 12
Discussion Questions 13

2 Sociocultural and Intersectional Factors Underlying IPV: Centering Black and Brown Women 15
Feminism Revisited 16
  Race, Feminism, and Intersectionality 17
  Intersecting Differences in Mainstream Feminism 19
  Immigrant Women of Color and Intersectionality 20
Intersectional Feminism, IPV, and Black Women 21
Case Study: Betty and Omar 21
  Betty's Intersectional Context 22
Case Study: Maria and Anthony 23
  Maria's Intersectional Context 24
IPV and Spirituality: An Intersectional Frame 26
Case Study: Brenda and Sue 27
  Brenda's Intersectional Context 28
Conclusion 30
Intersectional Factors and Safety Planning: Discussion Questions 31
Discussion Questions 32

3 Women's Formative Experiences and Exposure to IPV in the Family: An Object Relations Framework 33
Elements of Object Relations Theory 34
Object Relations Theory and IPV in Familial Context 35
Socioemotional Processes of Living with IPV 36
Exposure to Violence 37
Case Study: Kathleen 38
  Presenting Problems and Issues 38
  Kathleen's Relationship with Winston 39
  Kathleen's Relationship with Her Children 40

v

       Kathleen's Formative Experiences   40
       Case Conceptualization   40
       Sociocultural Factors   42
       Course of Therapeutic Interventions   43
   Recommendations to Clinicians   45
   Discussion Questions   46

4 Adolescent Males' Exposure to IPV: Practice Issues   49
   An Overview of Adolescent Male Development   49
       Exposure to IPV   51
       Community Context   51
   Case Study: Bryant   52
       Presenting Problems and Issues   52
       Familial Concerns   53
       Bryant's Relationship with Ebony   54
       Case Conceptualization   54
       Course of Therapeutic Interventions   56
       Sociocultural Factors   59
   Recommendations to Clinicians   59
   Discussion Questions   61

5 Mothering and Motherhood in the Context of IPV   63
   Traditional Positioning of Women and Mothers   63
   The Psychological Impact of IPV on Mothers   65
       Motherhood and Pregnancy   66
   The View of Mothering and Children's Welfare   67
       Raising Children under Fire   68
       The Role of Secrets within IPV Family Systems   69
       Ruptured Mother–Child Relational Processes   71
   Excerpts from a Qualitative Interview with Janet   72
       Reflections of Janet's Narrative   74
   Excerpts from Clinical Practice   75
       Clinical Assessment   76
       Suzanne's Therapy   77
   Conclusion   80
   Discussion Questions   80

6 Toxic Masculinity and Men Who Batter   81
   Social Learning Theory   81
   Contextual Features of Toxic Gender Issues   82
   Toward an Exploration of Toxic Masculinity   83
   Toxic Masculinity and Racial Injustice   87
   Toxic Masculinity and IPV   89
   Believability in Work with Abusive Men   91
   Implications for Clinical Practice   92
   Conclusion   95
   Discussion Questions   96

7 A Self-Psychological Frame for Working with an Abused Woman 97

Self-Psychological Ideas 97
Physical and Psychological Abuse 99
Case Study: Carmen and Angel 100
    Presenting Problems and Issues 101
    Carmen's Relationship with Angel 101
    Abusive Interplay between Carmen and Angel 102
    Court Processes and Ancillary Human Services 103
    Carmen's Relationship with Her Children 104
    Carmen's Formative Experiences 104
    Case Conceptualization 105
    Course of Therapeutic Interventions 107
Recommendations for Clinicians 110
Discussion Questions 111

8 Men's Work: A Call to Action Concerning Violence against Women and Girls 113

Reflections on a Calling to IPV Work 114
Men's Social Location and Service Delivery to Women/Girls 114
Men's Personal Ownership and Self-Awareness 116
The Duality of Alliances in Clinical Practice 117
On Becoming an Ally in Interrupting Gender-Based Violence 118
Some Implications of #MeToo 120
Living beyond the Binary of Male Supremacy 121
Men Who Advocate for Gender Equality 124
Implications for Psychotherapeutic Interventions 125
Conclusion 126
Discussion Questions 127

9 Shared Vulnerability: Countertransferential Reactions, Supervision, and Self-Care 129

Supervision 130
    Components of Supervision 131
Organizational Challenges to Implementing Supervision 135
Unpacking Countertransference Reactions and Feelings 135
    Annie's Supervisory Process 136
    Educational and Clinical Supervision with Annie 137
    John's Supervisory Process 140
    Clinical and Supportive Supervision with John 141
    Burnout and Vicarious Trauma 143
Self-Care and Rest-Care 146
    Being Kind to One's Self by Knowing and Doing 146
    Healing One's Self through Knowing 147
Conclusion 149
Discussion Questions 149

Appendix 1: Key IPV Terms 151
Appendix 2: A Biopsychosocial Assessment Framework for IPV Cases Involving Cisgender Women 153
  Definition 153
  Biological Factors 153
  Psychological Factors 154
  Social Factors 154
Appendix 3: A Biopsychosocial Assessment Framework for IPV Cases Involving Cisgender Men 157
  Definition 157
  Biological Factors 157
  Psychological Factors 158
  Social Factors 158
  Exploratory Process for Assessing Precursors to Violence/Abuse in Intimate Relationships 159
References 161
Index 169

Acknowledgments

The consistent support and encouragement that I have received from friends and colleagues allowed me to complete the arduous journey of writing this book in the midst of a pandemic. First, I must say thank you to the clients I have had the privilege to work with in my clinical practice and my colleagues who provided inspiration for pursuing this project. I must thank the abused women and child witnesses to intimate partner violence (IPV) whom I have worked with throughout my career; they have taught me how to recognize and understand the saliency of survivorship and resilience in the midst of relational risks and vulnerability, which in turn has made me a more empathic clinician. I want to acknowledge Dr. John Aponte, a dear friend, colleague, and mentor, who introduced me to batterers' intervention work over twenty years ago, and who was a constant source of support until his untimely illness. My work with Dr. Aponte taught me how to understand culpability in the context of helping men address the perils of patriarchy and their childhood abuse histories. Ethelena Bailey Persons provided excellent clinical supervision during the beginning phases of my work with abused women, which provided a solid frame for understanding the complex dynamics of IPV.

My students at Silberman School of Social Work who have enrolled in my class on working with victims of violence have provided invaluable feedback concerning course content and processes, which has served as part of the impetus for writing this book. Dr. Mary Cavanaugh, dean of Silberman School of Social Work at Hunter College, offered support and assistance relative to my efforts in writing this book. Dr. Gary Mallon, associate dean of research at Silberman, also motivated me to move forward with my desire to write a book on a topic that I am passion about. To my Silberman colleagues—thank you for engaging me in discussions on the topic of IPV, particularly when students are interested in researching this area in professional seminar classes.

Special thanks to Mark Kerr and Courtney Packard at Rowman & Littlefield, who have been extremely cooperative and supportive in my efforts to make this book a reality. I give thanks to Kathleen O'Brien, former associate acquisition editor at Rowman & Littlefield, who offered tremendous guidance as I was writing the proposal for this book. I must also extend gratitude to the staff at Rowman & Littlefield who provided helpful editorial feedback and insights regarding the premise of the book.

The ongoing support I received from my family was vital and allowed me to move along. Thanks to Jelani Bandele, Susan Moses, Lorna Johnson, and Dr. Manny Gonzalez and many others who checked in on me regularly to make sure that I was well. This was affirming and empowering given the presence of COVID-19 and the anxiety surrounding it. Undoubtedly, I could not have completed this book without the persistent support of the aforementioned individuals, who motivated me to work more intensely and creatively.

Preface

This book will contribute to the clinical and advocacy efforts of professionals who are committed to helping the fractured lives of clients affected by intimate partner violence (IPV; also known as domestic violence, gender-based violence, wife abuse, partner abuse, and relational abuse). I argue that clinical work should be informed by the premise that patriarchy, sexism, antifemaleness, and gender inequality predispose men to use power and control to dominate the lives of their female partners. The book focuses on how men's abusive behaviors impinge on the psychological functioning of women and children. In addition, I hope this book will inspire professionals who have not worked with abusive men to offer therapeutic services to abusive men so that they will comprehend the myriad ways their abusive behaviors impact others and themselves. This noncarceral process centers on their culpability and at the same time helps them work on the parts of themselves that were broken due to childhood problems and other social and familial ills that may have surrounded their formative and adult experiences.

The considerable practice experience I have obtained in providing therapeutic services to women, children, and men throughout my career was a tremendous source of inspiration for writing this book. And the provision of clinical supervision to clinicians working in the area of IPV has equally contributed to my clinical growth and expertise. My professional journey in this field of practice has made it possible for me to remain conscious of my gender; I had to remain mindful of my affinity group (i.e., the culture of men), which is responsible for the maintenance of male privilege, a pivotal factor that underpins men's violence against women. Furthermore, questions regarding my effectiveness abounded during my initial professional connection to IPV work. I considered whether I could withstand hearing stories of violence that were narrated by both the abused and the abuser without becoming judgmental and overwhelmed. I questioned whether my gender identity had any material effects on limiting abusive men from advancing power and control in intimate relationships. Paying attention to these questions and concerns allowed me to own the array of ways I continue to benefit from male privilege within the structure of patriarchy, underscoring just how critically important it was (and is) for me to consistently examine what it means for me to be a male ally in the fight against gender-based violence. Consistent supervision and peer support provided opportunities for me to unpack my thoughts and remain introspective about how patriarchy has shaped my life. Consequently, this type of self-inventory continues to inform my clinical and advocacy practice with clients.

Writing this book led me to similar themes: my aim was to center how women and children are psychologically impacted by men's violence and simultaneously address how heterosexual men are psychically injured by using violence as a means to oppress their partners. Undoubtedly, I contemplated the possible effects my gender and cultural socialization could have on writing this book. Seeking consultation from my professional networks about my introspection afforded me the opportunity to process my feelings and thoughts regarding the desire to construct a narrative that would truly speak to the themes I have heard during my clinical work and my research. These experiences, combined with my gender and cultural socialization, enabled me to bring a clinical frame for addressing the resulting psychological effects of IPV—without minimizing the fact that violence against women is a crime and that a criminal justice response can still be a viable intervention to stop an abuser's behavior.

All of the aforementioned experiences inspired the book's conceptualization and culminated in the following goals: (1) to contribute clinical content in work with victims, children, and perpetrators of IPV; (2) to illustrate the interplay between macro and micro issues in clinical practice; (3) to expand the pedagogy of IPV so that practitioners can become more clinically attuned in employing interventions that help women, children, and men work through the emotional effects of partner abuse; (4) to explore sociocultural factors and their significance for the helping enterprise between clients, clinicians, and advocates; (5) to offer proposed strategies for abusive and nonabusive men to alleviate and prevent relational violence; and (6) to explore the importance of supervision and self-care/rest in the context of work with IPV clients.

Exemplars of clinical case formulation that integrate the following constructs—object relations theory, self-psychology, and cognitive behavioral and narrative therapies—are explored throughout this book in order to increase knowledge of how to assess and intervene clinically and behaviorally with victims and abusers. This book has nine chapters, each written for graduate students pursuing degrees in social work, psychology, mental health counseling, marriage and family therapy, and allied human service programs, but the content of the book is also relevant to practitioners working in the field of domestic violence, health, school social work, criminal justice, and private practice.

Chapter 1: The Traditional Framing of Intimate Partner Violence

To make sure readers do not engage the book in an ahistorical fashion, the first chapter focuses on the important legacy of the Duluth model (Pence & Paymar, 1993), which postulates that violence against women in the context of intimate relationships is primarily predicated on men's use of power and control to dominate and oppress them. The chapter suggests that this model continues to be useful because it provides a sociopolitical analysis that enable practitioners to understand the gravity of gender-based violence: violence is underlined by patriarchy, sexism, and misogyny, which predispose abusers to perceive female partners as objects belonging to them. One goal of the chapter is to help readers understand that historical and contemporary sexism have shaped the ethos of our society. The devaluation of women is evident in the lack of pay equity, employment discrimination, and sexual harassment, all factors influenced by male privilege. The ecological model of social work practice (Germain &

Gitterman, 1995) is used to ground the chapter given its supposition that people are unable to thrive in society when there is a poor fit between themselves and their environment, a view that is consistent with a set of realities associated with violence against women in the home and in the society at large.

Chapter 2: Sociocultural and Intersectional Factors Underlying IPV: Centering Black and Brown Women

A "one size fits all" understanding of domestic violence ignores the reality of what it means to live in a multicultural and multiracial society where black and brown women's sociocultural differences tend to locate them on the margins (Crenshaw, 1995). Chapter 2 asserts, for example, that sociocultural factors (e.g., race, social class, religiosity/spirituality, ethnicity, and culture) can affect women of color in relation to their conception of being victims of their male partner's abuse. This perspective implies that although a critical feminist lens is useful for examining the nexus between battering and women's social location in society, an intersectional standpoint is also useful for capturing the experiences and worldviews of women from marginalized groups. The reason is that intersectionality helps shift our thinking away from a "one size fits all" outlook, and instead shows how interlocking influences related to race, ethnicity, immigration status, and culture affect gender identity among women from culturally diverse groups (Crenshaw, 1995). Marginalization and discrimination are social maladies impinging upon women of color, especially if they are poor, and the presence of intimate partner violence in their lives can create complexity as they engage in meaning making (i.e., how one organizes one's views about life choices, events, and circumstances) about the safety of themselves, their children, and even their abuser. Given the prevalence of police shootings of unarmed black and brown men, for example, many abused black women find themselves having to think about whether their spouses may be killed or brutalized by the police if law enforcement intervention is warranted. Crenshaw (1995) asserts that it is impossible to omit race and racism from the lives of black and brown women faced with violence because they are often consumed with wanting the violence to end without causality to the men who abuse them.

Chapter 3: Women's Formative Experiences and Exposure to IPV in the Family: An Object Relations Framework

This chapter examines the ways abused women's formative years are affected by witnessing IPV in the home (Celani, 1994; Garfield, 2005; Mills, 2003). This facet of abused women's histories tends to be ignored during the provision of service delivery, mainly because women access services when they are in crisis and are seeking help for themselves and their children. Creating safety and addressing the gamut of practical needs takes precedence over exploring and understanding women's formative experiences. This chapter uses a psychodynamic frame that suggests that girls' early exposure to violence in the family has the potential to impact their development. Object relations theory posits that children need to feel unconditional attunement from caregivers who create a "holding environment" devoid of risks (Winnicott, 1965). The outcome of this dynamic between parents and children is the development of children's self-efficacy, an important attribute for establishing, negotiating, and sustaining interpersonal relationships. The presence of IPV between parents during childhood, however, can interfere with the capacity to establish a holding environment (a parent–child relationship consisting of unconditional love, consistency, and maternal stability) for young girls (Winnicott, 1965). Furthermore, witnessing parental violence during childhood means young girls may internalize representations of their mothers as victims and of their fathers as abusers, and they may interpret IPV as normative, unless early intervention to counteract this internalization is offered (Aymer, 2008a; Krane & Davies, 2007; Winnicott, 1965). Such an internalized split speaks to both negative and positive associations girls may have about their parents, and such a split in early development needs to be resolved so that girls can forge a path that leads to a "healthy" understanding of relational conflict (Winnicott, 1965).

Chapter 4: Adolescent Males' Exposure to IPV: Practice Issues

This chapter covers boys' exposure to domestic violence and explicates how they attempt to process their familial conditions. One goal of the chapter is to help practitioners comprehend the differential effects (depending on the boy's emotional maturity) of IPV on boys who have witnessed their parents' aggression and fights. It illustrates how emotional scars from childhood exposure to domestic violence affect boys' self-development and their relationship with their parents. Becoming protectors of their mothers by exercising violence and aggression toward their fathers, for instance, is a relational element motivated by the corrosion of familial trust, depression, hypervigilance, intrusive thoughts, and anxiety (Aymer, 2008a). This underscores the fact that boys' early abuse histories can truncate the attachment processes with their parents, because fear of parental fatalities can elicit feelings of impending abandonment and loss, which in turn can result in traumatic reactions (Aymer, 2008a; Herman, 1992). Engendering trust, vitality, and nurturance in children is critical for bolstering their attachment infrastructure with parents (Bowlby, 1988).

Chapter 5: Mothering and Motherhood in the Context of IPV

This chapter examines the seeming formidable task women experience as they attempt to keep themselves safe and simultaneously be attuned to the needs of their children. It suggests that staying safe requires abused mothers to navigate a perilous relational terrain the produces anxiety, trauma, and depression, all of which can undermine their role as mother (Bancroft et al., 2012; Herman,

1992; Lavendosky et al., 2000; Peled & Gil, 2011). This chapter elucidates the psychosocial sequelae of mothers' coping and living with persistent coercive control and violence, highlighting how being a mother and a victim creates a complex narrative of parenting. The chapter speaks to the importance of recognizing that exposure to violence in the context of mothering and motherhood can have grave consequences for mothers and children, thus requiring healing for both in order to recover from the cycle of violence.

Chapter 6: Toxic Masculinity and Men Who Batter

Chapter 6 brings to light the relationship between the positionality of male abusers and toxic masculinity. Male abusers often embody toxic masculinity, an attitude that relies on a projection of strengths, toughness, stoicism, and even male belligerence. Such a persona is deeply embedded in the ethos of patriarchy and is reinforced by "the boy code," which underpins the male sense of invulnerability (Pollack, 1998). One of the goals of this chapter is to ground the reader's understanding of the power inherent in how many boys internalize the narrative of male supremacy, as well as to provide an analysis of how gender politics, hierarchies, and role definitions buttress their negative attitudes about women and girls. In addition, it addresses the need to assess how men's and boys' early association to "the boy code" values and ideas can shape their cognitive and affective understanding of problem solving, love/affection, masculinity, use of aggression, and "unhealthy" expression of emotions, which are characteristics of toxic masculinity that contribute to the victimization of women and girls.

Chapter 7: A Self-Psychological Frame for Working with an Abused Woman

This chapter focuses on trauma and the self-psychological lens, arguing that abusive actions can lead to despair and induce trauma reactions in women who feel their lives are under siege. Herman (1992) posits that traumatic events induce self-doubt and weaken people's sense of worth and humanity. Abused women can present traumatic symptoms, including anxiety, hypervigilance, tension, poor self-esteem, depersonalization, and depression (Bancroft et al., 2012; Herman, 1992; Lavendosky et al., 2000; Peled & Gil, 2011). Depression and anxiety, for instance, can corrode the psychic energy women need to leave their abusers. In addition to coping with traumatic symptoms, women often feel a pronounced sense of terror when they consider leaving their abuser due to the escalation of violence and its potential lethality (Campbell, 2004).

Chapter 8: Men's Work: A Call to Action Concerning Violence against Women and Girls

Men and boys chiefly perpetuate violence and abuse against women and girls in heterosexual relationships. Women have been the primary agents of change in preventing and addressing gender-based violence; their stubborn advocacy has led to the birth of the battered women's movement and the creation of shelter services for abused women and their children. The voices and advocacy of men regarding the interruption (advocating against gender-based violence with women's organizations, etc.) of women's and girls' victimization have been largely missing from public discourses. The #MeToo movement has raised questions about why men have failed to speak out against the sexual harassment of women. This chapter discusses the need for men to become involved in decentering systems of domination that marginalize and oppress women and girls. As advocates, counselors, clinicians, and researchers, men can become allies in the fight against violence, committing to action that challenges other men who may not feel they can contribute to an antiviolence agenda.

Chapter 9: Shared Vulnerability: Countertransferential Reactions, Supervision, and Self-Care

This final chapter emphasizes practitioners' need to understand their subjective experiences with either being a victim of abuse or using violence and aggression in their relationships, particularly when working with IPV cases. Practitioners may struggle when providing services to victims, children, and abusers as they listen to painful feelings and traumatic reactions. Research indicates that practitioners experience anxiety and fear as they attempt to engage, assess, and work with abused women and abusers (Tyagi, 2006). This is especially the case when practitioners' feelings about their own abusive histories are unresolved. To this end, the chapter discusses the utility of countertransference, stressing the emergence of shared vulnerability originating from the practitioner's abuse history, a process that can facilitate the development of emphatic responsiveness and understanding (the capacity to listen to difficult emotional content and offer support without being judgmental) in the client and the practitioner. Like countertransference, self-care implies that clinicians must be attuned to how they are being affected by the work, professionally and personally. Finally, the chapter argues that supervsion is an important component of clinical work that can facilitate professional growth and address issues of self-care.

Final Thoughts

The COVID-19 global pandemic has evoked fear and gratitude in me during the completion of this book. Fear, on the one hand, stems from remaining concern about my mortality and thinking of how the ensuing sufferings and fatalities are impacting the world. Gratitude, on the other hand, stems from maintaining my physical safety and developing the emotional stamina to continue writing this book in spite of my individual reactions to the effects of the pandemic. Amid all of this, it was disquieting to learn that crisis calls to the national domestic violence hotlines from abused women have escalated, an unintended consequence of the shelter-in-place policies of government authorities (throughout the United States), aimed at minimizing the spread of the virus. Requiring citizens to stay at home indefinitely by definition places women involved with abusive men in a dangerous and vulnerable position because IPV thrives when victims are isolated and disconnected from friends and families. Hearing about the increased incidences of IPV during this very challenging and anxiety-producing period reinforced my commitment to this work and enabled me to reflect on the services women will need to cope with the traumatic stress associated with the pandemic crisis, and IPV. Aside from the effects of IPV, mental health experts have already indicated that the emotional distress from COVID-19 will require psychosocial care for many people. Given this supposition, clinicians may need to bring a deeper understanding of trauma and emotional distress as they evaluate the psychological needs of women faced with IPV while under quarantine. For example, it would be important to gain insights into how these women grapple emotionally with the dual reality of attempting to remain safe from being infected with the SARS-CoV-2 virus while also attempting to remain safe from their partner's violence. Upon the completion of this book, I remain hopeful and optimistic that we will get through the pandemic, and as a community committed to working with abused women, we will provide psychosocial healing to address the layers of trauma connected with their lived COVID-19 abusive experiences.

CHAPTER 1

The Traditional Framing of Intimate Partner Violence

It would be unwise to engage this topic in an ahistorical fashion, despite the fact that this text is written to address current clinical work with clients affected by intimate partner violence (IPV). History provides context, texture, meaning, and depth about phenomenological events; thus, this chapter gives an overview of how gender-based activism and organizing (specifically, the feminist movement and the battered women's movement) have informed the current tone and tenor of how practitioners, researchers, and policy makers address the problem of intimate partner violence. The chapter begins with the person-in-environment (PIE) paradigm, used in the field of social work to conceptualize the myriad ways ecological variables affect individuals and their communities, especially those that are disproportionately marred by negative social and political forces. The rationale for using PIE to ground facets of this chapter is that it underscores how policies, laws, and social mores have intruded on the lives of women.

Furthermore, an overview of historical marital relationships is explored to add context to how patriarchy has had an adverse impact on women's lives through the legitimacy it gained from law and society. To this end, the chapter also elucidates that in the United States the institution of marriage has historically subjugated wives—that is, they were expected to yield to their husband's control—reminding practitioners working with IPV in the twenty-first century that using power and control relationally has been a longstanding problem. The chapter observes that cultural shifts in heterosexual marriages could not have occurred without two very influential social movements—the feminist and battered women's movements—both of which revolutionized society's attitudes and values about gender-based violence and the centrality of equity for women and girls.

The chapter concludes by discussing the enduring legacy of the Duluth model (also known as the power-and-control model), created by Pence and Paymar (1993), and the cycle-of-violence model (Walker, 1979). That both frameworks continue to evoke controversies in some sectors of the IPV field and that their utility in work with both survivors and abusers continues to gain traction among systems of care reinforce the saliency of their historical and contemporary dominance in how we think about the narrative of IPV as well as potential ways to help women and men.

Person-in-Environment Perspective

Utilized in social work practice to assess the degree to which societal flaws (e.g., sexism, patriarchal ideas, racism, poverty, and other forms of social injustice) restrict people's capacity to adapt to their social contexts (Germain & Gitterman, 1995), PIE is an ecological framework that is chiefly concerned with people's ability to thrive and grow within society. There has to be a goodness-of-fit in order for people to feel nurtured by society: they should receive support and protection that buffer them from distress and injustice, and this has the potential to foster self-growth. Furthermore, the PIE construct posits that difficulties confronted by people are influenced in part by ecological stresses and challenges, and in turn it is expected that practitioners and clinicians will evaluate their clients' coping based on their maladaptive functioning within the environment. As constructed by Germain and Gitterman (1995), PIE focuses on a "stress coping paradigm that takes account of the characteristics of the person and the operations of the environment, as well as the exchanges between them, it fits well with social work mission, the ecological perspective, and the life-modeled practice that is derived from it" (p. 10). Broadly speaking, the mission of social work is to promote well-being in the human organism by advocating for the public good and justice. Likewise, social workers work vigorously to reform social and political systems whose policies are regressive and antithetical to the human condition. PIE recommends that professionals be cognizant of the consequential outcomes for people who reside in an environment in spite of a lack of fit without judging or blaming them; instead, the impetus in practice should be on political advocacy to maximize people's socioemotional circumstances.

The Relevance of PIE to IPV

From the perspective of social work, the person-in-environment (PIE) frame is relevant to the discussion of IPV because it points to contextual sociopolitical factors such as policies, laws, and norms that impede women's lives, especially those affected by partner violence/abuse. PIE is compatible with the sociohistorical activism that has buttressed the battered women's movement, shaping the traditional framing of violence against women as both a private and a public problem requiring societal intervention. From the standpoint of PIE, it is important to view IPV as an oppressive problem girded by other gender-based ecological problems (e.g., sexual assault of women and girls, employment discrimination), and these problems hamper women from experiencing goodness-of-fit; women are compelled to navigate social and familial circumstances laden with angst and trepidation due to inequality. An important point is that a lack of goodness-of-fit related to ecological challenges for women, including workplace sexual harassment, employment discrimination, pay inequity, and blatant disrespect for their humanity as manifested in daily "catcalls" and the presence of a rape culture, fosters gender-based vulnerability (i.e., feeling targeted based on one's gender and social location in society) and fear. Gendered ecological stressors are undoubtedly rooted in aspects of antifemaleness, a worldview held by many men and boys committed to asserting their supremacy over women and girls. Employing a PIE lens to gender-related oppression enables practitioners to see that violence against women and girls occurs on a continuum: women are faced with a wide range of abusive behaviors (e.g., physical, psychological, and cyber-sexual harassment and sexual abuse) at home, in the streets, in workplaces, on college campuses, and online (Hines et al., 2021). PIE cautions us from assigning blame to people, an approach that is acknowledged in service provision with women and girls affected by the consequences of hegemonic forces that can produce fear, anxiety, and at times trauma. The point is that in order to understand goodness-of-fit (or lack thereof) for women and girls, it is prudent to evaluate how sexism has shaped an uneasy reality for them. Efforts to address a lack of fit in society for this group have raised awareness about IPV and other gendered problems, thus leading to laws and policies intended to improve and change women's lived experiences within society and intimate relationships.

A Historical Overview of Marital Relationships

Traditional expectations about the positionality and roles of heterosexual cisgender men and women within society have been constructed by standards relative to what are considered normative patterns of relating and behavior for the sexes (i.e., the value placed on men as having higher hierarchical roles within marriages and families and women's lack of importance within these same contexts). These core societal values are influenced by patriarchy and are rooted in the DNA of U.S. society, and they influence the multitude of ways we interpret, perceive, and process relational and interpersonal dynamics among women and men, especially on intimate levels. Patriarchal ideals have shaped the historical contours of marriage; that is, the positioning of wives as the property of their husbands granted men authority and responsibility for protecting women (Allard, 2005). The mores of conventional marriage unconditionally subjugated women and regulated their lives; thus, dynamic features of marriage and all forms of IPV (i.e., physical, coercive control and economic, psychological, sexual, and verbal assaults) became inextricably linked. Sack (2004) and her colleagues postulate that because the laws governing the institution of marriage imbued men with rights and privileges over their wives, IPV reform was difficult. Moreover, Sack (2004) indicates that prior to legal intervention regarding violence against wives in marriages in the 1970s, a violent act would have to be considered "serious" (p. 1662). As violence against wives shifted from "legal approval" to "toleration," the implication was that husbands would be granted immunity from prosecution on grounds of marital privacy and preservation of domestic harmony (Sack, 2004, p. 1662). Likewise, "because husbands could be held responsible for their wives' conduct, it was believed that they had the right to control their wife's behavior, through physical violence if necessary"

(p. 1661). The legal system supported the physical suppression of women in marriages because of the rights men held, and thus sanctioned all the maltreatment of wives. This view lasted until the 1970s. In spite of this, organized efforts of members of the battered women's movement and public attention to the problem of IPV played a role in helping some states conceptualize violence against women in marriage as a crime (Sack, 2004).

Further, as the law acknowledged the perils of IPV within marriage, struggles to enforce the law occurred; Sack (2004) notes that police still had discretion to assess the problem by talking with abusers and at times recommend that they "walk around the block," an attitude that minimized the seriousness of the problem (p. 1662). Thus, men's sense of ownership of women within the institution of marriage has its roots in U.S. jurisprudence. And therefore, legal reform concerning IPV could not have taken effect because the early legal framework conceived marriage as a private matter that assumed the supremacy of husbands and the pronounced influence they possessed within marital unions. Allard (2005) asserts that "the Anglo-American legal tradition initially viewed women as property" (p. 198). Such a notion stripped women of their inalienable rights, fostering a gendered view of the world colored by the dictates of patriarchy (i.e., risk and vulnerability stemming from male superiority).

Social Movements and Feminism

Social movements in the United States continue to imprint our collective consciousness about injustices that hobble the lives of diverse groups of people and their communities. Although the genesis of social movements varies from group to group and from problem to problem, at the heart of all movements is the need to eradicate oppression and advance human and civil rights for the oppressed. The civil rights movement of the 1960s, for example, forged a path for African Americans that would enable them to gain some measure of equality and fairness under the law (Alexander, 2010; Aymer, 2018; Davis, 1983; Karenga, 1983; C. West, 1993). Unleashing potent critiques about white supremacy, demonstrations, and nonviolent resistance were tactics used to demand equal rights and justice for African Americans (Aymer, 2018; Davis, 1983; DeGruy, 2005; C. West, 1993). This point is corroborated by Karenga (1983), who asserts, "The Civil Rights Movement, which was essentially integrationist, gave Black people in the U. S. their first major accomplishments of the decade" (p. 126). Arguably, the gains made by and the effectiveness of the civil rights movement motivated other groups, such as women, who began to work to expose systemic gender inequality and other social forces fueled by patriarchal ideals. hooks (1989) has stated that "patriarchy is a political–social system that insists that males are inherently dominating, superior to everything and everyone deemed weak, especially females, and endowed with the right to dominance through various forms of psychological terrorism and violence" (p. 18). Similar to the quest for civil rights for African Americans, the women's movement understood that justice and equal protection under the law were elements women needed in order to realize their full rights in social and familial domains. Advocates also knew that the onset of any movement designed to topple gender-based marginalization and inequality would challenge the social order that men are used to, because within a patriarchal paradigm many men (especially white heterosexual cisgender men who are at the levers of political/social/economic power) are invested in continuing the narrative of male supremacy. The notion of feminism often conjures up in some men, irrespective of their social and cultural identities, the idea that women are on a quest to annihilate them. In other words, feminism and the women's movement are often perceived as threats to those men committed to the culture of patriarchy. Such a mind-set is similar to how liberatory endeavors (e.g., the end of enslavement or the civil rights movement) inspired fear in many white people who supported white supremacy (Alexander, 2010). Glaude (2016) eloquently states that

> White people aren't fearful of black people simply because they're white. That fear has a history. It has shadowed American life ever since we reconciled our commitment to democratic principles with the institution of slavery. That reconciliation required, among other things, white people to believe their lives mattered more than others—that the benefits and burdens of democracy did not extend to black people. They were slaves or, at best, interlopers in this grand experiment to democracy. (p. 83)

Correspondingly, in her discussion of white fragility, DiAngelo's (2018) thesis emphasizes how many white people experience pronounced anxiety, fear, and discomfort when they have to confront narratives of black people's oppression and sufferings, which are the result of white supremacy. Both authors remind us that it can be unsettling and troubling for many white people to face white supremacy because of the positionality they have within society, which confers a sense of privilege and entitlement. Yet, for marginalized groups, efforts to bring about social and political change must be accompanied by articulating and politicizing their oppression. For women, equality could not occur without constructing a counternarrative explicating the perils of male dominance and its psychological, social, and political impact on their welfare.

The advent of the women's movement that was underpinned by feminism led to the creation of laws that moved society closer to the equal treatment of women. Traditional gender-based expectations for women linked to child rearing, homemaking, and caring for a husband were no longer perceived as the exclusive domain of womanhood. Opening up this new psychosocial vista for women enabled them to have options that would potentially grant them full participation and parity in the home and at the workplace. In addition, an important consequence of feminism and the women's movement was that they unmasked the caustic impact of male privilege. Litigation about issues such as pay equity, employment discrimination, and sexual harassment were geared to protect women's worth and value. Such endeavors improved women's lives, but may have elicited dissonance in many men, who may have felt a loss of and connection to male supremacy, which was how they cognitively and affectively understood their social location in the world.

Features of the Battered Women's Movement

Influenced and inspired by the women's movement, the battered women's movement also charted a course for society in the 1970s, raising awareness and educating society about the pernicious effects of IPV. The movement relied on years of organizing and protesting by the women's movement to address gender animus—based on the aforementioned points regarding societal and legal conceptions of marriage. Drawing on the work of the women's movement, the battered women's movement argued that violence against women in intimate relationships should not be understood as a private matter because of its injurious effects, a view espoused by second-wave feminists, who added that the American family should not be viewed exclusively as a private entity given the potency of hegemony (Evans, 1979). This perspective suggests that we should cease observing the family as a private system due to its reductionist view of women, and instead see it as a public and political entity requiring scrutiny (Evans, 1979; Schechter, 1982). Hence, the private and public nexus of the family gave rise to the well-known phrase "the personal is political" (Eisenstein, 1984; Evans, 1979). Such an outlook helped the battered women's movement frame battering as both a public and political problem (Bush, 1992).

The battered women's movement developed a wider lens for society to view how oppressive behaviors accompanied by violence contributed to the vicissitudes of women's social and intimate experiences, and in turn this requires society to lift the veil of denial and avoidance and expand knowledge of the presence of violence within intimate relationships, in marriages, and in the family at large. This was a formidable undertaking in light of the traditional view suggesting that women were appendages of their husbands. According to Bush (1992), the battered women's movement posited that

> battering is the result of gendered power structure of intimate relationships, not a private problem caused by deviant husbands or unresponsive wives. Rather, ideology that viewed wives as subordinate to husbands, a criminal justice system that ignored the violence and blamed the woman, and the cultural denial of power relations in the family were identified as roots of the violence by the BWM. (p. 593)

Such a definition debunked the notion that violence against women was based on a private quarrel between intimates; it spoke to how institutional culpability and denial condoned the victimization of women in the context of partner violence by framing the problem primarily through the prism of family or marital difficulties. Continual organizing and social activities by grassroots feminists and survivors of IPV helped define partner abuse as a social problem in the late 1970s and early 1980s (Pleck, 1987; Schechter, 1982). The members of the battered women's movement felt that the violence between men and women was chiefly related to "gendered power relations" (Bush, 1992, p. 593). The differential of power between men and women as constructed by society and internalized by men accounts for a relational imbalance, in that men exercise gratuitous dominant behavior in order to achieve desired outcomes from their female spouses. Dutton (1995) points out that "all men can potentially use violence as a powerful means of subordinating women" (p. 168). In a similar manner, hooks (1981, p. 99) asserts that men subscribe to what she refers to as "a patriarchal social order," in which they exercise a generalized belligerence to control women, and this reinforced the need for and the importance of conceptualizing IPV as an insidious problem that erodes women's self-worth, and at times can lead to homicide. Thus, the following traditional tenets of manhood should be considered in thinking through what it means for men (especially white heterosexual cisgender men) to be socialized in a patriarchal world:

- Manhood means entering a world of male supremacy.
- Manhood means accruing privileges based exclusively on gender identity.
- Manhood denotes perpetuating some degree of misogyny, consciously or unconsciously.
- Manhood means using male privilege and male entitlement to navigate interpersonal and intimate relationships, especially with women.
- Manhood means never having to think about how one's privilege affects self and others.
- Manhood implies consciously or unconsciously employing psychological defense mechanisms such as denial, avoidance, intellectualization, and rationalization when issues of misogyny and sexism are unearthed by others, especially women.
- Manhood signifies stoicism.
- Manhood means being devoid of emotions and affect.
- Manhood means "always" being in control of oneself.
- Manhood means being in control of intimate relationships.

The battered women's movement changed the landscape of how society perceives, conceives of, and talks about IPV, a portrait of emerging social change in the United States stemming from political and community organizing. Still, the political momentum and impetus of the battered women's movement heightened public awareness of the ways the aforementioned traditional notions of manhood contribute to the gravity of IPV. Furthermore, all of this brought about the passage of the Violence Against Women Act (VAWA) of 1994. The law ushered in a new vision of IPV: the government was now responsible for the safety of women, altering the advocacy-oriented processes led by grassroots organizers (Garfield, 2005). Garfield notes that "under VAWA statutory provisions violence against women is defined as primarily acts of domestic violence and sexual assault" (p. 2). All women, regardless of social class, racial background, and religious affiliation, are entitled to protection and safety, and to this end male abusers are held legally accountable for abusive behavior toward their wives and domestic partners.

The Power-and-Control Model of IPV

Prior to VAWA, various community-based organizations and social agencies serving abused women had been offering shelter services to women suffering violence in their relationships and families. This was done to empower and promote safety for women and children residing in battered women's shelters. Furthermore, criminal justice involvement regarding IPV existed as early as 1982; police were authorized by law to treat violence between intimates as "any misdemeanor or felony assault" (Bush, 1992, p. 594). At the same time, a push for a mandatory arrest policy regarding abusers was part of the sociopolitical activism originating in the jurisprudence advocacy inspired by the battered women's movement. Bush (1992) noted that "during the 1980s, many local jurisdictions adopted mandatory arrest policies at the behest of local shelters, sometimes in concert with local women's commissions" (p. 594). One jurisdiction known for its coordinated community response to IPV was Duluth, Minnesota, which launched the Domestic Abuse Intervention Project (DAIP) in the 1980s (Shepard & Pence, 1999, pp. 3–4). Many cities were influenced by the Duluth model because it was effective in coordinating law enforcement, communities, victims, and abusers. The model offered a coherent and consistent way for service providers to conceptualize and work with IPV cases, emphasizing that men use power and control to oppress their female partners. Notions of power and control in the context of understanding IPV enabled counselors, advocates, clinicians, and others to grasp the problem from a sociopolitical vantage point. An important hallmark of this paradigm is holding men accountable for their abusive actions without assigning blame to women for remaining in violent intimate relationships in spite of danger. Shepard and Pence (1999) state, in their reflections about lessons learned from their work, that "as women crowded into shelters, their stories revealed a disturbing pattern of specific actions on the part of legal and human service practitioners that seemed to collude with men's violence and intensify women's vulnerability to domination by violent men" (p. 8).

Prior to the creation of the Duluth model, shelter services offered refuge to women; advocates provided services to women and educated them about using the criminal justice system to address their victimization. Organized and engaged community-coordinated activism from the battered women's movement provided fertile grounds for Pence and Paymar (1993) to conceive of the Duluth model and advance the lexicon of power and control that is now synonymous with IPV discourses. The model is an educational one, intended to shift men's thinking about the perpetuation of male privilege that emanates from the teachings of patriarchy. Men learn via educational groups that exercising power and control induces discomfort, fear, and anxiety in women, and consequently, the presence of these dynamics in intimate relationships can ultimately lead to physical violence and even fatalities. Alternatively, the model can be used to help abused women gain insight into the abusive dynamics with their husbands and male companions during therapeutic work.

The Power-and-Control Wheel

The continuing presence of the Duluth model in discussions about IPV and the delivery of behavioral health and social and mental health services to women and men has been a sobering reminder that at the core of abusers' violence is

The Traditional Framing of Intimate Partner Violence 9

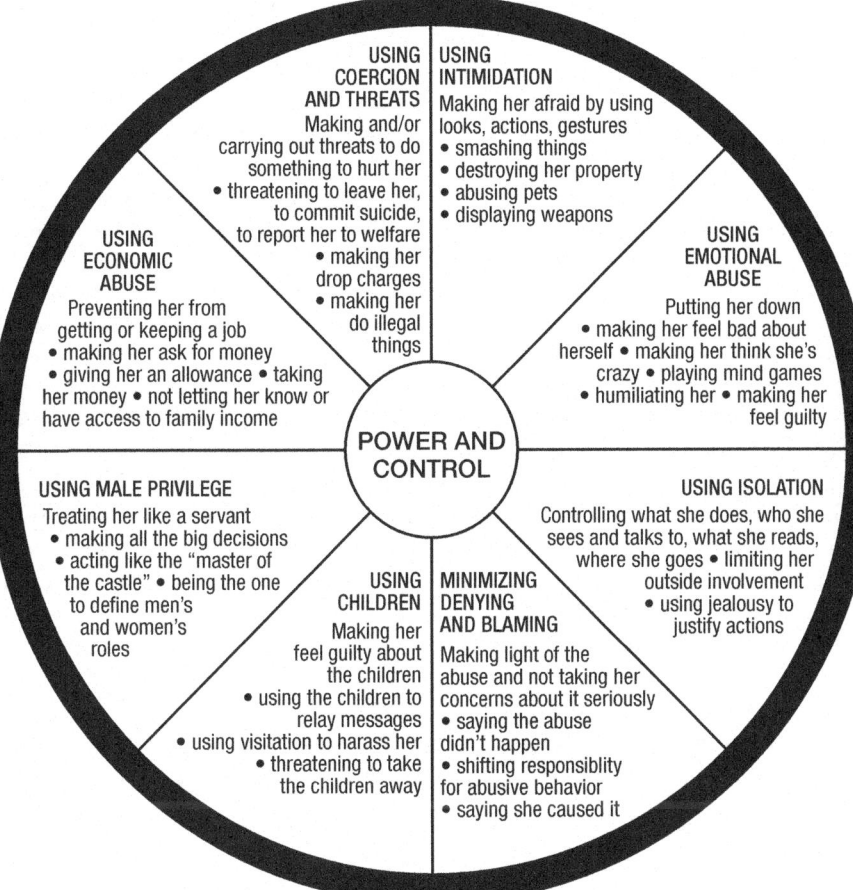

Figure 1.1 The Power-and-Control Wheel.
Source: Pence, E., & Paymar, M. (1993). *Education groups for men who batter: The Duluth model.* Springer.

the desire to control their victims. There are eight aspects of the wheel (fig. 1.1) depicting events and actions germane to abusive strategies batterers use in intimate relationships. In the middle of the wheel are the words *power* and *control*, signifying men's attitude and corresponding need for dominance over women they purport to love and care about. Pence and Paymar's (1993) intention behind the conception of the power-and-control wheel was to show how the coercive elements are parallel to the experiences of people subjected to oppression. The wheel suggests that like other "isms" (e.g., racism or anti-Semitism) sexism is an omnipresent sociopolitical problem impinging on the self-worth of women in all domains of human functioning. Pence and Paymar expand on this by noting, "They are the tactics employed to sustain racism, ageism, classism, heterosexism, anti-Semitism and many more forms of group domination" (p. 2). That men and boys are taught patriarchal principles, and live in social-cultural contexts supporting these principles, explains why many utilize male aggression to achieve a sense of conquest over women intimately and relationally.

The following headings constitute the power-and-control wheel (fig. 1.1): Using Male Privilege; Using Economic Abuse; Using Coercion and Threats; Using Intimidation; Using Emotional Abuse; Using Isolation; Minimizing, Denying, and Blaming; and Using Children. Using the wheel can be beneficial to men in batterers' intervention programs as well as women attending support groups for survivors of IPV. Clinicians have also used it in individual therapy to educate their clients about the sociological and political underpinnings of IPV. Unpacking various elements of the wheel in service provision can have differing meanings for men and women. For men, understanding the implicit sense of entitlement from which their privilege originates could promote insights into how this way of thinking leads to problematic interpersonal interactions with women and others: "patterns of abuse may be so ingrained in his history and cultural experiences that it seems second nature to him" (Pence & Paymar, 1993, p. 2). Eliciting men's thoughts and feeling about male privilege based on patriarchy can hopefully foster a critical consciousness relative to the limiting effects of this attitude on their roles as husbands, partners, fathers, and lovers. Similarly, discussing the idea of male privilege in survivors' groups for abused women can heighten awareness of how this belief system in men, rooted in patriarchal expectations, mutes women's voices, denies them personal agency in their intimate relationships, and devalues their humanity. Exploring these issues can help mitigate abused women's internalizing and blaming of themselves for their abusers' harmful behaviors.

The Cycle of Violence

In the late 1970s, Lenore Walker coined the term *cycle of violence*, based on qualitative interviews with abused women. Walker (1979) argued that violence against women in intimate relationships is a cyclical process, and that understanding this "helps explain how battered women become victimized, and how they fall into learned helpless behavior, and why they do not attempt to escape" (p. 55). The cycle of violence has three distinctive phases: first is the tension-building phase, the second phase is the acute battering incident, and the last phase is kindness and contrite, loving behavior (p. 55).

The initial phase of the cycle (see fig. 1.2) is marked by aggression and tension: the abuser may engage in name-calling (e.g., women may be referred to as poor mothers or terrible lovers) and may be critical of how the woman spends her free time or with whom she interacts. The abuser's behaviors can instill terror in the woman and debase her self-esteem, in particular in the face of his coercive temperament. He might accuse her of having an affair or even raise questions about whether her friends may be influencing her to be unfaithful to him. In spite of his accusations, the woman remains nonconfrontational, possibly conceding to his appraisal of her behaviors and motives, a strategy to appease his ego and prevent him from escalating and becoming violent. In the

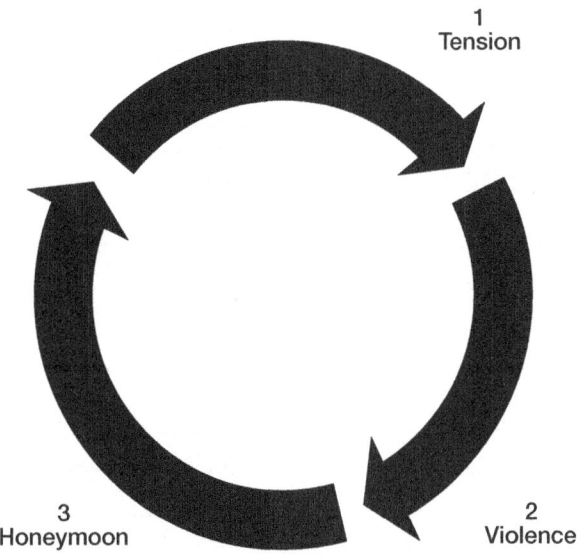

Figure 1.2 The Cycle of Violence.
Source: Walker, L. E. (1979). *The battered woman.* Harper & Row.

service of staying physically safe and alive in the midst of this type of relational turbulence, the woman remains silent in order to "keep the peace." During this phase, the demeaning behavior of abusive men is often a precursor to more dangerous acts of violence, such as hitting, slapping, grabbing, and even lethality, all derived from an escalation of tension unique to each relationship. Walker's (1979) formulation suggests that women involved in the cycle of abuse use the psychological defense of denial to cope with their feelings of helplessness, and stresses how the subordination of women as promulgated by society reinforces the ways they respond to abusive relationships. The escalation of minor incidents of violence often means the woman finds herself in a precarious abusive situation, sometimes resulting in death.

Acute battering occurs during phase two of the cycle of violence, and it encompasses the dynamic energy and tension that were present during phase one. The behavioral system of abusive men is to release anger, rage, and frustrations to establish a milieu of fear, terror, and anxiety, causing women to shiver emotionally. Whether the men are conscious or unconscious of their intentions to create instability, they use violence to construct intimate relationships that are saturated with coercion, which allows them to feel a sense of conquest over the women they claim to love. In addition, in phase two verbal attacks are also pronounced, and this also contributes to the injurious effects on women. Walker's (1979) research reveals that the acute battering phase can become more torturous depending on the duration of the relationship.

Following episodes of violence in the second phase, the third phase of the cycle consists of kindness and contrite, loving behavior, which many men demonstrate. Accordingly, Walker suggests that the third phase offers respite and a sense of peace for couples existing in a vortex of aggression, control, and violence. Surrounded by apologies and seeming care, love, and empathy, this period offers a modicum of hope for women in that they believe the systemic abuse perpetrated by their male partners will end. The man's apparent concern for the woman's well-being, his display of emotions for appropriating violence vis-à-vis the relationship, and his seeming interest in atoning for his actions often motivate the woman to forgive and be optimistic. Some men may ask for a second chance, promise to control their anger, and pledge to cease using violence to solve relational discord. This period elicits a sense of desperation in some men—making them feel they are unable to exist without being in a relationship with their respective partner—and they may even threaten to hurt themselves should the relationship end. An attitude of this kind can leave some women feeling worried about their partner's welfare, and can create sympathy, making women feel that their partners are genuinely interested in coexisting in a violence-free relationship.

In the context of society, abused women are exposed to a message from their immediate community, their family, and society at large reminding them about the importance of working on their marriages, that they should remain in their marriages in spite of fights and arguments, and that the decision to leave an abusive union is indicative of a moral failing. Messages from these social entities—along with the behavioral reactions (i.e., contrite apologies and a fear of losing one's partner) from their abusive partners—reinforce the idea that women should understand the plight of their abusers. All of this is an outgrowth of "respectability politics," which is associated with vestiges of traditional gender norms that accentuate a reverence for marriage. The seeming calmness of the third phase of the cycle of violence can give women false optimism and hope, evoking the desire to preserve the domestic partnership. Walker cautions us that this period does not last very long because it repeats itself over and over, resulting in a great deal of tension and violence, with only limited room for a calm, loving, nonviolent union. Thus, this phase of the cycle becomes hazardous for abused women and children, as violence and tension can become a ubiquitous reality within many family systems.

Conclusion

Social and political actions by advocates (mentioned above) have changed how IPV is understood and processed by society. Ecologically speaking, these actions produced protests and advocacy to combat the systemic marginalization of women. That attention was directed to the problem of IPV, and the general plight of women, underlined the enormity of ecological challenges that prevented women from feeling fully safe in their homes and in society in general. As a society, we understand that violence against women is no longer an intimate problem, or simply an instance of marital discord that should be resolved by the couple. We also recognize that women should not be held responsible for their partners' violence, an important outcome of the work of the women's movement and the battered women's movement. In particular, activism centering on IPV has enabled many sectors of society to comprehend that IPV is a sociopolitical issue and a crime, which has led to the creation of laws designed to protect women and children—highlighting a recognition that IPV is as much a public matter as a private one. Still, the strength inherent in the sociopolitical actions noted previously is that other entities, including academia, the law, and the media, have shaped how IPV is framed. Media coverage of partner abuse (e.g., the O. J. Simpson case in 1994, the Tracey Thurman story in 1985, the Lisa and Joel Steinberg and Heather Nussbaum case in 1987, the Rihanna and Chris Brown incident in 2009), albeit painful to watch, has reinforced just how prevalent violence is in women's lives.

The power-and-control model continues to affect how advocates, practitioners, and clinicians think about the role of patriarchy in society, and how it alters women's functioning as a social class. At the same time, the cycle-of-violence model continues to be used in practice, helping clinicians focus on the subtle and life-threatening patterns in abusive relationships. Drawing on these models and on my many years of experience, I present IPV as a complex psycho/social/political/relational problem that must be understood from a multitheoretical perspective. This book brings into focus an ecological and clinical frame for working with victims, children, and abusers, and this would not have been possible without the historical groundwork laid here.

This chapter uses an ecological frame to view women's lack of fit within their environment, historically and currently. Women have challenged and politicized their lack of fit in order to forge a liberatory struggle through an array of social and political circumstances, such as community organizing, activism, and legislation. With regard to IPV, the women's movement paved the way for the battered women's movement; without these movements, the reforms that exposed the systemic neglect of women in the law and in the provision of social services would not have occurred. Implicit in this chapter is that the traditional framing of IPV matters; it would be wise for clinicians to situate their clinical work at the intersection of sociopolitical ideas and psychological processes, and to recognize that women's emotional and behavioral health cannot be addressed without addressing the presence of gender-based justice in all aspects of their lives.

Discussion Questions

1. What thoughts have emerged for you after reading this chapter?
2. What are your thoughts on marriage historically and its connections to IPV after reading this chapter?
3. Are these new or existing thoughts?
4. How will these thoughts shape your view of the ensuing chapters of this book?
5. What were some salient points you took away from this chapter?
6. What aspects of the chapter resonated for you regarding your clinical sensibility to IPV cases?

7. What aspects of the chapter resonated for you, given your ideas about contextual factors related to IPV?
8. In general, what facets of the chapter are applicable to your view of clinical or advocacy work?
9. How has this chapter added to your knowledge base?
10. What are your reactions to the intersection of social movements that have been fueled by issues of racial inequality and gender-based oppression?
11. What are some advantages of using a power-and-control analysis in work with IPV cases?
12. What are some disadvantages of using a power-and-control analysis in work with IPV cases?
13. What are some advantages of using the cycle-of-violence model to help women and male abusers?
14. What are some disadvantages of using the cycle of violence to help women and male abusers?

CHAPTER 2

Sociocultural and Intersectional Factors Underlying IPV
Centering Black and Brown Women

Living in the United States, where religious, cultural, racial, linguistic, ethnic, gender, sexual, and political diversity matter, means that professionals providing services to women and children exposed to intimate partner violence (IPV)—as well as to male abusers—need to grasp the standard approach of conceptualizing the problem (i.e., men's violence against women is predicated on their use of power and control). At the same time, service providers must be acutely aware of the sociopolitical and cultural variables that buttress the social identities of victims and abusers of color, both of whom are on the margins of society. This chapter stresses the importance of this, contending that too often practitioners reflexively analyze the problem of IPV from a one-dimensional point of view, omitting how overt and covert issues of social injustice impinge on the humanity of black and brown women in spite of the existence of IPV. Although this chapter recognizes that all women suffer under patriarchy, it centers black and brown women, acknowledging that the lived reality of black and brown women is devoid of privilege, which means that they must contend with gender and racial oppression. The absence of white privilege moreover means that black and brown women who embody other social differences (e.g., linguistic, immigrant, religious, or LGBTQ+ identities) are subjected to multiple oppressions. Such a point should always be embedded in IPV analyses, advocacy, and therapeutic intervention. Because space does not allow for an exhaustive interrogation of every social variable that affects black and brown women, this chapter addresses the nexus among IPV, race, sexual orientation, religion, immigration, and ethnicity that informs the narratives of this group.

The concept of intersectionality is used to argue that the mainstream feminist movement should pay more attention to how gender-based inequality interacts with other forms of oppression and adds to the complexity of black and brown women's reactions to social injustices, including IPV. Three abbreviated IPV cases are discussed in this chapter, and these cases demonstrate how the strong interactions among clients' cultural identities are relevant to how they understand their circumstances and the larger social context they inhabit with their abusers.

Feminism Revisited

The prolific feminist scholar bell hooks (2015) reminds us that "feminism is a movement to end sexism, sexist exploitation, and oppression" (p. 1). By definition, movements necessitate the examination of social and political problems affecting people (e.g., LGBTQ+ groups, people of color, immigrants, women) whose lives are often decentered and omitted from the dominant discourses. Because patriarchy adversely affects women regardless of their cultural, ethnic, racial, and socioeconomic or immigrant status, hooks argues that feminism should be conceptualized as a movement because it is opposed by institutions committed to the paradigm of patriarchy. Entrenched in societal views, practices, and behaviors, sexist mores and norms devalue women and rob them of their human and civil rights. hooks disagrees with the notion that sexism is predicated on individual acts of bias against women; instead, she argues for a larger perspective that allows us to see that sexism is a systemic problem underlying all facets of our society, and that this conception offers a more complex portrait of how societal systems impinge on women's lives. Patriarchy is the core of sexism, and hooks (2015, p. 1) contends that it is critical for students of gender-based politics to understand the link between them. Attitudes shaped by patriarchy often imprint the psychic reality of men and boys and prevent many of them from seeing women and girls as equals. To adhere to patriarchal attitudes is to engage in the rejection of women, and for many men and boys, this fortifies their egos and sense of maleness. Institutionalized projections of the values inherent in being a man in U.S. society lead to the "othering" of women. Orenstein's (2020) book on boys and sex amplifies a multitude of ways young men resort to "othering" by using sex, gender, and male privilege to objectify and oppress young women.

In combating the marginalization of women, feminism will always need to oppose images, laws, and policies that seek to undermine the gains women have achieved in their quest for equality of the sexes. Feminism and feminist thinking will always reflect phenomenological factors, including political ideology and worldviews, religion linked to politics and fundamentalism, the evolution of mind-sets concerning what constitutes a fair and equal society for women, and shifting ideas based on demographic fluidity (issues of pluralism). The point is that in the twenty-first century, the struggle for women's equality must address issues of race, culture, immigration, transgenderism, and lesbianism that were either absent from or not at the forefront of the feminist agenda at the beginning of the movement. This view is found in the work of many feminist writers, who have pointed to the need for more inclusion and greater appreciation of diversity within the mainstream feminist movement, which has been dominated by white cisgender heterosexual women whose ideological views are different from those of women of color (Carruthers, 2018; Cooper, 2018; hooks, 2015; Kendall, 2020; Mills, 2003; Sokoloff & Dupont, 2005).

Race, Feminism, and Intersectionality

To be a woman who is black or brown in the United States signifies a set of meanings that are associated with white supremacy and gender-based prejudice. This is in contrast to white heterosexual cisgender women, who must deal with their whiteness through the lens of gender-informed bias. And though some may contend with other sociocultural variables (e.g., sexual orientation, gender identity, social class) that intersect with their whiteness and gender, white supremacy and racism, which focus on "whiteness," hold a different and powerful meaning for black and brown women given the potency of racism in the United States. Conversations and practices about feminism, be they in academia or in politics, can no longer be exclusively white but must include black and brown women, whose entire lived experiences are raced and gendered. Oluo (2018) draws attention to this:

> Feminist movements, for example, often fail to consider the different needs and challenges that many women of color face when they differ from what white women face. I've done a fair amount of work in support of reproductive rights, and I'm still surprised at how often reproductive rights groups claim that they are fighting for reproductive rights for all women, yet consistently ignore the documented racial bias in the medical field that keeps many women of color from accessing reproductive healthcare, regardless of [the] law. (p. 78)

According to Oluo, in the gaze of the mainstream feminist movement, sociopolitical issues germane to women of color tend to be invisible. In contrast, focusing on the experiences of black and brown women could ease the tension and discomfort they often feel when mainstream white cisgender heterosexual women's agendas take precedence over theirs. Though some mainstream white cisgender feminists indicate this may be changing, black feminist writers feel there is much work to be accomplished, given the current state of race relations in the United States, and based on the leadership of Donald Trump, the forty-fifth president (DiAngelo, 2018; Carruthers, 2018; Cooper, 2018; Garfield, 2005; hooks, 2015; Kendall, 2020; Taylor, 2016). The realities of black and brown women, shaped by racism, race, immigration, social class, and other sociocultural factors, should be pivotal to the mainstream feminist agenda, a viewpoint that hooks and other feminists of color have espoused (Crenshaw et al., 1995; hooks, 2015; Hull et al., 1982). A concerted attempt to include an intersectional perspective in mainstream feminism would truly reflect the lives of all women. By the same token, Crenshaw et al.'s (1995) groundbreaking research on intersectionality provides a framework for this and has played a tremendous role in shaping current discourse regarding the social location of black and brown women vis-à-vis issues of sexual assault, rape culture, intimate partner violence (IPV), and the #MeToo movement.

What is important about the construct of intersectionality conceived by Crenshaw (1995) is that it asserts the importance of contextualizing the experiences of women of color, especially those who are black. It is not ahistorical in its conceptualization, given the laws and policies that originated in enslavement and white supremacy, which have intruded on the lives of black people in general and on the narratives of women of color in particular. The weight of race and racism in the hypothesis of Crenshaw cannot be minimized when we examine how gender-based discrimination affects the lives of black and brown women. Crenshaw affirms that it is imprudent to examine black women's lives exclusively through the lens of sexism. The interlocking nature of these categories (i.e., racism, race-related stress, poverty, sociocultural variables) is virtually impossible to divorce from feminism when addressing the needs of black and brown women. And yet the resilience of such women is informed by their capacity to employ coping behaviors to survive and thrive in hostile social environments. Crenshaw (1995) writes, "My focus on intersections of race and gender only highlights the need to account for the multiple grounds of identity when considering how the social world is constructed" (p. 358). Indeed, the social construction of the world for black and brown women is qualitatively different from the world known to mainstream white heterosexual cisgender feminists. In addition to enduring "otherness" originating from sexism and patriarchy, black and brown women are compelled to navigate social structures where white supremacy, xenophobia, and other "isms" devalue their lives. For instance, the portrait of black women in society is oversaturated with stereotypical, racialized images: angry, strong, domineering, oversexed, aggressive, and the like. The research of Stephens and Phillips (2003) situates these images in both historical and contemporary contexts, and they offer the following typologies associated with black women: "The Jezebel, the Mammy, the Welfare Mother, the Matriarch, the Diva, the Gold Digger, Freak, Dyke, Gansta Bitch Sister Savior, Earth Mother, and Baby Mama." A full discussion of each image is beyond the scope of this chapter, but it makes sense to summarize how these images affect black women and influence how society responds to black women.

The enslavement narratives of black family structure and the need for survival can explain the phenomena of the Matriarch, the Mammy, and the Jezebel roles/images, which were prevalent during the period of enslavement. First, the Matriarch role/image was adaptive and occurred out of the necessity that black women had to maintain the family unit in the face of physical assaults and violence that pervaded black masculinity (e.g., lynching and the commodification of black men's bodies) (DeGruy, 2005; Staples, 1982). In contemporary society, black women are perceived as emasculating black men because they tend to be disproportionately heads of households, another adaptive factor given the high under- or unemployment rate for black men in U.S. society (Alexander, 2010).

The Mammy archetype stemmed from the social positioning of black women who worked for slaveholding families as caretakers of children and consolers of slave mistresses who may have been experiencing marital/family discord (Staples, 1982). The Jezebel image, however, depicted black women as overly promiscuous, a perception of slave masters that justified the rape and sexual assault of enslaved black women (Bontemps, 1969; Staples, 1982). These images should not be construed as irrelevant images of the past. They are instructive for our cultural awareness of—and sensitivity to—how history has marginalized these women. Because the enslavement of African people is one of the United States' original sins, we must recognize that these historical portraits of black women linger in the American psyche and therefore intertwine with society's projections and knowledge of them.

The other aforementioned archetypal images (the Welfare Mother, the Diva, the Gold Digger, Freak, Dyke, Gangsta Bitch Sister Savior, Earth Mother, and Baby Mama) from Stephens and Phillips's (2003) typology evolve from contemporary perceptions designed to objectify black women's existence. For example, the music industry promotes misogyny against black women through hip-hop and rap music that vilifies their humanity and places them in sordid music videos that fetishize their bodies. The misogyny of the music industry and the young urban black men who are the primary creators of hip-hop and rap music conspire to devalue the dignity of young black women by allowing the profit motive to supersede their self-respect. That privilege was not accorded to black women, and that their existence historically was not revered but castigated, enables society to debase their lives. A precursor to this is their history of enslavement, in which their objectification was commonplace, and such a legacy arguably remains in the imagination of our society, unconsciously informing how we respond and interact with them (either as objects or subjects) in society. Lending credence to this notion is the image of the angry black woman, a common stereotype signifying that this group is aggressive, obnoxious, illogical, and imperious. Anger is a valid emotion, but when it is applied to black women it becomes fraught and serves to blunt their subjectivity and sense of agency. The enslaved (men, women, and children) were expected to always demonstrate jovial and happy affects in order to maintain the comfort of the slaveholders. Expressions of other emotions were not permitted because they would be deemed threatening and conspiratorial (Johnson, 1982; Staples, 1982).

Intersecting Differences in Mainstream Feminism

The narrative truth of enslavement may not resonate personally or racially for all women of color, depending on their country of origin. Ethnicity, culture, and immigration may be more pronounced in the minds of Latina and other women in terms of how they see the world and its geopolitical dynamics. Even with differences among women of color, the one commonality that can be acknowledged is that they are nonwhite or consider themselves as such in a society that venerates women who are white. Nonwhite women in U.S. society (and globally as well) are classified as other because they do not carry the designation of being white and female—two categorizations synonymous with possessing inalienable rights and privileges. Moreover, other subjective differences, such as having a queer identity, can complicate the standard of whiteness and femaleness in the United States due to the primacy of the heterosexism and homophobia, which encroach on the rights of LGBTQ+ communities. That is, a white lesbian woman, for instance, will encounter homophobia at some point in her life; however, she will still benefit from protective coloration—her whiteness, which the world has been taught to revere.

Although there are black and brown women who embody a queer identity and may see parts of the world in ways similar to white gays, trans women and men, and lesbians, their sociopolitical experiences have created a narrative that is qualitatively different than their white LGBTQ+ counterparts. Carruthers (2018), a black feminist activist and writer, discusses the intersectional reality of queer black women:

> Black feminists have coined the terms in theorizing about the multiplicity of our experiences and expertise: "double jeopardy," "triple oppression," "interlocking oppression," and "intersectionality." No one experiences the world through a single identity. Understanding and expressing what it means when one's race, class, gender, and sexuality simultaneously shape one's political values is part of a long tradition of being a Black woman who is queer or transgender or both. (p. 6)

Carruthers's portrayal captures the complexity of black women's circumstances, yet it can be applied to other women of color whose ethnicity and linguistic and immigration differences situate them on the fringes. Carruthers's claim is important because it helps us dispense with the idea that women of color are engaging in what some people refer to as the "the oppression Olympics" (i.e., a generalized sense that women of color feel they are more oppressed than others) as they assert and remind mainstream feminists that sexism and patriarchy must be understood through the prism of interlocking aspects of other forms of oppression.

Immigrant Women of Color and Intersectionality

The experiences of immigrant women of color are not always central to mainstream feminist debates. This present period in the history of the United States makes it necessary for the feminist movement to focus on the pervasive anti-immigrant attitudes directed at these women and their children. That countries of color were targeted by the Trump administration's anti-immigrant policies and attitudes, and that women and their children are disproportionately affected by such policies, provides a basis for infusing the voices of this group into contemporary feminism's agenda. Draconian immigration policies geared to separate women from their children are a feminist issue, given the social construction of motherhood and the significance of the mother–child relationship in children's growth. Addressing the rights of these women to remain with their children, and to seek refuge from gender exploitation (in their countries of origin) such as sexual assault, IPV, and economic instability, reinforces their vulnerability as well as intersecting with racism and xenophobia. This is another thread common among women of color who are afflicted by patriarchy and misogyny and yet must also deal with other social forces that impinge on their lives. Crenshaw's (1995) notion of political intersectionality enables us to understand how politics and policies intersect with the lives of poor and vulnerable women whose existences have been deemed insignificant by the people who hold power and authority. Political intersectionality vis-à-vis current immigration debates produces a culture of fear and helplessness among women who have no political leverage to effect a different response from the government due to their undocumented status.

Intersectional Feminism, IPV, and Black Women

The rationale for the above discussion is that intersectionality should always inform the notion of feminism, in particular as it relates to black and brown women. Black feminist writers and researchers have corroborated this idea, stressing that racism and feminism have pierced the lives of black and brown women and that this has manifested in gendered, race-based anxiety (Carruthers, 2018; Cooper, 2018; hooks, 2015; Oluo, 2018). In addition, black feminist scholars Hull and colleagues (1982) write:

> The reason racism is a feminist issue is easily explained by the inherent definition of feminism. Feminism is the political theory and practice that struggles to free all women: women of color, working-class women, poor women, disabled women, lesbians, old women—as well as white economic privileged heterosexual women. Anything less than this version of total freedom is not feminism, but merely female self-aggrandizement. (p. 49)

This view allows us to further understand the pointlessness of feminism if it does not actively address the multiple social and cultural narratives of all women. A more critical inference that can be drawn from such a conjecture is that the subjective reality of black women suggests that they must manage the confluence of racism, sexism, and other factors that marginalize their existence; therefore, the feminist movement, accustomed to centering a certain class of women and their issues, should now de-emphasize that position in order to create space for women of color. As a practitioner working with IPV clients and attending meetings and conferences, and as an academic teaching a course on violence against women, I find that fostering conversations about intersectionality forces individuals to confront their class and white privilege, which can be a point of self-reflection regarding unearned advantages over others, another facet of oppression. Being aware of this point can stimulate useful discussions about the nuances of oppression that are within ourselves and our activism.

Case Study: Betty and Omar

Betty, a client I worked with in therapy, encapsulates how race envelopes life as an abused woman. An African American woman married to Omar, Betty presented interesting dilemmas early on in my practice. Betty sought help to deal with Omar's abuse and appeared to have been in crisis at the time. Following agency protocols geared to ensuring physical safety, I explored Betty's concerns by focusing on the need for her to secure an order of protection, to develop a safety plan for herself and her children, and to reach out to the police in the event of an episode of violence. As a psychoeducational process, this was a routine practice method for women who were accepted for services with the organization I worked for. Safety-planning strategies (a discussion with women about what types of practical information and personal documents would be needed in the event they had to leave the abusive situation) were taught via in-service seminars and workshops on IPV 101, which emphasized that the physical and emotional safety of women and children were of paramount importance. In principle and in practice, safety-planning strategies laid the groundwork for therapists to preserve the victims' safety, an essential service delivery approach given that IPV creates a precarious existence for women and their children. Arousing anxiety at the beginning of the process, Betty revealed she did not feel any of the preceding options made sense to her. She spoke of wanting the abuse to cease, but she did not want to leave Omar, and she was not comfortable involving the police in her family situation. Betty's concerns appeared linked to common hesitations other abused black women had conveyed to me about leaving their abusers. Further exploration uncovered that the issue of race, her commitment to her community, and her multiple consciousnesses (how she perceived herself as a black woman who must cope with gender-based and race-related bias) seemed to have affected the meaning she attributed to her victimization.

Betty's Intersectional Context

Recognizing that both race and sexism matter, I respected Betty's view by inviting her to share her thoughts about the content associated with the safety-planning process. Remaining unwavering about being in a violence-free relationship, Betty conveyed she wanted to sustain her family. This is where the issue of race and gender cohered: she spoke of the splintering of black families observed in her neighborhood due to divorces, unwed unions, and other social difficulties. Also, she struggled with the idea of contacting the police for help, noting that the brutalization of black men by law enforcement is rampant and deadly at times, and as such she was concerned that Omar would either be killed or abused should she avail herself of police intervention. Nevertheless, Betty expressed an interest in separating from Omar temporarily as a way to secure a respite from his abuse.

The importance of Betty's reactions is reflected in Garfield's (2005) work. She posits that black women's reactions to IPV are significantly different from the traditional conceptualization promulgated by mainstream feminism. Moreover, Garfield reveals that this group does not interpret physical abuse as violence, but believes that racist behavior is akin to abuse. This underscores that black women's lives are intersectional; that is, in spite of Betty's abuse, she expressed empathy for Omar by talking about the gravity of policing, race, and black men's mortality. Betty's feelings can be applied to the work of Du Bois (1953), the eminent black thinker who postulated that in order for black people to survive under white supremacy, they must develop what he referred to as "double consciousness." This is a view of life that recognizes that black people's circumstances cannot be divorced from the historical and contemporary racial oppression that continues to hobble their self-worth. As a precursor to intersectionality, the notion of "double consciousness" permitted black individuals to have an affective and cognitive comprehension of the reality of living in a society that purports to promote justice and equality for all groups but continues to embrace systemic racism, which obstructs their civil and human rights.

Moreover, Betty's attitudes about maintaining her marriage were another example of cultural/racial loyalty ties that intersected with her gender, and were emblematic of her experiences with facing the ubiquitousness of racism. I framed this in a previous publication as "shared vulnerability," which "means that many African Americans have some level of psychological consciousness about the potential of physical and psychic danger of living in a society that has a history of racial animus toward them" (Aymer, 2016, p. 375). That the safety-planning strategies illuminated her relational empathy (for herself and her husband) reflected the impact of historical and present-day racial oppression and how they may have informed the meanings Betty attributed to her abusive relationships. C. M. West's (2004) research about black women and partner abuse speaks to the extent to which their narratives should be placed in a historical sociopolitical context, so we may comprehend their experiences relative to their communities. West writes that "some events continue to live in the collective memory of African Americans, including sexual violence during slavery in the form of rape, forced breeding, and coercive medical experiences, such as the 40-year government sponsored Tuskegee study that withheld treatment from African Americans diagnosed with syphilis" (p. 1491). Here is the relevance of such an assertion in the twenty-first century: cultural memories (whether historical or contemporary) based on systemic injustices do not fade, and viewed through the lens of West's claim, black women's reluctance to enlist the help of institutions to address partner abuse may in part be affected by their knowledge of the systemic oppression and bias that disproportionately affect black men (C. M. West, 2004, p. 1491). In addition, West points out that "memories of lynchings and police brutality make some Black women reluctant to report their abusers to a larger system that they perceive as discriminatory" (West, 2002).

Case Study: Maria and Anthony

Maria, a Latina woman, sought help from a victim assistance organization in her community at the suggestion of her priest after she told him that Anthony, her husband, had physically attacked her and threatened to report her to immigration authorities. Initial interviews with her revealed the following: she was a mother of three toddlers, her English was poor, she was undocumented, her primary means of financial support was linked to Anthony, and she had fled her country of origin to escape repression. Except for her two undocumented sisters, who also resided in the United States, Maria had limited familial support. Anthony's family (mother, father, and siblings) treated her fairly well by ensuring she had food for herself and the children. Maria was approximately twenty-seven years old when I interviewed her. Although it was not an ideal approach for clinical practice, an interpreter was used because of Maria's lack of proficiency in English and the agency's lack of bilingual and bicultural clinicians.

As previously noted, exploring safety issues with all women inflicted by IPV was—and is—a normative practice employed by the agency I worked for. The dangerous reality of IPV is such that women face physical and emotional injuries, including threats of homicide (Campbell, 2004). Since IPV can cause fatalities, safety-planning practices are commonplace in service provision. Assessing for severity of risks associated with Maria's relationship used similar questions to those in Betty's case in order to engage Maria on issues of safety, risks, and vulnerability. In particular, the following questions were explored:

- What types of things would facilitate safety for her and her children?
- How safe does she feel in Anthony's presence?
- What would it mean if she had to leave Anthony and not share her whereabouts with family or friends?
- What would it mean for her to pursue an order of protection?
- What would it mean for her to pursue shelter services?
- What would it mean for her to call the police?

Asking Maria these questions led to apprehension and distress, which was conveyed by the interpreter, who summarized that she did not want to leave Anthony, that her family was important to her and she could not leave them, and that she is afraid of the police and the courts. Central to the interpreter's remarks was that Maria was anxious and fearful about her undocumented status and did not want to do anything to endanger her stay in the United States. In other words, she was afraid of any step that would affect her abusive situation. It was evident that she felt contacting the police or pursuing an order of protection would motivate Anthony to contact immigration officials. Also, she felt the authorities (courts, police, and the shelter system) would deport her if she made herself visible by securing assistance to deal with Anthony's abuse. The idea of being deported brought up her previous abusive relationship with a boyfriend, who presumably was still living in her country of origin, illuminating in part why she fled to the United States to preserve her physical safety. Issues of anticipatory shame and disappointment emerged in that she believed deportation would lead to her family ridiculing her for not being able to remain in the United States and for not being able to preserve her family.

Maria's Intersectional Context

Like Betty, in order to assess Maria's abusive relationship with Anthony, it was important to consider her context. Her gender, ethnicity, and immigrant status were relevant to her overall sense of self as a Latina woman, and this meant it was challenging to separate the danger she faced from IPV from other parts of her personal and cultural characteristics. In particular, she had to contend with her lack of facility with English, lack of acculturation, and fear of deportation—all of which added context, texture, and meaning to her understanding of being in an abusive relationship with her husband. Research indicates that IPV among Latina women cannot be separated from the rest of their subjective experiences, which is why an intersectional analysis should be used by practitioners (Lohman & Maldonado, 2014; Reina & Lohman, 2015). Maria's undocumented immigration status was a major source of anxiety during the safety-planning interview. Her feelings and concerns were linked to the ways Anthony weaponized her immigration status, using it to maintain coercive control. That he would refer to her as an "illegal alien" who should be removed from the United States was a tactic designed to intimidate, engender fear, and induce emotional distress.

This corroborated Dutton et al.'s (2000) findings that immigrant status is a tactic of abuse used by abusers to instill submissiveness in their female partners. For many women, deportation means returning to a social milieu where opportunities for upward mobility are limited or nonexistent; in Maria's case, it brought up unresolved anxiety of past experiences with IPV in her country of origin. Reina and Lohman (2015, p. 480) emphasize that Latina women's "unstable residency" is a factor that can add psychosocial stressors to partner abuse. By definition, "unstable residency" for these women can mean economic dependence on their abusers, and the possibility of not having their basic needs met can influence how they process their victimization (Reina & Lohman, 2015). Such a sentiment was expressed by Maria, who was unemployed due to her undocumented status and dependent on Anthony to support her and her children. The following excerpt from a different qualitative study captures the essence of Maria's feelings: "You know I wasn't working and I was taking care of my girls so I didn't look for jobs for a while. So, I was dependent on him and that stopped me. Five years went by before I decided to look for help. I first looked for help with a friend because I was desperate. I wasn't working and I wanted to find a job" (Reina & Lohman, 2015, p. 485). This quote exemplifies the insidiousness of economic dependence within IPV, and this form of dependence impedes women's agency and prevents them from having access to a world apart from the abuser. Beyond the financial gratification that is derived from being employed, employment enables people to establish relationships with coworkers, with whom they can develop social networks that facilitate connections to an array of issues, entities, and circumstances that inevitably increase their sociocultural literacy. Relational connections originating from being employed have the potential to reduce isolation, a common tactic used by abusive men to separate women from friends and families. An abused woman who goes to work with a black eye or marks on her face, for instance, is more likely to receive questions about her physical welfare, and this could stimulate her to reflect on her situation and perhaps avail herself of assistance. This is in sharp contrast to an unemployed abused woman, whose primary connection is to her children and her abuser, and who has limited access to outsiders who could act as mirrors with which she could examine herself (Alvarez & Fedrock, 2016).

Maria's lack of acculturation and immigrant status may have informed how she thought about her rights as a woman within her marriage. The idea of contacting the police for assistance was disquieting, and a corollary to this outlook seemed to have been underpinned by cultural values, including *simpatia* and *familismo* (Alvarez & Fedrock, 2016). In the literature, researchers assert that these cultural values (in the absence of IPV) can influence Latina women's perceptions of their roles and themselves in relation to their spouses and families. *Simpatia* reflects the idea that women are expected to be responsive to the needs of their husbands, remain submissive, and foster understanding within the marriage (Faulkner & Mansfield, 2002). Furthermore, *familismo* speaks to the primacy of the family and the need to consider it over one's individuality (Faulkner & Mansfield, 2002). In addition to these cultural values, seeking assistance from the police signified danger for Maria: she was not only fearful of being deported, but she was also fearful that calling them would result in the deportation of her undocumented sisters, with whom she is extremely close. Maria spoke of her cultural knowledge of policing, that in her country of origin she witnessed the maltreatment of poor people by law enforcement, and this seemed to have complicated her concept of policing in the United States. Maria's formative views of law enforcement were not dissimilar from the experiences of black and brown women living in the United Sates who have witnessed police brutality in their communities and gratuitous violence against unarmed black and brown men and women (Aymer, 2018). The implications of cultural values and fear of the police were compounded by Maria's inability to read and speak English and her lack of acculturation.

Maria' s case is not representative of all Latina immigrant women—no group is monolithic. Within groups there are differences and circumstances that can mediate cultural worldviews. What can be garnered from Maria's case, however, is that there are commonalties that can be applied to other Latina immigrant women, especially those who are poor and live on the margins of society. Related to this are structural problems (e.g., race, gender, and social class) within the United States that affect being an immigrant (documented or not), which serves to create a reality entangled with bias, racism, class stratification, and xenophobia. It is important to note that women bring their idiosyncratic experiences from their country of origin, and this can color how they interpret their immigrant experience. All of this reinforces the point that a universal understanding of service provision for battered women is unhelpful because it lacks an intersectional orientation, and thus omits the voices of marginalized women. The problematic nature of this is echoed by Sokoloff and Dupont (2005), who declare that "the intersectional approach provides ways to legitimate the experiences of women who have been marginalized and hidden from the dominant cultural discourse about battered women" (p. 49). This assertion encourages practitioners to appreciate the intersecting circumstances common to marginalized women (as well as the differences in their cultural backgrounds); for example, the vexing issue of policing was intertwined in Maria's and Betty's narratives.

IPV and Spirituality: An Intersectional Frame

There are a number of women for whom spirituality intersects other facets of intersectionality. This is at best minimized and at worst completely ignored in clinical practice where the focus is on IPV. Mental health clinicians are not routinely trained to develop knowledge in this area of practice. This can lead to a lack of appreciation for a client's spiritual or religious sensibility when they are faced with crises. Teaching clinical social work content to students and a course on violence against women has enabled me to recognize the gaps in students' knowledge about the relationship between clinical work and an apparent religious or spiritual orientation that some clients embrace—or reveal—in therapy. Knowing that I am mostly preparing students to serve an urban disadvantaged and marginalized population (largely black and brown clients who tend to subscribe to some form of spirituality) has emphasized the need for my students to be exposed to an intersectional perspective. Further influencing my pedagogy were lessons learned from my clinical work with predominantly abused women of color prior to entering the academy, in particular that a number of them relied on their faith as a means of coping with their abusive partners. This teaching approach is supported by the research of Van Hook (2019), who maintains that practitioners should understand the spiritual dimensions of their clients' lives. Practitioners should explore whether or not a client embraces spirituality/religion, which can create a more holistic understanding of a client's functioning. Underscoring such an approach to practice is Van Hook's (2019) position that "spirituality shapes issues of meaning and purpose, how suffering and healing are understood, and appropriate ways to resolve life struggles" (p. 320).

Case Study: Brenda and Sue

Brenda, a thirty-five-year-old woman who considered herself a biracial black woman of color, came to therapy to deal with abuse from her female partner, Sue. Brenda has one child from a male partner with whom she was involved before meeting her lesbian partner. Brenda grew up in a Christian home; she was baptized and attended Sunday school regularly. She is a deacon in her church, a position requiring her to attend to the needs of congregants who are vulnerable. She is also involved in hospitality issues, ushering and welcoming people to Sunday worship services. Brenda's partner, Sue, considered herself an atheist and had a difficult time reconciling she was in an intimate, loving lesbian relationship with a dedicated Christian. Brenda's coming out process to her family was not turbulent; she felt supported and understood. Because the church has been a dominant force in her life, she thought it would be useful to share her sexual orientation with her minister, who was affirming and supportive. Based on her perception that some deacons were closed minded, she disclosed her sexuality to only a limited number of them.

Working with Brenda in therapy revealed that she was in a relationship with a white woman who abused her physically and emotionally. Brenda's partner justified the abuse by accusing her of being unresponsive to her needs and putting the needs of her church before their relationship. Although the abuse had been occurring for some time, the presenting issue that prompted Brenda to seek help was the fact that her partner threatened to "out" her at work by revealing her sexual orientation to her boss, a source of conflict for Brenda, who had decided to keep her sexual orientation private: she considered her workplace a hostile, homophobic setting. She was afraid of losing her employment—a terrifying thought that conjured up poverty and hardship, which she had endured in her formative years. The first several sessions centered on Brenda's fear of her partner's abuse and her fear of losing her job. A more careful look at her fears indicated that Brenda's career enhanced her self-esteem and offered financial security, which had been missing from her childhood. Furthermore, Brenda felt that her church had nurtured her as she struggled with her cultural identity; she drew meaning and purpose from embracing her spirituality.

Brenda's Intersectional Context

Brenda sought help in order to address the abuse in her relationship in terms of its impact on her social and emotional functioning. Her therapy sessions revolved around this concern and provided an opportunity for her to explore and talk about issues that intersected with her abuse. Writers focusing on intersectionality and women of color in the context of partner abuse have noted that their victimization should be treated with the same importance as other parts of their lives (Crenshaw et al., 1995; Sokoloff & Dupont, 2005; Kasturirangan et al., 2004). There are multiple realities associated with the vicissitudes of these women's existence; they should not be reduced to the exclusive category of "abused victims" or "abused women." Doing so obscures their perspective on what abuse is and how it has affected their lives from myriad vantage points. Crenshaw (1995) affirmed this: "Thus, when the practices expound identity as 'women' or 'person of color' as an either/or proposition, they relegate the identity of women of color to a location that resists telling" (p. 357). To a degree, therapy enabled Brenda to verbalize her IPV narrative as well as to explore how it intertwined with her identity, socialization, and grasp of the structural oppression that inevitably shaped her racial, gender, and religious values.

Her identity as a biracial, black woman of color was a source of angst growing up: this imprinted her and affected her self-esteem. And although she found solace in living in a predominantly black community and being a member of and attending a black church, it seemed that she still struggled with self-esteem issues. In talking about herself, she spoke of being too dark for white people to see her as being biracial and spoke of not being black enough when she was in the presence of black people. It is interesting that Brenda's acceptance by her white partner elicited complex feelings about race and identity given the sense of rejection she felt from whites growing up. She struggled to understand why she fell in love with a white partner, knowing that her biracial status as a child caused others to reject her. In pondering her feelings in therapy, Brenda admitted she had ambivalent feelings toward her partner due to the racialized rejection she experienced as a child. Root's (1994) work on the emotional well-being of mixed-race women revealed that remnants of antimiscegenistic views still hover over our society due to white supremacist attitudes. This same research pointed to the fact that the psychological distress of mixed-race women is a by-product of internalized oppression from society. Indeed, Brenda's self-identity development was not innately maladjusted; rather, she internalized societal messages stemming from systemic oppression and white supremacy (Root, 1994). In turn, this internalization shaped her concept of her relationship with her partner, creating a dynamic where she functioned with a sense of inferiority, a possible outgrowth of her reverence for and conflict with white privilege—a position her partner held and that Brenda was denied even though one of her parents is white. This was a nuanced feature in their relationship; it was not unearthed until she was able to explore all aspects of her story via therapy.

bell hooks (1992) stressed that race and racism permeate all domains of black being and survival, expounding on the fact that "'whiteness' is the privileged signifier" (p. 167). The relevance of this point is that Brenda's sense of otherness (based on racial stereotyping and racial oppression) may have been unconsciously accentuated by the privilege connected to her white partner's life. Being able to talk about this in therapy was freeing but also evoked feelings of shame and inadequacy, validating hooks's claim that "collectively black people remain rather silent about representations of whiteness in the black imagination" (p. 169). Still, Brenda was fearful of broaching her feelings with her partner for two reasons: first, the contentiousness of their relationship made it difficult for them to talk about most issues, including an issue such as race; second, Brenda did not feel her partner would understand her feelings. To an extent, the second factor may have been credible: hooks states that "some white people may even imagine there is no representation of whiteness in the black imagination, especially one that is based on a concrete observation or mythic conjecture" (p. 168).

The aforementioned issues intersected with Brenda's religious beliefs and could not be disentangled from the rest of her life, especially her relationship with her abusive partner. Research on the interactions between women's spiritual lives and IPV has gained traction over the last twenty years, in part because the problem affects women from a range of cultural and ethnic groups, some of whom have a religious or spiritual orientation (Boehm et al., 1999; Giesbrecht & Sevacik, 2000). Relevant to this body of scholarship is that women gain purpose and meaning in their lives as they attempt to survive IPV (Bent-Goodley & Fowler, 2006; Gillum et al., 2006). An important insight from these studies is that some women's faith and religious journey facilitates protective, adaptive coping, a way of managing the challenges of living with violence.

Brenda, who considers herself a Christian, believes in a higher power and placed a great deal of emphasis on her faith in order to deal with her abusive union. Notions of higher power and faith correlated with Brenda's belief in God, teachings she received from her mother, her church, and her weekly attendance at Sunday school during her childhood. Ending her abusive relationship with Sue was predicated on her belief in daily prayer and self-reflection, which may have also facilitated her coping behaviors, a process in which she was able to gather her thoughts about what it meant for her to leave a relationship she cared about and wanted to salvage, knowing that it was becoming physically toxic. Speaking to her pastor (who also referred her to therapy) and some of her fellow deacons brought her closer to her faith as a Christian, reinforcing hope and permitting her to reflect on the existential psychological threat she felt from Sue's abuse. It is worth mentioning that Brenda wanted to end her abusive relationship without the involvement of outside authorities such as the courts and the police, a rationale similar to that of Maria and Betty. It was worrying to call the police for assistance because as a woman of color in a lesbian relationship she anticipated how issues of homophobia, racism, and gender bias could have been perceived by the police, potentially exposing her to injustice. Her anxiety about engaging the police on top of having to deal with the abuse speaks to the multiplicity of issues that many women of color must deal with to survive potentially hostile societal circumstances (see, e.g., Aymer, 2018; Garfield, 2010; Oluo, 2018).

Therapeutic work honored all aspects of Brenda's situation and respected her need to examine her life in a holistic manner. IPV and issues of race and religion had tremendous import for her, and as a result the helping process had a strong intersectional angle. The absence of physical danger or potential lethality allowed the work to move in a direction where the saliency of these issues could be explored in terms of their importance in Brenda's life. With considerable support during (once-a-week) therapy sessions, which lasted for approximately a year, Brenda dissolved the relationship with her partner, moved out of the apartment, received financial assistance from her church to secure her own apartment, and remained active in all aspects of her church.

Conclusion

This chapter has discussed the concept of intersectionality and its utility when working with women of color grappling with IPV. Black feminist and womanist writers have argued for years that it is critically important to employ an intersectional lens to conceptualize the sociocultural locations and experiences of black and brown women. Influenced by this body of work, scholars, advocates, and clinicians have begun to bring an intersectional framework to IPV discourses, in particular with women of color, in order to prevent reductionism when analyzing their social realities. This chapter argues that such a framework helps practitioners see the problem of IPV and women of color through a much broader lens. The result is to avoid the "one-size-fits-all" paradigm common among some practitioners, who may (consciously or unconsciously) subscribe to what Mills (2003) refers to as "white mainstream feminist thinking" (p. 65). Mills (2003) cautions us to reflect on white mainstream feminists' ideas of IPV, arguing that their thinking is laced with privilege and cultural bias that serves to promote the ways violence affects women, and that this omits the distinctiveness of violence on black and brown women. As an example of this point, Mills writes, "That privilege—to not have to be subjected to the intrusion of the criminal justice system, as people of color are, and to have a platform from which to speak and legislate as powerful white women—has prevented mainstream feminists from developing a method for reflecting on their own power; this has been especially true in the domestic violence context" (p. 63). This claim underscores the psychic tension Betty, Maria, and Brenda felt about seeking police intervention. Their private narrative truths as abused women intersected with their knowledge of the public narrative truths about policing and communities of color, immigrants, and the LGBTQ+ population. Although Betty saw the need for personal help from the police, she was acutely aware that policing of the black community and in particular of black men remains a troublesome issue. Likewise, Brenda struggled with the police relationship with the LGBTQ+ community, and she had concerns about what it would be like for her as a lesbian, biracial, black women of color to call the police on her white, lesbian lover. Homophobia notwithstanding, Brenda questioned who would be viewed as the aggressor when the police arrived at their apartment, a thought linked to the stereotypical and racialized images of black women as angry, strong, domineering, oversexed, and aggressive (Stephens & Phillips, 2003). In part, these attitudes reflect the conundrum faced by abused women of color, a sharp contrast to their counterparts (white, cisgender, heterosexual women) who do not carry a similar cultural and racial burden, freeing them to primarily focus on their own physical safety.

The chapter notes that abused women of color are diverse and have idiosyncrasies due to such sociocultural variables as social class, sexual orientation, race, and immigration status. And this population is subject to multiple forms of oppression as a result of living in hostile social environments that devalue their self-worth, which is inextricably tied to how they perceive all the facets of life. Thus, public debates on IPV, policy development, and clinical practice with women should always include substantive discussions on how systemic practices of dominance on macro (public) and micro (personal and intimate) levels intersect in women's experience of IPV. A major repositioning of this narrative requires mainstream white feminists to center the importance of "intersectional subordination" (Crenshaw, 1995 p. 359). IPV should not be assessed as a singular occurrence in the lives of women of color but as one of the many plights they endure, and should be viewed in light of patriarchy and white supremacy, which are manifested in daily gendered racialized microaggressions, heteronormativity, and xenophobia.

Safety planning is an important service that can facilitate a modicum of safety for all women dealing with partner abuse. But this process may not always consider the intersectional experiences of women of color. Betty's and Maria's resistance to this process demonstrated that safety concerns are not primarily focused on women of color and ignore the larger social, political, and cultural factors that are omnipresent in their lives. In response, the questions below are designed to promote safety as well as consider the intersectional experiences of women of color. They are not meant to be exhaustive, but rather they can be used to engage black and brown women about their lives, which are fraught with racialized, gendered victimization.

Intersectional Factors and Safety Planning: Discussion Questions

1. What does it mean to plan for your safety during this time in your life?
2. How do you feel about including outside authorities in your personal matter?
3. How possible is it for you to plan your safety given your undocumented status?
4. How possible is it for you to plan your safety knowing that you may need to leave your partner who is undocumented?
5. How possible is it to plan for your safety knowing that the children may have to leave their father?
6. What would it mean for you to call the police to obtain assistance during an episode of IPV?
7. What would it mean for your partner if you called the police for

assistance during or after an abusive situation?
8. What would it mean for your children and you if you called the police for assistance?
9. What would be a helpful plan for you to use to remain safe from your abusive partner?
10. To what extent are issues of race, culture, immigration, religion, or sexual orientation affecting your feelings about planning for your safety?

Finally, it is hoped that this chapter expands the reader's knowledge of and sensitivity to a population of women often omitted from the mainstream public conversations about IPV, unless those conversations are tinged with race and celebrity. For example, following the revelations of the abusive relationship between hip-hop artist Chris Brown and pop superstar Rihanna in 2009, IPV in the lives of black women became visible, and though this was important, the narrative of two celebrities was not representative of the vast majority of black and brown women, especially those who are poor and disadvantaged. The chapter advocates for the inclusion of an intersectional approach to IPV work at all practice levels so that the voices and truths of these women can be accurately addressed.

Discussion Questions

1. What reactions do you have to using the lens of intersectionality to understand the experiences of women of color with IPV?
2. Prior to reading the chapter, what were your thoughts about how IPV affects women of color?
3. What new insights have you learned about ways to attend to the service needs of women of color?
4. What ideas came up via reading the abridged case scenarios?
5. What specific therapeutic/direct service questions do you have about Betty, Maria, or Brenda?
6. What stood out for you about the ways structural issues of race, gender, and other forms of oppression adversely affect women of color?
7. What aspects of the chapter resonated with you the most?
8. What aspects of the chapter did not resonate with you?
9. What else would you like to know about the three cases from the view of intersectionality?
10. What observation have you made about intersectionality and the women's movement?

CHAPTER 3

Women's Formative Experiences and Exposure to IPV in the Family
An Object Relations Framework

The deleterious effects of intimate partner violence (IPV) are so severe that the need to create safety and offer immediate services (i.e., securing shelter services, planning safety strategies, and exploring criminal justice interventions) to women is of paramount importance to service providers. This is a service-delivery orientation geared to address the fact that many abused women tend to access help for themselves and their children during or after an episode of violence that has placed them in crisis. This chapter argues, however, that although the provision of crisis intervention services makes sense given the variety of needs many women demonstrate when they avail themselves of help from human service organizations, it is equally helpful to examine the ways their formative years may have been marked by either witnessing or knowing about violence in the home. The chapter does not imply that all abused women were exposed to IPV during childhood; instead, it invites practitioners to pay attention to those women who may have had such experiences. It also argues that it is important to recognize internalized representations of patriarchy and sexism as normative factors in women's formative years.

The chapter elucidates aspects of object relations theory, a relational psychodynamic approach that explains that human development is predicated on children's internalization of early relational interactions with their mothers/caretakers (parents and caretakers are referred to as "primary objects") and the social environment (Cooper & Lesser, 2008). Winnicott (1965), a major object relations theorist, postulated that interactional dynamics between children and their caretakers result in what he called "the facilitative environment," which plays a key role in shaping children's psychological development. Underpinning this chapter are the following themes: What messages have been instilled in some young girls as a result of growing up in the midst of abuse/violence but who nevertheless interpreted their parents as still in love? What does it mean for young girls to have anticipatory anxiety (i.e., worries about one's physical and emotional safety) that a fight is inevitable due to dynamic patterns of aggression, hostility, and physical violence between their parents? A case of an abused woman who sought psychotherapy will be presented and elements of object relations theory applied to illustrate the impact that both familial and societal internalizations have had on her psychosocial functioning.

Elements of Object Relations Theory

Within object relations theory, mothers or maternal others are significant objects in molding the character and personality development of children (Winnicott, 1965). These important objects in the infant world provide care, holding, and responsiveness, and, as Winnicott explains, these significant objects create a *holding environment* devoid of risks, enabling the infant to feel physically and psychologically safe. A holding environment in the parent–child matrix can be understood as the physical and psychic conditions mothers/caretakers establish that reinforce emotional caring and responsiveness, and as such this forms the basis for healthy attachment. In turn, this provides an emotional guardrail for children to negotiate and sustain adult interpersonal and intimate relationships. Object relations theory also includes the idea of the "good enough mother." Mothers provide "the ego support" (i.e., the demonstration of good maternal judgment that provides a secure base for healthy maturation) necessary to protect the infant from external harm that would truncate maturational growth (Winnicott, 1965, p. 37). In Winnicott's formulation, good enough mothering involves bolstering the ego development of children (i.e., facilitating adaptive qualities in children to help them function within the environment) through validation of their personhood. "The good-enough mother meets the omnipotence of the infant and to some extent makes sense of it" (p. 145).

Applicable to Winnicott's (1965) ideas are the *true self* and the *false self*, which are a product of the relational dynamics between child and parent. On the one hand, the true self emerges from nurturance and maternal consistency in children's development that can cultivate healthy development. On the other hand, the false self occurs in children in the absence of parental attunement, a significant quality needed to enliven the child's omnipotence and psychic energy. In his seminal work on emotional intelligence, Goleman (1995) writes:

> Prolonged absence of attunement between parents and child takes a tremendous emotional toll on the child. When a parent consistently fails to show any empathy with a particular range of emotions in the child—joys, tears, needing to cuddle—the child begins to avoid expressing, and perhaps even feeling, those same emotions. In this way, presumably, entire ranges of emotion can begin to be obliterated from the repertoire for intimate relations, especially if through childhood those feelings continue to be covertly or overtly discouraged. (p. 101)

The point is that misattunement leads to the false self (due to the development of an inauthentic persona) that reflects parental failure during early development, limiting how the child interacts emotionally with others during adult interactions.

Premised on the centrality of the qualitative aspects of children's relational and emotional processes with their mothers/caretakers, object relations theory holds that such interactions are internalized. It is the provision of parental care and connections and the milieu with which the child is associated that produces "internal objects" (mothers/caretakers) (Klein, 1964; Segal, 1974). Klein felt that the psychic development of children was based on the internal representations of their external realities. Another dimension of object relations theory centers on internalized good and bad object relationships that emanate from interactions with people and the environment. Fairbairn (1954) postulated that bad object experiences in the child stem from his or her internalization of negative experiences (i.e., physical abuse or emotional neglect) with parental figures. Instead of viewing parents as responsible for such negative experiences, the child engages in self-blame, and this creates a psychic split whereby the child avoids acknowledging parental badness because this could potentially impede attachment to his or her parents. The abused child, or a child exposed to IPV, for example, might blame her- or himself for the parents' abusive behaviors—as opposed to recognizing that the unacceptable and unjust basis for parents' actions are related to their own sense of badness. Furthermore, children have the innate capacity to internalize good aspects of their mother/caretaker based on feeling loved and protected by her. This subjective state occurs for the child, and it facilitates ego strengths (Goldstein, 2001). All of this is corroborated by Cashdan (1989), who indicates, "The inner world of the child was a world of human relationships" (p. 5). As a result, these relationships provide the psychological template for how children deal with familial others and the social environment.

Object Relations Theory and IPV in Familial Context

Because it is unfamiliar to some therapists and service providers who work with victims of IPV, object relations theory may not have much resonance. But this approach can offer a therapeutic framework for attending to the psychosocial needs of clients and examining the relationship between the presenting problem of IPV and the client's formative history. Object relations theory is derived from other forms of psychologies, including Freudian and ego, and it emphasizes that children's early relationships with primary objects inform character development and their sense of themselves and others with whom they interact. Cooper and Lesser (2008) refer to object relations theory as a relational construct promulgated by "American and British psychoanalysts" (p. 89). Some professionals and students who are just becoming acquainted with the construct may find it difficult due to the awkwardness of the language (e.g., the use of the term *object* to describe individuals), which can appear "mechanistic and distancing" (p. 89). Critiques notwithstanding, I feel that object relations theory remains a relevant framework that clinicians can use with some abused women to help them make possible connections between early childhood issues and current circumstances. That is, exploration of women's early familial internalized objects and experiences can potentially stimulate introspection, enabling them to have a deeper understanding of their psychology and an awareness of their idiosyncrasies. A cornerstone of this theory is that internalizations are a central part of self-development during children's formative experiences. Celani (1994) argues,

> Memories of external objects become internalized or introjected when the child is able to remember the characteristics of her parents even if they are not physically present. These internalized objects are made of packages or groupings of emotionally similar memories of events that actually took place in relation to the parents. For instance, the child groups together memories of being cared for by the mother into a single "good mother" internal image. These groupings become more detailed as the child develops, and they can be called upon when needed. (p. 48)

Relevant to this assertion is that it can be useful for abused women to know that internalizations of partner violence associated with their parents can affect selfhood as a child and an adult. Furthermore, the rationale for employing an object relations lens is that abused women can have a sense of how their formative exposure to IPV may be interfering with their current psychological functions. Likewise, clinicians can assess the needs of and respond to the emotions of women in a holistic way without assigning blame or minimizing the abuser's culpability. Additionally, because much of object relations theory makes clear that internalizations are a critical part of self-development, cultural factors marked by gender norms (rigid gender roles informed by traditional societal values) should also be understood as internalizations leading to self-object representation.

Socioemotional Processes of Living with IPV

Because much of object relations theory makes clear that internalizations are a paramount part of self-development, multidimensional variables such as familial, societal, psychological, sociopolitical, and spiritual factors should also be understood as internalizations leading to self-object representation (i.e., through parental figures), which contribute to the growth of women and girls. An attempt by clinicians to comprehend women's biopsychosocial history requires the following: exploration of early attachment relationships with parents, communication processes, the traditional construction of heterosexual marriages and family life, the possibility of teen dating abuse circumstances, the development of roles, and myriad peculiarities related to family functioning and dynamics, including the gendered messages concerning boys and girls conveyed by parents, family members, and society. What is important to weigh in this context is how the aforementioned aspects of women's lives contribute to their overall development and how they perceive their immediate sociocultural environment and society at large. A key observation of this chapter is that the meanings society assigns to womanhood, based on traditional standards and to some extent on contemporary ideas about gender, also influence women's positionality within families and in intimate relationships. From the standpoint of family relations and lifestyles, a pivotal factor to reflect on is the distribution of power in traditional nuclear families: women frequently hold a lower status than men. The conventional mores of society shape the essence of family life, and thus the manifestations of women's roles and authority within the family are often rigidly defined and largely determined by gender-informed expectations. Many girls growing up in traditional families are raised to be subservient to men; others growing up in progressive households are raised to believe they are equal to men. Still, some women in heterosexual relationships have been socialized to think that being in a marriage or committed relationship means that they should take care of their male partners emotionally. Other women think about intimate relationships in terms of egalitarianism. Ways of knowing and being for many women in relationships with men are the result of systemic sexism, gender bias, and standard socialization. This gendered reality is synonymous with the worldview held by other marginalized people, notably black men and women who must comport themselves in an acceptable manner to mitigate biased treatment (e.g., brutality and killings from the police), an expectation rooted in systemic racism and marked by the racialization and otherness of their daily experiences (Butler, 2017; Garfield, 2005; Kendall, 2020). Thus, both racism and sexism negatively color the existence of the oppressed, and because of the accommodations needed for emotional and physical survival, the pain and anxiety caused by this process can lead to feelings of marginalization, which arguably surrounds the lives of disenfranchised people.

Exposure to Violence

IPV in the family and its impact on women faced with partner abuse and their societal conditions should receive attention when clinicians attempt to evaluate women's coping processes. Research reveals that girls growing up in IPV homes tend to exhibit internalizing behaviors (e.g., depression and somatic complaints) in contrast to boys, who are more likely to demonstrate externalizing behaviors (e.g., fighting, acting out, and drinking alcohol) (Hughes, 1988; Jaffe et al., 1985; O'Keefe, 1996; Wolf & Korsch, 1994). These findings, albeit inconclusive, suggest that girls' internalizing behaviors could be precursors to mental health challenges. Indeed, this finding underlines the need for clinicians to be cognizant of how the phenomenon of IPV shapes girls' early abuse histories and contributes to the growth of adult women. It is not surprising that internalizing reactions evident in girls are indicative of how family and society mute their voices: they are prohibited from acting out in anger, aggression, and other antisocial behaviors. These same behaviors are common in their male counterparts who have also witnessed IPV at home. That the traditional expectations of femininity stress the importance of "patriarchal formation," denoting that women's and girls' place in the world should conform to behaviors and attitudes that are consistently ladylike, demure, coy, or feminine, is indicative of social mores designed to promote the subjugation of women. To step out of "formation" is to violate practices and norms that are not in line with gender-based conformity, and in turn this may yield ridicule and even ostracism from society.

From a familial standpoint, some girls' internalization of feelings may be related to their identification with mothers who also internalize such feelings as depression and anxiety due to partner violence (Herman, 1992; Sipe & Hall, 2013). Gilligan (1982) states that girls' psychological development is heavily influenced by a strong identification with their mothers, a critical aspect that nurtures self-development. This sociorelational observation is amplified by Gilligan, who notes, "For women and girls, issues of femininity and/or feminine identity do not depend on the achievement of separation from the mother or on the progress of individuation" (p. 8). And in this regard, identification is based on attachment to one's mother—a process in which an affective-relational bond fosters psychological growth through learning and imitation. As a consequence, clinical attention should be given to an abused mother's internalizing behaviors and how this may serve as a model for daughters who present similar internalizing reactions.

Case Study: Kathleen

Kathleen, a thirty-five-year-old Catholic Irish woman with long brown hair and gray eyes, is married to Winston, a forty-one-year-old biracial man who is also Catholic. She met him while they were undergraduate students; they have two boys, ages nine and ten, who were diagnosed with autism and are receiving mental health services. Kathleen's relationship with her husband is challenging; arguments and physical fights have become daily occurrences. The last episode of violence prompted her to call the police, and Winston was arrested. She has an order of protection, and he must stay away from her. Winston was granted the right to supervised visits with the children. Kathleen sought therapy to deal with what she described as long-standing depression.

Presenting Problems and Issues

Kathleen noted her depression appears to be related to her marital problems, and as such, the therapist made every attempt to create a supportive therapeutic alliance with Kathleen as she revealed that she felt sad about the current state of her marriage and wished she had not involved the police in her family affairs, though she was afraid and felt unsafe after her husband choked her and threatened to kill her—so calling the police seemed a viable way to protect herself. Kathleen spoke of experiencing physical and emotional abuse from Winston during their honeymoon, and a pattern of abuse subsequently surfaced and created considerable tension in their relationship.

The initial session afforded Kathleen the opportunity to talk about herself, her children, and the marriage. Kathleen is an educator who loves her work, but her ability to be available to meet the needs of her students was affected as she became preoccupied with escalating problems at home. She refers to herself as pleasant and joyous prior to Winston's abuse. Patterns of emotional and physical abuse in the marriage have led to feelings of depression and a sense of disappointment in herself for endangering the marriage. This seems to have particular resonance for Kathleen because her parents maintained their marriage in spite of arguments and fights. Emotional and physical abuse notwithstanding, Kathleen expressed love for Winston because there are times when he makes her feel wanted and important—when he is not abusive or violent.

Kathleen's Relationship with Winston

Prior to dating Winston, Kathleen described herself as a shy, reserved young woman who didn't feel she mattered to other people. She was a good student and interested in building a career as an educator. Her first date with Winston was fun and exciting: she laughed intensely from the jokes he shared, and she felt enlivened by being in his presence, hoping she could establish an intimate relationship with him. It was after a year and half of dating that Kathleen began to feel controlled by Winston, who wanted her to come home directly after work and would accuse her of being interested in other men if she was unreachable after work. She did not ascribe any real meaning to his behaviors (she did not consider him abusive or controlling), but she remained cautious, acquiescing to his wishes.

The multiracial reality (Winston is a black man) of Kathleen and Winston's marriage was a source of conflict for some family members who did not approve of their union. Winston felt rejected by such a sentiment and made this known to Kathleen. Talking about this issue proved to be a challenge for the couple. Kathleen felt she had to constantly reassure Winston that she wanted to share her life with him, yet this did not appear to alleviate the sense of rejection he felt from her family due to his race and gender. After the birth of their first child, the members of the family who were unhappy with her decision to marry her husband became more tolerant, offering a glimpse of her family's approval. In contrast, Winston's family embraced Kathleen and supported their relationship. Kathleen acknowledged she struggled with the positive regard she received from Winston's family in light of her family's disapproval. This caused compensatory reactions (e.g., she tends to reassure Winston that she loves him regardless of her parents' feelings) when they talked about the impact of her family's condemnation of them as a multiracial couple.

Kathleen described Winston as loving and caring most of the time. He has a good sense of humor and makes her laugh, qualities that attracted her on their first date. His humor often introduces levity to tense moments when they talk about anxiety-provoking issues such as their cultural differences. And yet over the course of the relationship, she has observed his generalized anger and believes this causes him to become controlling and rigid. Arguments stemming from differing views of managing money and disagreements about how things should occur in the marriage escalate into name-calling and screaming. She becomes quiet and withdraws emotionally from Winston, and although this disposition appears to deescalate tension at times, she considers the eventuality of his abusiveness in light of the history of control and abuse she has tolerated.

Kathleen's Relationship with Her Children

Their children have been present directly or indirectly during arguments and fights. Even though Kathleen has not seen any maladaptive behaviors that she can trace to the abuse at home, she expressed concern about their vulnerabilities given their autism diagnosis. She has encouraged them to talk about their feelings concerning problems at home with her as well as with the therapist treating their autism. According to Kathleen, both boys relate reasonably well to their father and seem to love him in spite of his abusive reactions and behaviors toward her.

Kathleen's Formative Experiences

Growing up in an Irish Catholic family meant that Kathleen attended Mass regularly with her family and was taught to be kind to people who were less fortunate. She attended Catholic school throughout her childhood and adolescence. She volunteered twice per week during her adolescence at the local soup kitchen affiliated with her church. She was adored by her four brothers, who were overly protective of her; a strong emotional bond was forged among them, making her feel special within the family. She felt close to both parents; however, there was a strong attachment to her father, who was overprotective of her. He prevented her from dating, stating his distrust of boys, who he felt were only interested in sex, and conveyed his dislike of such an attitude. Both parents imparted the view that Kathleen should graduate from high school and become a wife and a parent. According to Kathleen, her mother idealized this type of family structure, and the narrative of marriage and having children was an ordinary part of their conversations. Her parents also spoke with her about the importance of behaving "ladylike," and that having self-respect would make her a good wife.

During her childhood, Kathleen's family appeared to be well adjusted. But she recognized her parents' marital problems—they fought and argued regularly. Her mother was a traditional homemaker who was expected to cater to her father. Fights and arguments would erupt if her father felt her mother was not cooking his favorite meals or maintaining the home in a particular fashion. Talking about familial problems was not the norm in the family, so Kathleen never discussed her reactions to her parents' discord with her siblings. Denying her husband's controlling abusive behaviors, her mother often told Kathleen that her father was a "good man" who cared about his entire family. And although she believed this message, Kathleen felt some confusion because she witnessed considerable emotional friction and physical abuse between them.

Case Conceptualization

Kathleen's husband's long-standing controlling and abusive behaviors undoubtedly affected her. The assessment process illuminated that until the terror and fear induced by Winston's recent abuse (he threatened to hurt her in the course of a series of volatile arguments) that incited her to call the police, her tendency was to hide her marital problems from others, including family and friends. Although seeking assistance from the police provided a measure of safety for Kathleen, the guilt and anxiety she felt concerning Winston's arrest and the court order preventing him from staying in the home were palpable. The police and court interventions resulted in Winston's physical separation from the children; Kathleen felt the court-ordered supervised visits were emotionally damaging for the children. She appeared sad and disappointed in herself for imperiling the stability of her family, a mind-set that has its origins in her formative experiences and in her socialization as a girl growing up in a patriarchal society and a male-dominated family where the existence of her parents' violence did not dissolve their marriage.

First, in the discussion of object relations theory (above), it was noted that early infant/child development cannot occur without relational connections to others: children internalize parental/caretaker messages and dynamics, and this creates the infrastructure of the maturational process (Goldstein, 2001). The sense of regret for involving the police in her IPV situation was influenced by the self-object experiences she had in her family of origin, where the primacy of family stability overshadowed any apparent dysfunctions, even violence and aggression. The psychic reality of her own marriage reflected her childhood internalization experiences: the wholesome ideas her parents taught her about marriage and family during her childhood, along with witnessing the abuse between them in silence. Applying object relations thinking to clinical work with Kathleen brings into focus the need to recognize resonant familial/formative internalizations, which have formed the ways she understands herself in relation to others, especially her husband. Thus, it may have been discordant for Kathleen to call the police for help because of the internalized familial object representations (i.e., her mother was a traditional homemaker who placed her husband at the center of the family; she endured his abuse and did not reach out to the police), which have fashioned the ways she processes relational aggression, conflicts, and an unhealthy marriage. The manner in which her mother dealt with an abusive, problematic marriage was inculcated in Kathleen, and it probably emphasized martyrdom in service of her husband and children. Clinical writings and research maintain that an ensuing effect of internalized self-object representations is the psychological weight it has on adult interpersonal relationships and the judgments people make about their situations (Cashdan, 1989; Goldstein, 2001).

Second, internalizations of sociocultural issues can be placed in a context similar to the introjections (i.e., taking in the emotional qualities of the caretaking systems) of familial relationships. Internalizing regressive gendered ideas and thoughts that devalue women can certainly affect how a woman makes sense of her life. Regressive gendered conditions in society mean that women are exposed to ideas and images suggesting they are less than men for a variety of reasons, including the significance of male supremacy. Like many women, Kathleen has been exposed to explicit and implicit gender bias and its concomitant difficulties throughout her life, beginning with gendered scripts she was subjected to in her family of origin, and this may have unconsciously played a role in eliciting disappointment in herself for calling the police and having to face the potential breakup of her family. The nexus of familial and societal messages brings powerful internalizations explaining Kathleen's (and that of other women as well) seeming desire to sacrifice her need for safety in her marriage, a cultural belief buttressed by rigid gender norms. hooks (2015) contends that

> Since our society continues to be primarily a "Christian" culture, masses of people continue to believe that god has ordained that women be subordinate to men in the domestic household. Even though masses of women have entered the workforce, even though many families are headed by women who are the sole breadwinners, the vision of domestic life which continues to dominate the nation's imagination is one in which the logic of male domination is intact, whether men are present in the home or not. (p. 2)

The point is: women learn about the meaning of living in a society where men (especially cisgender white men) receive societal nurturing and where women must navigate structural inequality. Research on the impact of marginalization on African Americans, for example, has made similar claims, noting that it is important to assess and understand the significance of racism as an "invisible" introjected factor that impairs the well-being of "African Americans living in urban settings" (Aymer, 2010b, p. 24; Mayo, 2004). This analogy reinforces that sexism is also an invisible interjected reality, which impacts women's daily existence.

One of the tenets of object relations theory is that mothers and caregivers (objects) create what Winnicott (1965) refers to as a holding environment to nurture children (objects). The holding environment can be characterized as the process by which love, consistency, continuity of care, and emotional presence are inculcated in the relational spheres between the caregiver and object. In an optimal situation, the holding environment would be devoid of ruptures and traumatic situations because they interfere with the burgeoning selfhood. The concept of mothering in the formulation of object relations theory does not imply perfection; instead, mothers just need to be "good enough" in order to protect and promote the well-being of children (Greenberg & Mitchell, 1983, p. 196). Kathleen knew her parents' relationship was fraught; this may have impeded her perceptions of object-relatedness (communications and interactions that were exempt from abuse) between her parents. With this in mind, it is fair to infer that a holding environment surrounded by IPV presents a distorted image of parental relationships to children, and such internalized conditions can impair self-esteem and influence future adult intimate relationships. Formative exposure to IPV presented a distorted image of intimate relationships for Kathleen, given the idealized image she had of her father, and thus created a template for how she understood her relationship with Winston, whom she may have also idealized.

Sociocultural Factors

Kathleen's formative relationships with her parents and her siblings were marked by consistent love, validation, and praise—all of which fortified her ego, in particular because she was the only girl among her brothers (who loved and adored her). This was emblematic of the holding environment (per Winnicott's formulation) she experienced. Yet falling in love with a man of color ruptured parts of her family unit and generated considerable stress and anxiety, and for this reason, she questioned the perceived bond she had with her family. Although Kathleen did not refer to her family as biased or racist, she characterized them as unprogressive due to their disapproval of her marriage.

In essence, her family's reactions to the choice she made to marry outside of her cultural reference group created echoes of insecurity throughout the marriage, a reality Kathleen was keenly aware of and spoke about during therapy. She also spoke about loving her husband regardless of his race, and at the same time she had a yearning for her family's approval. Making sense of her conflict surfaced the dichotomy between the acceptance and love she received as a child (which supplied the building blocks for her development) and having to manage the emotional rejection from her family, who taught her to accept and relate to people from other cultures during her childhood, a value that shifted due to her interracial marriage. Object relations theory suggests that people can experience considerable angst when their internalized childhood experiences (e.g., Kathleen growing up in family where the implicit message was that she would marry someone from her own cultural background) result in circumstances that are different from the hopes and wishes of their social environment. Her family's disapproval of her marriage made it possible for her to reflect on their acceptance of her in its totality, thereby enabling her to examine her motivation to marry outside of her culture even though she had a sense it would be problematic for the family, and she expressed a pronounced sense of disappointment in her parents' lack of acceptance of Winston.

Course of Therapeutic Interventions

Although the presenting problem that motivated Kathleen to seek therapy derived from being a victim of IPV, she expressed a need to explore and address a range of feelings linked to her family, marriage, and children. The first phase of treatment was to make sure that Kathleen felt physically and emotionally safe, which is paramount to working with abused women (Kress et al., 2008). Although she felt upset and anxious about the abuse she experienced a month prior to starting therapy, she felt relatively safe because she had secured an order of protection, and the court ordered her husband to leave the home. Although the outcome of the court's decision brought Kathleen some measure of psychic safety, it also caused her to question if she should have chosen this type of intervention because it separated the children from their father. Clinical work was designed to help her process such feelings and gain insights into all aspects of her life. An object relations frame increased her understanding of how early self-object representations informed current functioning and current relationships, without making her feel that such a familial dynamic interplay completely explained Winston's abuse or her desire to remain with him before contacting the police.

It was helpful for Kathleen to understand why she tolerated Winston's abuse for several years prior to calling the police, a point she lamented during therapy. It was helpful for the therapist to affirm the fear she felt as a result of his abuse and control in order to diminish the effects of self-blame, a common reaction among abused women. Relevant to this intervention was Herman's (1992) seminal work on the recovery processes from traumatic events. Herman shows that the effects of trauma on women induce a range of psychological reactions, including terror and diminished sense of psychic and physical safety. Still, Kathleen's internalized self-object experiences as a child, along with internalizing societal messages about patriarchal ideals, were key to understanding why she tolerated her husband's abusive behavior. Therapeutic work with Kathleen centered on her attachment to dysfunctional internal objects (namely, her parents), and the degree to which such experiences hindered her capacity to recognize she could still be a "good enough" mother to her children and a "good person" even if she did not tolerate the abuse. Her internalized emotional attachment to the dynamic processes between her parents offered a model that she could use to (consciously or unconsciously) rationalize her marital troubles (Bowlby, 1988). In addition, clinical work helped her reflect on patriarchal standards and the potency of their impact on the manner in which she may have viewed her abusive relationship with Winston. The goal was to underline via therapy (from macro and micro frames) that her motivation to preserve her marriage (thereby tolerating her husband's actions) stemmed largely from the linkages of familial and societal internalizations, all of which were dysfunctional introjects.

Working with Kathleen for approximately a year opened up ways for her to cease self-blame and diminish guilt. This was possible because in many ways the therapeutic space can emerge as a "holding environment," giving clients like Kathleen a sense of stability, consistency, hope, empathy, and compassion, and (following object relations theory) this in and of itself can be quite curative, for it often provides a counterfamilial and counterpsychological narrative for clients. As noted above, the holding environment is imbued with maternal attunement, love, and affection, factors pertinent to the growth of children (Winnicott, 1965). Thus, the clinical process promoted psychological holding undergirded by trust and caring; Kathleen began to process multiple dimensions of her self and explored the feelings associated with being a victim of IPV, a mother, a wife, and a woman with a familial history whose lived truths have been marked by sexism. Many of the feelings revealed by Kathleen were difficult for her to process: she spoke about still loving Winston, her love and dislike for her family based on how they reacted to her marriage, feelings of disappointment with herself for tolerating the abuse, and questioning her competency as a mother. The capacity of the therapist to contain such charged emotions was another characteristic of the holding environment. Goldstein (2001) writes,

> Another important characteristic of a therapeutic holding environment is the worker's ability to contain the client's turbulent feelings and impulses. In order to do this, the worker must be able to help clients to get in touch with and

verbalize their feelings, to understand the client's symbolic communications and his or her attempts to put his or her feelings into actions, to refrain from counter-reacting to the client, and to set reasonable limits on disruptive, inappropriate or extreme behavior. (p. 157)

Containment with Kathleen necessitated the use of active listening (i.e., paraphrasing and offering encouraging statements to elicit clarity about emotional issues) and supportive feedback to allay the range of emotions caused by her abusive relationship, and to build her ego functioning. There were moments in therapy when she became boisterous, expressing her anger and disappointment for staying in the marriage. The therapist supported her need to express herself without interrupting her process, a clear departure from living with a husband whose controlling behavior muted her voice. The therapeutic hope was for Kathleen to connect with a self-object experience (her therapy and the therapist) so that she could feel less broken from the pain of her abusive marriage and address familial and societal internalizations that have influenced her life cycle trajectory. Reinforced by Celani (1994), this outlook in the therapy was designed to attend to what he refers to as the "*'hopeful self,'* which acts as an antidote to the pain and despair of the abused self, and deprived children and adults learn specific techniques that stimulate and strengthen their hopeful selves" (p. 127). The end of clinical work denoted progress for Kathleen: she felt less stressed and anxious in the absence of IPV and felt reasonably comfortable about her decision to call the police for assistance. She remarked that her actions were in the service of her children's and her own safety. Gaining insights into her inner life using early object representation (the formative images and messages she obtained from her parents and family) permitted her to examine unconscious thoughts and reactions that had been omitted from her explicit awareness of herself. Likewise, knowing her affect and thought process were also informed by society's construction of gender norms alleviated the belief that how she responded to her husband was based primarily on her own emotional schema.

Recommendations to Clinicians

Women facing IPV access various services, depending on a variety of issues, including the severity of their physical injuries, the needs of their children, and the precariousness of living with an abusive partner. For this reason, it is unhelpful to consider a one-dimensional service delivery method for assisting abused women; they are not monolithic in the ways they process and deal with their partners' abuse and its impact on their lives. But it is unquestionable that abused women are not comfortable with and accepting of IPV, and therefore at some point many will avail themselves of some type of service to combat violence at home. That said, the following are object-relations-oriented ideas that can be employed in clinical work with clients:

- Listen and reach for what age the client became aware of her parents' violence.

- Tune into her feelings and thoughts about her earliest memory of knowing that her parents' violence may have been impacting her (internalization of parental ruptures).
- Explore types of messages the client received from her parents regarding their discord.
- Explore family-of-origin dynamics to determine to what degree a woman has been impacted by her parents' violence.
- Focus on interactional patterns among and between family members to assess for psychological ruptures stemming from IPV.
- Examine the degree to which a woman's parents were capable of being attuned (i.e., parents' ability to tune into the subjective and affective states of children) to her in spite of the presence of their abuse.
- Address issues of childhood safety (emotional and physical) and how this reality may have shaped a woman's psychological health.
- Help the client process feelings about each parent in an attempt to illuminate the potential for ambivalence regarding "good and bad object interpretations of one parent over another."
- Explore what constitutes a healthy relationship from a woman's point of view.

As a site of psychological growth, healing, and recovery from abuse, the creation of the therapeutic relationship—along with infusing the noted object-relations-oriented ideas in the therapy—helped Kathleen understand how familial and societal internalizations contributed to her psychosocial functioning. Indeed, this process brought introspection that improved self-esteem, clarified questions about her reactions to Winston's abuse, and stressed that such reactions were illustrative of a relational power imbalance based on gender. Such a psychodynamic and sociocultural systemic approach to clinical work is supported by Herman (1992), who remarks, "the therapist's role is both intellectual and relational, fostering both insights and empathic connections" (p. 135). Finally, it is important to note that the clinical work captured in this chapter is no more or less important than any other type of service designed to help abused women. Instead, aspects of object relations theory are used to anchor the interpersonal, cultural, and intrapersonal dynamics of this one case, a sharp contrast to other textbooks, where there is a tendency to focus on macro factors and where the application of practical services to address the needs (e.g., shelter, legal, and social services) of women is primary (Hines et al., 2021; Sipe & Hall, 2013; Mills, 2003).

Discussion Questions

1. What parts of Kathleen's narrative expanded your knowledge of her subjective reactions to coping with IPV?
2. What struck you when thinking about Kathleen's relationship with Winston?
3. What was your assessment of multicultural dimensions of their rela-

tionship in relation to the feelings Kathleen wrestled with?
4. What thoughts do you have about Kathleen's early attachments to her siblings?
5. Other than what you have read in this case, what additional questions might you have about Kathleen's self-object representation (the dynamic reactions between Kathleen and her parents given the presence of IPV) based on her family?
6. How has your knowledge of societal internalizations (messages and ideas about masculinity and femininity) shaped your view of the case?
7. What was useful about this case conceptualization and course of treatment?
8. What facet of the case and the course of treatment might inform your practice with women impacted by IPV?
9. If Kathleen was your client, how would you have responded to her lingering ambivalent feelings toward Winston?
10. What were your reactions to Kathleen's intimate feelings for Winston in light of their violent history?
11. What lingering questions are you left with after reading this case study?
12. Overall, what was the most compelling aspect of this chapter?

CHAPTER 4

Adolescent Males' Exposure to IPV
Practice Issues

Witnessing the victimization of one's mother or hearing her scream for her life during the physical assault of one's father is anxiety producing for boys growing up in homes where violence is common. The effects of living in such familial circumstances and managing the emotional challenges of adolescence can be formidable. Through the use of a case study, this chapter addresses the ways intimate partner violence (IPV) affects the mental health of an adolescent young man, and makes the point that young men living in families riddled with fights and arguments between parents are more susceptible to exhibiting maladaptive behaviors in interpersonal relationships. The case illustrates how one young man struggled with anxiety and depression as well as other symptoms associated with trauma.

The chapter asserts that exposure to IPV is further compounded by environmental and sociodemographic factors (e.g., poverty, community violence, inequality, and oppressive forces), important facts for practitioners to be mindful of, especially when they are assisting black, brown, and poor young men who may have to deal with violence at home while coping with daily risk-inducing social maladies such as racism, poverty, and inequality. Finally, elements of cognitive behavioral therapy (CBT) are explicated throughout the case discussion, highlighting their therapeutic importance in helping the young man develop coping skills to buffer his early history of abuse, which affected his psychological functioning.

An Overview of Adolescent Male Development

Gender identity formation is an important hallmark of adolescent growth, and as a normative dimension of this stage of development, young heterosexual cisgender men are confronted with a host of questions, feelings, and concerns about who they are and who they are becoming in relationship to their parents and peer groups. Pertinent to this process are changes in physical appearance, such as muscular growth and the development of puberty and sexual characteristics as well as changes in tone of voice, all of which signal a shift in how young men begin to perceive themselves in relation to others (Blos, 1962, p. 8). And although adolescence ushers in many outward and physical changes in some boys, it must be acknowledged that other changes may develop at a slower pace, and as such feelings of inadequacy can occur, albeit temporarily (Mishne, 1986).

Parental responsiveness and nurturance are central to the well-being of adolescents; indeed, this provides the emotional base needed to facilitate ego development (e.g., the emergence of self-esteem, judgment, and self-efficacy) in boys (Blos, 1962). Parents demonstrate love, nurturance, good judgment, interpersonal skills, and moral reasoning to fortify the maturation of the child. In particular, adolescence in some heterosexual males can symbolize manhood, albeit in an incomplete way, emphasizing biological and physiological shifts in development. Parental care therefore helps young males move through the transition from childhood to young adulthood, a facet of parenting wherein values and standards about life are conveyed, both intentionally and unintentionally. This fosters attachment to parents and produces love, consistency, and a strong sense of belonging that can enable young men to maintain the innocence of childhood needed in the midst of traversing this developmental pathway (Erikson, 1968).

Adolescence is also denoted by a pronounced desire to separate from parents in order to increase autonomy and independence. In this regard, separation can involve showing romantic interests in individuals of the same or opposite gender based on emotional or physical attraction. Relying heavily on peers for validation and affirmation is another significant indicator of growth during adolescence. Connections to peers serve to counteract parental teachings, which helps the adolescent expand his developing perspective about his place in society. Research refers to this dynamic as a repudiation of authority figures in an attempt to establish self-understanding and identity (Blos, 1962; Erikson, 1963; McKenzie, 2008). As an example, traditional masculine identity development during adolescence is affected by observations of and interactions with other young and adult men, whose sense of reality has also been informed by familial and patriarchal influences. The potential for patriarchy to penetrate adolescent males' identity formation is inevitable, and their proclivity unwittingly to engage in and express sexist behaviors is due to its potent systemic influences.

Notwithstanding the aforementioned reality, there are parents who attempt to raise boys with gender-nonconforming attitudes (e.g., the process of raising boys to respect girls and women and grasping the idea that relationships should be based on egalitarianism), with the hope of modeling the values of gender equality—the point is to decenter male privilege in order to prevent the propensity for embracing and supporting sexist behaviors. The writing of Orenstein (2020) supports this idea in that she argues, "Mothers and fathers (and any other adults in a guy's life) need to challenge the unwritten rules of socialization, the forging of masculinity through unexamined entitlement, emotional suppression, aggression, and hostility towards the feminine" (p. 228). Thus, young heterosexual cisgender men raised in gender-nonconforming families may still grapple with ambivalence when they are confronted with gender-based oppressive behaviors and misogyny in other males. Fear of being ostracized and the strong influences of patriarchal "groupthink" can explain, in part, the ambivalence young men may feel, and as such they may appear unaffected while hearing or observing sexist commentary about women and girls from their contemporaries. What is important in this regard are two points: (1) oppression of women is systemic and has penetrating effects on men and boys; (2) a prerequisite for self-acceptance by other males, especially during their formative years, is to remain indifferent to hearing gendered debasing remarks and commentaries in order to comply with loyalty to patriarchy. The significance of gendered self-acceptance in young men and boys facilitates male bonding, and consciously or unconsciously this can culminate in notions of maleness and masculinity rooted in patriarchal principles and animus toward women and girls.

Exposure to IPV

Familial context embedded in partner abuse inevitably affects the psychosocial maturation of children of all ages (Davies & Cummings, 1994; Devany, 2009; Rosenbaum & O'Leary, 1981). Particularly, the externalization of aggression and violence is a common behavioral reaction observed among male adolescents who have been exposed to parental fights and violence (Aymer, 2008a; Ehrensaft et al., 2003). The socialization of boys and men in U.S. culture does not readily allow for the expression of emotionality. Instead, it permits "acting-out" negative behaviors such as the use of aggression and violence to deal with feelings of depression, sadness, anxiety, and confusion due to exposure to IPV. Ehrensaft et al. (2003) argue that the use of violence to solve interpersonal conflicts among friends and girlfriends is pervasive among male witnesses of IPV. Likewise, Aymer's (2008a) research illuminates that this type of externalization of aggression and violence is representative of how adolescent males cope with a range of feelings (e.g., sadness, anxiety, and depression) given the significance of parental abuse in their lives. Research subjects in this study coped directly or indirectly with witnessing IPV between their parents while still attempting to deal with the feelings associated with adolescence. Attending school, completing homework assignments, developing a focus on one's academic pursuits, or cultivating a social network are socioemotional milestones that can be undermined by living in the midst of IPV.

Community Context

Social class notwithstanding, adolescent males do not live in a vacuum, and thus developing relationships with peers can nurture interpersonal growth. Sociodemographic/environmental variables and the impact they have on young men is an important part of the practitioner's knowledge about the intersecting relationships between managing violence at home and dealing with risk factors such as poverty, community violence, and inequality. Privileged adolescent males (i.e., white heterosexual cisgender young men), by virtue of their socioeconomic status, may have a host of protective factors, such as better schools, the absence of widespread community violence, and the availability of community and familial resources to alleviate some of the distress due to their exposure to IPV. In contrast, adolescent males of color must deal with marginalization irrespective of social class. Police brutality, white supremacy, poverty, substandard housing, inferior schools, and community violence are risk factors that young black and brown men living in an urban context must confront. Risks of this magnitude compound how young black and brown men process and cope with IPV at home. This claim is bolstered by Rutter (1990), who posited that the multiplicity of risks present in children's worlds can have a major influence on their recovery from hardship. In essence, having a grasp of young men's coping reactions to and their understanding of what it means to be exposed to their parents' violence should be understood through the prism of both risk and protective community variables, because these can help practitioners assess issues of vulnerability and resilience.

Case Study: Bryant

A slender-built, light-skinned young man with short curly hair and a nose ring, Bryant is a sixteen-year-old African American adolescent who was enrolled in an after-school program where he met with his coach and revealed that his parents fought regularly and that he was concerned about his younger siblings, ages ten and eleven. Prior to this revelation, Bryant's coach reached out to him after observing his disengagement from recreational activities at the center. The coach invited Bryant to meet with him because he appeared sad. Although it took Bryant several days to connect with his coach, he decided to talk with him after witnessing a recent fight between his parents, and this prompted a referral to a clinical social worker, who met with Bryant weekly for approximately one year.

Presenting Problems and Issues

The goal of the first session was to build a rapport and provide a safe space for Bryant to talk about himself and his familial concerns. Therapy sessions with the social worker uncovered the following: Bryant attends a large urban high school populated by black and brown students, he considers himself an athlete, he has several close friends who also play sports, and he is romantically involved with his girlfriend, Ebony, age sixteen. Bryant is doing fairly well in school and plans to attend college. He is involved in an after-school program located in his community to meet friends and play sports. Although he likes this setting, Bryant is experiencing some challenges making many friends with other young men; they tease him about his physical size, making him feel uncomfortable about himself. Some kids refer to him as skinny and weak and question his athletic prowess, a point of conflict for Bryant, who believes he is a very good athlete. In spite of being subjected to teasing from his peers, Bryant feels the after-school program is a "cool" place because he can socialize with peers and engage in an array of social activities.

Bryant resides with his mother and father in a dense urban community surrounded by violence and chaos. His parents are employed: his father works as a technician for the telephone company, and his mother is a teacher for a private school. Expected to play a role in caring for his younger siblings, Bryant indicates he can only attend the after-school program two days per week. On the other days, he is expected to stay at home with his siblings, a role that is a source of conflict between him and his parents. Bryant understands that the rationale for babysitting his siblings stems from economic insecurity in his family system. His parents are unable to pay for child care five days a week. Yet he would prefer to attend the after-school program five days per week. On the days that he is babysitting his siblings, he has to stay in the apartment—a precaution to reduce his exposure to community violence; this has fueled considerable tension between him and his parents, especially his father. He often feels trapped in his home when he is babysitting his siblings. The lack of safety in Bryant's community due to community violence is another reason for his active participation in the after-school center, which provides safety and a viable place for him to socialize with friends.

Familial Concerns

Appearing anxious, Bryant spoke about his parents' relationship, saying that they are good people who love each other, but they fight and argue constantly. He recalled hearing his mother crying and his father yelling at her during his early childhood and adolescence. Upon his return from the after-school program, there have been instances when he assumed his parents were fighting because of the disheveled and chaotic appearance of the apartment. Bryant's siblings have asked about the fights between their parents, and according to him this has triggered feelings of helplessness. He spoke of overhearing his father using expletives and derogatory statements toward his mother and threatening to kill her if she did not stop nagging him (his father's homicidal threats were reported to the police). Bryant cried at this point, wondering whether his father was really capable of killing his mother.

Bryant feels closer to his father, whom he characterized as loving. His father praises his basketball skills and encourages him to excel in school so that he can obtain meaningful employment after college. His father also inquires about Ebony, who Bryant believes pesters him sometimes. Despite this, Bryant expressed some fear of his father based on the fights and the aggression evident between his parents.

Regarding his mother, Bryant listens to her regularly defending his father's abusive actions. Bryant has never questioned his mother about the fights and arguments. Instead, he tries to remain polite and respectful of their privacy. Yet he expresses confusion about why his mother uses the stress at work that his father may be experiencing as a justification for his use of violence. Bryant's mother helps him with his homework and makes sure he is doing well in school. He has translated this into her love for him, and likewise he explained that he loves his mother, despite her seeming rationalization of his father's abuse.

Bryant's Relationship with Ebony

Although Bryant and Ebony have been dating for about one year, the relationship has been periodically turbulent. As a self-described "jealous type" who tends to be accusatory when he notices other young men admiring Ebony, he becomes emotionally distant, blaming her for paying attention to these men. He has not admitted to using physical abuse in the relationship, but he has acknowledged provoking tense and heated arguments in response to his jealousy. Yelling, screaming, and using expletives in his communications with Ebony at times create a pattern causing her to apologize defensively in order to assuage his insecurity related to his perceptions that other young men are flirting with her. Bryant does not understand that his thought processes may in fact elicit anxiety in Ebony, especially when he becomes extremely angry when he cannot reach her via text. Moreover, this further compounds her anxiety, as he often believes she is cheating, a distorted view emanating from his need to control her. His coercive control compels Ebony to provide explanations to justify her availability (or lack thereof) to alleviate his insecurity.

Bryant spoke of not taking precautions during sexual intercourse with Ebony. Upon further exploration, he expressed a dislike for using protection, a point of contention causing Ebony to disclose her fear of becoming pregnant. Bryant's episodic use of condoms creates vexing conversations between them in that he believes Ebony should use contraceptives, whereas she believes he should also use protection, making it clear she will refuse to have sex unless this occurs. Even though he states he does not want Ebony to become pregnant, and even though he claims he understands her feelings and concerns, Bryant contends that she should use contraceptives, without comprehending his role and responsibilities as a willing participant in having sex. Bryant's behavior is consistent with Dutton and Golant's (1995) research on male abusers, who demonstrate "intimate rage," an attitude that insulates them from taking ownership for their abusive and controlling behaviors (p. 37).

Case Conceptualization

It was apparent that Bryant was grappling with many issues originating in his exposure to his parents' violence: he felt sad, confused, and depressed, and his use of coercive force with his girlfriend seemed clearly influenced by his familial history. The assessment process revealed that his adolescence was an important factor in understanding his behavior and feelings toward himself and others. And in this sense, it was useful psychosocially for evaluating the vicissitudes of his experiences, in that the connections between his parents' violence/discord and other risks, including economic insecurity and community violence, affected his way of understanding his lived circumstances. The contours of assessing his functioning included how witnessing his father's violence was shaping his identity formation and implicitly translated the message that violence against women was acceptable (Blos, 1962; Dutton & Golant, 1995; Orenstein, 2020).

Gendered attachment to other men (e.g., lessons learned from the interactions of and connections with the ethos of manhood that are rooted in norms of patriarchy) enables young men to wrestle with questions pertinent to their grasp of masculinity and manhood. Bryant's attachment to his father was fraught with ambivalence, yet he felt a strong sense of connection to him. In terms of his development, we know from research that boys raised in two-parent families have an innate need to identify with fathers, whom they often see as models that they can emulate and thereby work through emotional struggles regarding their sense of maleness (Blos, 1962; Hunter et al., 2006). The violence at home may have been a perceived threat for Bryant relative to his relationship with his father; nevertheless, a reasonable relational tie appeared to have been forged out of their mutual interests in sports and possibly their gender, allowing them to talk about and play basketball. In general, Bryant's father seemed attentive to his personal life and his academic pursuits, creating a paternal bond that permitted him to overlook his feelings associated with exposure to IPV in the home.

Furthermore, the presence of IPV in Bryant's developmental trajectory resulted in an emotional split: he compartmentalized his parents' abusive narrative based on the individual relationship he cultivated with each of them. His father's abuse as narrated by his mother was a clear example of her rationalization, a defense mechanism designed to explain to her son, whom she may have been trying to protect psychologically, why she tolerated her husband's violence and maltreatment. IPV places women and children on the margins within families—mothers find themselves having to continue parenting in the face of all forms of violence (Aymer, 2019; Krane & Davies, 2007). A corollary to this point is that abused women have an innate need to protect the welfare of their children while attempting to cope with the perils of IPV. For this reason, Bryant's relationship with his mother was complicated emotionally, and her maternal desire to shield him from the truth of his father's abuse may have allowed him to have empathy for her, even if he remained confused about her rationalization of his father's abuse. Blos (1962) amplifies this relational feature in families by arguing that adolescents who are conflicted about parental troubles develop what he called "defensive identification," implying that they intellectualize feelings relative to these troubles to adapt to and cope with them (p. 180). Similarly, the connections between Bryant's mother's defense of her husband's abuse and his father's inability to take responsibility for his abusive behavior culminated in Bryant having to deal with a sense of dissonance in his relationships with both parents, who he believes love him. Dissonance occurs when his observations of the gravity of violence that exist between his parents are inconsistent with how he feels about them, and their messages to him about the abuse, stated or unstated, are incongruent with his cognitive reality.

Bryant's exposure to his parents' violence offered an "emotional template" for how he currently treats his girlfriend, deals with conflict, and ultimately uses control to maintain emotional and physical power over her. Bandura's (1973) research on the significance of social learning implies that human behavioral needs are very much influenced by the ecological circumstances in which they are operating. Furthermore, Bandura indicates "aggressive identification reduces anxiety not by assimilating the external threat, but by appropriating forceful tactics that can ensure better control over the environment" (p. 89). The use of coercion to dominate his girlfriend made Bryant feel in control, albeit maladaptive, and this may have reinforced his concept of masculine identity, a representational image he observed in his father's reactions to his mother. It is worth noting that Bryant projected a hypermasculine demeanor during therapy sessions, and his treatment of his girlfriend mirrored his observations of his father's abusive aggression. This supported Ehrensaft et al.'s (2003) research, which shows that learning from important others that violence is a legitimate means of solving problems during early development indicates to adolescent males that it is acceptable to use violence in intimate relationships.

The enactment of Bryant's controlling behaviors (Bryant's sense of powerlessness was manifested in his embrace of combativeness and hostility in dealing with his girlfriend) was psychologically indicative of several factors: his exposure to his parents' violence and his lack of insight into how his experience influenced him affectively and cognitively. His sadness, anguish, helplessness, and anxiety were indicators of complex/chronic trauma. Kinniburgh et al. (2005) assert that "there is growing consensus that early onset and chronic trauma results in an array of vulnerabilities across many different domains in functioning: cognitive, affective, behavioral, physiological, relational and self-attributional" (p. 424). Correspondingly, another feature of complex trauma is the inability to regulate emotions, starting with the ability to identify, process, and understand them (Cook et al., 2005). In Bryant's circumstances, complex/chronic trauma was exemplary of the fact that he had to cope with the pernicious effects of violence between his parents, and at the same time he had to navigate the unpredictable and consequential effects of community violence. The aforementioned researchers remind us that supportive parents play an important role in helping children regulate their feelings in the midst of traumatic circumstances by ensuring they have a grasp of and awareness of their emotions, and given the pervasiveness of violence in Bryant's home, it is questionable if his parents were attuned to aspects of his emotional life.

Course of Therapeutic Interventions

Bryant attended weekly psychotherapeutic sessions where the focus was on the psychosocial meanings of his exposure to IPV and his relationship with Ebony. Although he seemed more amenable to talking about his parents' violence, the therapist's framing of his exposure included how it had affected his relationship with Ebony. Helping Bryant develop coping skills through the use of cognitive behavior therapy (CBT) was the primary goal for him in therapy. CBT was employed because of its emphasis on helping clients with faulty cognitions in negative behavioral outcomes that impede relational dynamics between themselves and other individuals. A primary focus of the clinical work centered on helping Bryant examine how his exposure to his parents' abuse caused difficulties in his self-concept and ruptured his intimate relationship with Ebony. Bryant, who in some sense attempted to comprehend the utility of his father's violence, aggression, and belligerence, struggled with several questions: Why did his mother stay with his father? What could he (Bryant) do to defend his mother? Why did his father continue to abuse? These questions marked Bryant's cognitive schemas, a CBT notion suggesting that the external environments (social and familial) to which children are associated play a determining role in how they take in social conditions as well as how they process and understand them. An amplification of this point is made by Diemes et al. (2011), who state: "Schemas form the basis of both 'healthy' personalities and those of individuals with psychopathology" (p. 150). The thought processes of children, for instance, contribute to this process in that their knowledge of events around them, coupled with the manner in which they construe and evaluate these situations, can create distortions or inaccuracies. Bryant was undoubtedly left with significant distortions based on witnessing his parents' violent relationship—notably, that spousal violence is normative.

Designed to offer support and clarify cognitive distortions, psychoeducation, a facet of CBT, was employed to debunk maladaptive ideas and views about IPV and its prevalence within Bryant's family. Employing this approach allowed Bryant to express a range of emotions, including guilt for tolerating his father's abusive behavior and ambivalence about loving his father in spite of the abuse. This was done gingerly and in an age-appropriate manner in order to engender psychic safety (i.e., offering empathy as opposed to inducing more shame and guilt as Bryant verbalized the distress he felt concerning his parents' abusive relationship) so that he could hear and process his feelings and assimilate new information that would counteract his distorted perceptions of why violence was occurring in his family. A psychoeducation approach promoted introspection, and Bryant became more conscious of the variety of ways that his faulty cognitions about and responses to his parents' abusiveness aroused anxiety and other feelings in him.

Bryant worried a great deal about not protecting his mother, for he felt his father's abuse could have caused a fatality. Therapy validated his concerns and elucidated that his need to defend his mother is a common attitude held by other young men in his position, given the psychological distress connected to witnessing or knowing that one's mother is subjected to violence by one's father. Research has revealed that adolescent males impacted by IPV "expressed aggressive and homicidal feelings toward their father" in order to feel a sense of control and to cope with anxious feelings (Aymer, 2008a, p. 658). In clinical terms, Bryant's anxiety was both adaptive and maladaptive given the abusive culture of the family. On the one hand, adaptation meant that the sense of worry he experienced about not being able to intervene prompted feelings of powerlessness. On the other hand, maladaptation meant that his desire to protect his mother, which seemed reasonable, would have occurred through perpetrating violence against his father. By addressing anxious feelings, Bryant expanded his understanding of the abusive and emotional interplay between his parents' problems and himself. This was a dimension in his therapy where he could engage in cognitive and emotional processing relative to his abusive family life.

CBT was also employed to help Bryant reflect on the abusive dynamics of his relationship with Ebony, and to interrupt the apparent cycle of violence he was re-creating. An important note that was pointed out to Bryant was that although he appeared to abhor his father's violence, somehow it became a part of his cognitive and behavioral systems, playing a role in how he dealt with relational challenges and problems with Ebony. The intimidation tactics he exercised in his relationship with his girlfriend were by-products of learned behaviors ingrained in negative relationship modeling he observed between his parents. In a behavioral sense, Bryant emulated his father by intimidating and using aggression to control his girlfriend, an explicit outgrowth of how formative events, especially for an adolescent male who by definition is still developing, can cause distortions in his functioning. All of this formed a complicated picture reinforcing a sense of weakness in Bryant whose perceptions of intimate relationship were punctuated with faulty cognitions about himself and his parents. In addition, cognitive distortions leading to imitating his father's violence were illustrative of how he processed personal distress with his girlfriend. Therefore, it was essential to offer psychoeducation to Bryant by focusing on the overall process of relationship abuse and its impact on victims and abusers in general.

Homework assignments, which are common in CBT, were given to Bryant in order to promote self-reflection in and out of therapy. For example, an assignment consisted of keeping a "feelings log" involving events that triggered a range of emotions in Bryant on a daily basis. The goal was to help him manage his emotions during periods of stress and frustration. The clinical rationale was that during instances of relational tension between his parents, Bryant did not observe any emotions in his father other than anger and rage; the therapeutic goal was for him to be able to perceive himself as an individual who possesses a full range of emotions that could be expressed in the absence of hostile actions toward others, including his girlfriend. Initially, this activity was a struggle for Bryant, and he reported that he could feel only two emotions, anger and sadness. Anger mirrored what he saw in his father and sadness reflected the feelings he observed in his mother, and this was indicative of his limited conceptions of expressing feelings and concerns. How Bryant processed his mother's defense of her husband's abuse, for instance, was an area of work in therapy, suggesting he felt she may have been protecting both him and his father. All of this may have prevented her from acknowledging the hurt and pain she suffered. After several sessions, Bryant developed greater ease in capturing a range of feelings in his log, including anger, sadness, frustration, happiness, and disappointment, which were related to his exposure to his parents' abusive relationship. New ways to react to his feelings and circumstances were processed via therapy. For example, Bryant learned that anger is an emotion that can be expressed to his girlfriend without exhibiting hostility, belligerence, and other forms of aggression. This was revelatory and enabled him to gain perspective on his distorted perceptions of his emotional life.

Bryant demonstrated functional coping in spite of the aforementioned psychosocial difficulties. Chief among his coping responses was his ability to be involved in the after-school program, play basketball regularly with his father, maintain good grades in school, maintain his friendships, sustain an intimate relationship with his girlfriend, and engage in therapy. His connections to these activities and individuals served to reduce the anguish he endured from living with familial turbulence and violence, which were imprinted on his sense of self and thus encumbered his mental health. As protective factors, these activities and individuals became a major part of Bryant's social support system in that they affirmed his being and strengthened his resilience. As Maruna (2001) stresses, "social bond theory suggests that varying informal ties to family, employment, and educational programs in early adulthood can potentially explain changes in criminality during life course" (p. 36). In addition, even though he had begun to mimic his father's abusive ways, it seemed that his openness in therapy and his capacity to relate to others contributed to adaptive coping and a desire to change his life course from a potential abuser to a caring and nonabusive young man.

Sociocultural Factors

In addition to dealing with violence in his family and in his community, Bryant had to contend with issues of implicit and explicit bias, an inescapable reality for young black and brown men living in the United States. Research pertaining to adolescents of color asserts that issues of race and racism often impinge on their psychological growth (Phinney, 2010; Scott, 2003). As Bryant's treatment focused on his familial situation and his escalating abusive relationship with his girlfriend, factors about his social identity and community violence were not fully addressed. It should be noted, however, that issues of racism and marginalization probably added to his anxious feelings because they are risk-inducing problems that disproportionately confront Bryant's demographic. For instance, he did note that the police racially profiled him on several occasions on his way to school and the after-school program. Emotional supportive feedback was provided to validate his feelings of outrage in light of the apparent race-related stress originating from such experiences.

As stated previously, preservation of life for Bryant depended on managing the violent terrain of his community by regulating his physical movements to and from his apartment. His parents' concerns regarding his safety prevented him from socializing with friends in the community. Attending school and the after-school program afforded Bryant safe spaces in which he could mingle with friends and peers; his parents felt they were less dangerous and that Bryant's life would be less precarious. Thus, in order to fully appreciate the seriousness of how exposure to IPV intrudes on the functioning of young men such as Bryant and understand their coping responses, it is critically important to be cognizant of the ways their social context may predispose them to other social toxins and therefore complicate their lives.

Recommendations to Clinicians

Clinical work with adolescent males affected by exposure to IPV should address a range of emotional reactions, including depression, anxiety, sadness, powerlessness, anger, unhappiness, and melancholy, which can impede psychosocial functioning. The following are clinical implications for working with adolescent males who have been exposed to IPV during their formative upbringing:

- Recognize and appreciate that adolescent development can be challenging, irrespective of exposure to IPV during childhood.
- Focus on the variety of ways IPV has affected their psychosocial development (e.g., academic performance, relationships with friends, intimate relationships, etc.).
- Evaluate how other social and community problems may compound their development and exposure to IPV.
- Explore if they have sustained physical injuries as a result of witnessing parental fights.
- Explore issues of split loyalty ties regarding their parents (i.e., the desire to collude with one parent over another, which can surface ambivalent feelings).
- Examine how IPV is viewed in the context of their emotional development to determine if it is understood as an adaptive or maladaptive behavior.
- Pay attention to whether they are currently using abuse or control in dating relationships.
- Explore their ideas around what constitutes healthy dating relationships.
- Examine the relationship between witnessing IPV directly or indirectly and the emergence of their gender identity formation.
- Normalize the expression of emotionality and validate the range of feelings (e.g., shame, embarrassment, guilt) that can emerge in talking about family violence.
- Focus on types of coping behaviors (e.g., avoidance, denial, rationalization) employed by these young men to deal with their exposure to parental fights and arguments.

In providing clinical care to young men impacted by IPV, these points can help clients talk about the psychological pain associated with witnessing violence and knowing that their parents are in harm's way. Clinical care can also help shift their cognitions about patriarchal ideas that may underpin their socialization and thus shape their relational connections to women and girls. In addition, having knowledge of the undermining effects of social problems (e.g., poverty, community violence, and the lack of resources present in communities) serves to contextualize the lived experiences of young men exposed to violence at home, a critical factor in assessing their coping behaviors. This therapeutic approach is one example of an adolescent male who garnered emotional support from therapy and was exposed to cognitive behavioral strategies that instilled hope and a desire to modify the pattern of his life, thereby preventing him from emulating his abusive father's violent behavior in adult relationships. Moreover, clinical work with this group can also focus on the internalizations of rigid gender-role expectations in terms of how issues of privilege are often synonymous with masculine identities, and the psychic hazards of subscribing to male dominance and conquest in interpersonal relationships.

Discussion Questions

1. What aspects of Bryant's case increased your knowledge of how IPV affects adolescent males?
2. How would you assess Bryant's exposure to IPV given his cultural context?
3. What stood out for you regarding Bryant's relationship with his parents?
4. How would you assess Bryant's relationship with his girlfriend, Ebony?
5. To what extent have sociodemographic factors affected Bryant's understanding of himself and his exposure to violence at home?
6. What surprised you the most about this chapter?
7. What else would you want to know about Bryant's exposure to IPV in order to garner a more complete clinical assessment?
8. If Bryant was your client, how would you engage with him around his ambiguous feelings relative to his abusive father?
9. Overall, what were the most important features of this chapter?

CHAPTER 5

Mothering and Motherhood in the Context of IPV

Mothers and their children living in the cycle of intimate partner violence (IPV) constantly wrestle with the threat of danger that comes from living with or being connected to abusive partners or fathers. Taking this into account, this chapter addresses what it means physically and psychologically for abused mothers to manage keeping themselves safe while remaining watchful over the practical and emotional needs of their children. Highlighting the unsafe relational landscape that abused mothers must navigate with their abusive partners, the chapter focuses on how this fraught existence forces women to stay safe so that they can parent their children. The chapter is premised on the fact that IPV adds another layer of emotional heaviness to parenting, given that all forms of dominance directed at women by their partners and spouses can lead to psychological ruptures (i.e., psychic strain in the attachment process) in the mother–child attachment system.

Based on a recent qualitative study, an account of how one mother (Janet) lives and copes with partner abuse while parenting her sons is presented. In addition, there is a summary of clinical practice with a mother (Suzanne) who sought psychotherapy following her divorce from her abuser. Principles of cognitive behavior therapy (CBT) to promote healing and recovery from the cycle of relational abuse are applied. Both scenarios represent experiences common to many mothers, whose coping responses to IPV include surviving while carrying out maternal functions (i.e., attending to the instrumental and psychological needs of children). Finally, the chapter explores the sociopolitical and psychological implications of motherhood and mothering against the backdrop of society's traditional positioning of women and through the prism of the changing landscape of family life, birth, and parenthood.

Traditional Positioning of Women and Mothers

Mothering denotes the behavioral and affective activities necessary to raise and nurture children. Likewise, *motherhood* speaks to the feelings and emotions of being a mother that bolster the parent–child attachment experience (Bowlby,

1988; Winnicott, 1965). Neither notion can be detached from society's "traditional positioning" of women: that is, they are expected to be mothers who will competently carry out the roles, responsibilities, and functions of raising children in spite of adversity. Linked to motherhood and mothering, the traditional positioning of women is an intrinsic part of society and has imprinted our collective knowledge of mothers, a point relevant to the general premise and tone of this book. So, turning our attention to society at large and its notions of family, it is understood that women are expected to be emotionally and psychically accessible to their children from conception throughout their developmental processes. Etched in the psychosocial worldviews of many mothers (cognitive and psychological schema) are the ubiquitous societal projections and images about motherhood and its relationship to girls' and women's lives, which appear in all facets of our culture. Womanhood and girlhood are correlated with motherhood, and the potency of messages that appear in movies, commercials, and fairy tales intrude on the imaginations of both groups. The "biological clock" metaphor, which can dominate the mind of women of a certain age and induces anxiety for many, represents in part the impact of societal messages regarding the centrality of motherhood in women's lives. Women who have no desire to undertake the role of motherhood may be left with feelings of inadequacy and self-doubt, in particular when they are placed in a position of having to rationalize or defend their decision. Such feelings have surfaced in my therapy practice with a variety of female clients who have expressed ambivalence and uncertainty about being mothers. Discomfort and even guilt have underlined therapeutic work with this group, especially when these women processed their lack of interest in becoming mothers. These clients revealed they have not felt emotionally drawn to motherhood, and they questioned the possible psychological pathology underlying their feelings and decisions (many have wondered if their lack of urge to be mothers is normal). Feminist writers posit that the social and familial expectations of being a mother are so strong that women who are uninterested in having children are ridiculed (D'Arcy et al., 2011). The point of all this is that differing values among women about being a mother should not be omitted from motherhood and mothering discourses. To do so is to reinforce a false narrative, giving the impression that all women have an innate yearning to become mothers simply because of their gender. To a great extent, this false narrative diverts our attention away from the socially prescribed images of what it means to be a woman. On the one hand, traditional patriarchal teachings create dichotomous realities for men and women in relation to family life, where men are expected to be breadwinners and women caregivers. On the other hand, the traditional spheres of motherhood and mothering may comport with other women's definition and grasp of their gender identity, albeit under the dominance of societal outlook and expectations. Feminist scholars claim, "Becoming a mother is a rite of passage in many women's lives" (D'Arcy et al., 2011). These same scholars note that the idea of becoming a mother exposes a woman to sociocultural and political matters such as social policies concerning pay equity and child and health care.

The changing expectations of family lifestyles and the changing position of women in society have brought innovative and new approaches (e.g., couples involved in surrogacy, couples identified as gender nonconforming) to becoming a mother. Couples and noncouples (e.g., lesbians, single-parent heads of household) can use surrogacy in pursuit of becoming a mother, which is a clear departure from the conventional way of becoming a parent. To subscribe to a static conception of motherhood and mothering in the twenty-first century is unwise: that lesbians or (male-to-female) transgender men may have a desire to or may actually become mothers and parents underscores the fact that an exploration of this subject adds complexities to our assumptions about gender, identity, roles, and social status relative to who can or should be mothers and parents. Current debates surrounding birth, parenthood, and family life are not new, not unlike the occurrences of single parenthood in the 1970s, which were viewed by proponents of the nuclear family as antithetical to the traditional institution of marriage and the American family (where the cultural norm was for children to grow up in two-parent homes consisting of a man and a woman). Many people who respected the nuclear family system were dismissive of single-parent head-of-household families, attitudes driven by cultural and racial bias, and this meant that motherhood and mothering for certain groups of women (black and brown women in particular) were maligned. Social class and race also explained this stance, according to Kawash (2011), who states, "Middle-class stereotypes dismiss poor, unmarried mothers as incompetent in their willingness or inability to use birth control or else as malicious schemers using children as a way to gain access to more welfare benefits" (p. 979). In other words, the meanings that have been ascribed to some mothers were based on their social, racial, and cultural position (D'Arcy et al., 2011). In a broader sense, this suggests that the idea of social location can also capture the circumstances faced by women who are victims of IPV and still hold the role and the responsibilities of motherhood. Some in society, disregarding the terror such a mother feels from being victimized, still question her competency when she remains in an abusive relationship. From the perspectives of family, culture, and politics, all of this adds nuance to the paradigm of motherhood, a reality that influences the lives of women.

The Psychological Impact of IPV on Mothers

The literature explicates that all forms of IPV (e.g., physical, emotional, economical) place women in a dangerous position and can obstruct their ability to parent their children (Krane & Davies, 2007; Lapierre, 2010). What is important about this claim is that rather than blaming women for not being "good mothers," it is essential to know that the presence of violence in their lives—regardless of whether they stay or leave the violence—has an impact on self-esteem and self-development. The traumatic stress associated with IPV predisposes women to engage in a negative devaluation of themselves that culminates in feelings of depression and anxiety (Bancroft et al., 2012; Herman, 1992; Mechanic et al., 2008). Advocates, practitioners, and clinicians should not underestimate how the psychosocial sequelae of abused mothers can contribute to mental health challenges; knowing this permits professionals to contextualize the many ways the abusers' tactics actually control the body, mind, and spirit of these women. Such tactics include physical, sexual, economic, and emotional abuse, creating a climate of control and subordination, which can induce feelings of fear and a sense of dread that can lead to depression. Research points out that depressive symptoms manifesting in an inability to sleep, chronic sadness, low energy, and a bleak view of life can be debilitating, in particular in the absence of medication or psychotherapeutic services (Celani, 1994; Goldstein, 1995). In a discussion of the extent to which violence in the family impedes mothers' functioning, Herman (1992) argues that it is parallel to the level of terror that triggers traumatic reactions and mars their sense of well-being. A central factor is that although mothers are subjected to maltreatment by their abusers, they still cope, which enables them to parent their children, and given their seeming resilience we should refrain from reprimanding mothers who are parenting in spite of IPV.

Motherhood and Pregnancy

It is clear from clinical practice and the literature that abused women experience physical and psychological ill-treatment from their abusers during all phases of the relationship, and as such violence during pregnancy should not be overlooked in light of the risk it represents in a woman's relational journey with her abuser. Moreover, we know from the literature that several factors can occur during pregnancy: violence can be more pronounced during pregnancy, or it may cease temporarily, during which time some women may feel some sense of relief (Campbell, 2004; Campbell et al., 2007). This temporary cessation of violence is analogous to Walker's (1979) "honeymoon" phase of the cycle of violence (noted in chapter 1), where men's seeming contrition about their abusive behaviors interrupts the sequence of abuse and thus offers a much-needed respite to victims. The honeymoon phase cannot obliterate tactics of psychological abuse that have enduring consequences on women's welfare, and this fact should produce empathy for mothers, especially those who are expecting. McFarlane et al. (2002) note that pregnancy is a difficult time for abused mothers because they face threats of homicide from the abuse. Indeed, the psychological toll of carrying a child under such conditions involves emotional pain and terror (Campbell, 2004; Herman, 1992). As conditions for survival, pregnant abused women must develop coping skills that will allow them to withstand abusive behaviors that could be harmful to themselves and their unborn children. Abused mothers, moreover, have to monitor their physical health by seeing their physicians, which may be hampered by the abuser's exercise of power and control. This type of control also places both the mother and her unborn children at significant risk.

The intersection of IPV and pregnancy shapes women's understanding of motherhood, and this can reverberate for those women whose pregnancy may have occurred due to unwanted sex (rape as a tactic of power and control) by the abuser, which is not an uncommon dynamic in IPV cases. That most abusers exercise coercive control to police their partner's body underscores how sexual assault and even rape are used to humiliate, subjugate, and induce fear in women. The narrative of pregnancy originating from sexual violation can complicate how women in abusive relationships feel about themselves and their unborn child. Having no desire to give birth to a child who was conceived from a rape, but being forced to do so by the abuser, can be traumatic for pregnant women. Furthermore, there are women who may have felt fearful of voicing their lack of desire to be mothers under such a condition. Implicit in these observations are the connections among IPV, pregnancy, and sexual assault/rape, which should serve to remind us that reproductive control can be a tactic of abuse in these relationships. Thus, for some women, becoming a mother can be fraught, and practitioners should create therapeutic spaces for abused women to talk about the full scope of their maternal experiences and the emotions associated with them.

The View of Mothering and Children's Welfare

Practitioners and clinicians, experienced or inexperienced, must think about how mothers of all socioeconomic, cultural, and racial backgrounds and sexual orientations deal with IPV while parenting children. Interestingly, this insight surfaced in my research on coping responses among adolescent males (between the ages of fourteen and seventeen) who witnessed IPV at home (Aymer, 2008a). Recurring themes shared by the young men in the study spoke to whether their mothers were aware of how IPV had affected them, and whether their mothers had taken steps to leave their fathers. Similar questions have come to light among students enrolled in my graduate-level social work class on violence against women: students expressed curiosity about the psychology of abused mothers raising their children in an onerous familial milieu. In addition, professionals who have participated in training seminars and workshops I have led have articulated similar sentiments. Underlying the groups' reflections was the question of whose rights should be protected when mothering is occurring in the context of IPV. Should it be the rights of mothers or the rights of children? At the heart of these observations was a genuine need on the part of trainees to understand this complicated facet of partner abuse and family dynamics, a professional curiosity influenced by the trainees' empathic reactions to both children and their mothers.

Still, for trainees working in fields of practice such as child welfare, hospitals, school social work, and shelters for abused women, issues specific to child safety bring into sharper focus the associated viewpoints of children who witness parental abuse as well as the fact that they exhibit a range of behavioral and psychological difficulties (Cook et al., 2005). Knowing about IPV within the family raises questions about the welfare of children and heightens the concerns of professionals who are legally mandated to report incidents in which children are at risk of abuse or neglect. Research indicates the professional child welfare community evaluates children's exposure to IPV as maltreatment, even if they have not been subjected to physical abuse (James, 1994; Mckay, 1994). Another attitude responsible for our thinking about the connections between children's exposure to partner abuse in the family system and child abuse and neglect is buttressed by concepts such as social learning theory, the cyclical nature of IPV, and intergenerational factors, all of which can lead professionals to make clinical conjectures about the psychological implications of witnessing IPV and children's emotional functioning (Bandura, 1973; Ehrensaft et al., 2003; Jaffe et al., 1990). These ideas and attitudes continue to influence child welfare social policies and practices (e.g., mandated reporting based on reasonable suspicion of abuse and neglect). As a result, licensed social workers, advocates, and other mental-health practitioners are required to protect the rights of children in IPV households. It makes sense for this group to examine their legal and ethical responsibilities, and pay attention to and evaluate what steps, if any, have been employed by abused mothers to address the problem, as opposed to reflexively attributing blame to their character or their apparent decision to stay in the abusive relationship. The strategies many abused mothers use for obtaining an order of protection or planning an escape route from their abuser, for instance, illustrate how they ensure protection and security for themselves and their children. Abused women's fortitude and resilience are characteristics they bring to bear to combat or minimize partner abuse—thereby emphasizing their will to remain safe for their children, a finding captured in my qualitative study on mothers' perceptions of parenting their adolescent sons in the context of IPV (Aymer, 2019). All mothers in that study spoke of ways they tried to remain safe, including calling the police and leaving the abusive relationship.

Raising Children under Fire

We know from mainstream feminist scholarship and research that although being a mother can bring joy and gratification to many women's lives, it also requires self-sacrifice, a view that society upholds and instills in the psychology of many women. Correspondingly, the lived circumstances of motherhood and mothering look and feel different for women from differing cultures: issues of race, culture, immigration, migration, sexual orientation, gender identity, and religious and political diversity inform how children are raised, educated, and cared for, especially regarding different access to financial resources, familial support, and social support systems. Raising children within patriarchy places enormous expectations on mothers to be omnipotent and "super" competent in general, which can elicit doubts and a sense of uneasiness. Uncertainty and worry about being a "good enough" mother can have particular resonance for women raising children under the fire of IPV, which is deeply entrenched in family dynamics and processes (Winnicott, 1965). Violence can occur at any time, leaving mothers psychologically and physically wounded, yet they may still have to project an image of "wellness" to foster stability and a sense of calm in their children. This is captured in qualitative data regarding several mothers' accounts of how violence affected their sons, who were grappling with revenge fantasies:

Barbara indicated that, "The children tried their best not make any noise around the house, especially my teen son, Mickey, who was protecting of me." This view was held by Maria, who said, "Yeah, 'cause my son would talk to me and tell me, like, 'I just I want to get a bat and bash his head in.' But that was just frustration in him . . . and me being his mother and him being my son, he felt he should defend me." Janet said, "My son jumped him [the batterer] and they started to fight, I know my son was tryin' to protect me." Moreover, Nia, Wanda, Maritza, and Melba felt their adolescent sons used "violence and anger" to fight their stepfathers' and/or fathers' abusive behaviors. Anna's son stated, "I can't take it no more mom. You let him beat you up and one day I am going to protect you. Am a kill that man. He beat you up and you cry all time. I need to protect you from him. Am a hurt him real bad and he have to stop beatin' on you all the time. I am so mad at him all the time." (Aymer, 2019, p. 10)

These exchanges between mothers and their sons demonstrate the resulting effects of IPV on children's emotional and behavioral functioning. What can be extrapolated from these narratives? That mothers have to manage their safety and prepare their sons to be functioning adults with the additional overlay of also helping them develop protective behaviors to regulate their apparent murderous rage toward their fathers and stepfathers.

The Role of Secrets within IPV Family Systems

As noted above, young men in my earlier study pondered whether their mothers were aware of how IPV impaired their functioning and what, if any, steps their mothers took to solve or stop the violence (Aymer, 2008a). Secrets within a family are not unique to those with mothers who face intimate abuse. Family therapist and scholar Boyd-Franklin (2003) writes that secrets are prevalent among families in general. In particular, Boyd-Franklin's research focuses on black families, and she points out that patterns of keeping secrets can prevent family members from knowing certain truths pertinent to their emotional development. Likewise, in some households, abused mothers may avoid talking directly to their children about relational abuse and familial turmoil. Children are left with troubling feelings about hearing arguments and seeing fights between their parents, but they may not be able to verbalize their worries due to a tacit acknowledgment of the silence surrounding the family. Adolescent males who were in the midst of their psychosocial development and who were trying to make sense of the world revealed that exposure to their father's abuse was extremely challenging and complicated (Aymer, 2008a). Though these young men had some positive feelings for their abusive fathers, they also grappled with the urge to hurt their fathers because they perceived their mothers as helpless and defenseless. Beaumont (2012) writes that "it is natural for a child to worry about his mother's well-being and happiness and to want to do whatever he can to help her" (p. 35). Central to this postulation, Beaumont makes the point that relational discord among parents provokes in children, especially boys, the need to physically and emotionally connect with their mothers in order to offer some measure of comfort to them, and to unconsciously assuage their own discomfort.

Women experiencing IPV in the family may engage in keeping secrets to protect the emotions of their children and preserve the family, possibly concealing feelings of shame and guilt related to remaining with an abuser. As an adaptive factor, keeping secrets of this kind can shield, albeit temporarily, young children from obsessing about the survival of their parents' relationship. A significant question for this age, when crises are preeminent in their lives, is this: Who will take care of me if my parents sever their relationship? This question is suggestive of anticipatory reactions to the threat of abandonment or even homicide. As a maladaptive factor, avoiding talking about parental violence could reinforce in children and adolescents that violence is normative in families, which can begin to shape their attitudes and create a model for what constitutes healthy intimate relationships. The powerlessness and unprotectedness that many children feel from knowing about or witnessing the abuse of their mothers should not be underestimated. Aymer (2008a) found that all of the young men spoke openly of the toxic effects of being exposed to their parents' verbal and physical fights, such as their use of drugs to numb their emotional pain, their use of violence in interpersonal relationships and intimate relationships with girlfriends—mimicking what they observed between their parents—and their preoccupation with their mother's safety, all of which led to poor academic performance. The overarching point was the heightened state of concern these young men felt regarding their mother's safety due to violence at home. In addition, knowing their mothers were attuned to their feelings was personally empowering, even when these young men felt their age, physical size, and gender overshadowed their mothers' outward lack of responsiveness to their emotional state (Aymer, 2008a). Mentioned previously, Aymer (2019) embarked on another study in which the data revealed that although mothers did not directly engage their sons on facets of the abuse narratives, they were cognizant of the ways IPV affected their sons, and this became an important impetus for them to leave the abusive situation. Mothers in this study made it known they did not want their sons to emulate their fathers' abusive behaviors, a clear indication that they wanted to interrupt the potential perpetration of the abusive cycle common in families where IPV is widespread. A lesson that can be discerned from exploring the dimensions of being a mother and a victim simultaneously is that the crisis mode some women find themselves in may be emotionally depleting, and as a result they may not be able to harness enough psychic energy to engage their children directly about how the abuse is affecting them, or even talk about plans to escape from the abuser (Aymer, 2019). As a reframe, however, keeping secrets may be understood as an unintentional dynamic that enables abused mothers to cope with IPV and its consequences for their children. This avoidant coping behavior should not be interpreted as a lack of receptiveness to their children's needs; instead, it may be understood as an abused mother's way of managing maternal guilt and regret stemming from societal messages about a mother's role in protecting her children from adversity. In light of this, blaming a mother compounds negative feelings about herself and her children. Thus, it is reasonable for service providers and therapists working with IPV cases to be cognizant of how the aforementioned findings are pertinent to children's exposure, and offer support in order to empower them.

Ruptured Mother–Child Relational Processes

The primacy of motherhood and mothering in children's growth is well documented in the psychoanalytical literature (Baker & Baker, 1987; Blos, 1962; Bowlby, 1988; Kohut, 1977; Winnicott, 1965). The premise of these theories is that children's maturation is predicated on strong attachment and relational dynamics with their mothers. In his analysis of motherhood, Beaumont (2012) writes,

> Mother is the gate through which all humans arrive in the world. Poetically viewed, her womb is an empty space, a nothingness in which all human life begins, and she offers her body to host this mystery of entry into Being. She accepts the risk of pain and death to give her children a chance to live. We know that early learning begins in the womb, so from the perspective of the fetus, Mother is the whole world, surrounding, embracing, holding, nourishing, and protecting. Everything beyond mother comes to the fetus filtered through her and a fetus has little chance to recognize what is or is not mother. (p. 39)

Beaumont is making the point that motherhood is a powerful role that is associated with external and internal processes geared to advancing life in the human organism. Similarly, Winnicott (1965) argues that there is no baby without its mother—another powerful observation pertaining to the centrality of motherhood and mothering in children's lives. Despite such claims, the role is imperfect and is riddled with challenges that negatively affect children. IPV adds to the constellation of challenges that can rupture mothers' relationships with their children.

Fleeing an abusive situation can cause an emotional breach in the parent–child relational orbit. As such, fleeing the abuser can take myriad forms: some women temporarily leave the abuser, while others leave permanently; for others, leaving can mean seeking refuge in a battered women's shelter for a limited period of time or relocating to a different state or country. For others, escaping the abuser means leaving their child with family. For some women, leaving temporarily means they return to the abuser due to fear, financial insecurity, and anxiety; others may return to their abuser because they want their children to have access to their father, or they may struggle with ambivalence about the relationship. Mothers have to consider such options, and this has an effect on how they interact with their children, exercise their maternal duties, and adjust to a role of motherhood that is laden with apprehension about remaining alive. The need to remain safe and alive is chiefly related to a strong maternal yearning that is an outgrowth of society's social construction of motherhood, denoting that it is incumbent upon mothers to be physically and emotionally available to facilitate the growth of their children (Aymer, 2019; Bancroft et al., 2012; Vatnar & Bjorkly, 2010). This view is reinforced by developmental theorists who argue that the process of connecting to caregivers, especially mothers, is crucial because parental interactions with children influence their social and psychological development (Bowlby, 1988). Furthermore, this process begins during infancy and continues throughout the life cycle. Bowlby's notion of "internal working models" is germane to the essence of this chapter: he suggests that there is a dynamic interplay between children's sense of themselves and their attachment (caregivers/mothers), which they internalize. These internalized behavioral and emotional parts of their parents enable children to anticipate their parents' actions and attitudes, and in turn this makes them feel attached, creating the pathways for adult relationships. Thus, as a psychological imperative, feeling securely attached to caregivers/mothers shapes children's overall development (Bowlby, 1988). And Herman's (1992) research underscores that "a secure sense of connection with caring people is the foundation of personality development" (p. 52).

Notwithstanding abused mothers' abiding regard for their children, research reveals that women are affected by the climate of oppression produced by victimization (Lavendosky et al., 2000). This study found that abused mothers' relationships with their children were marred; in particular, they felt frustrated with children who exhibited abusive behaviors similar to the abuser and demonstrated less maternal warmth to them. An observation inferred from the study was that the psychological and physical abuse that undergirded these mothers' lives impeded their capacity to be attuned to the emotional needs of their children. Findings from this and other studies reveal that the stressors induced by living in an abusive relationship can compromise the quality of attachment and interpersonal relatedness needed to provide a secure base for the mother–child matrix (Aymer, 2008a, 2019; Vatnar & Bjorkly, 2010). Aymer's (2008a) study on adolescent boys' exposure to IPV in the home, for instance, uncovered that they had ambivalent feelings toward their mothers for remaining with their abusive fathers. Admitting that their feelings strained their interactions with their mother afforded the young men the opportunity to speak about the split loyalty they felt: having feelings for their abusive fathers and feeling empathy for their abused mothers. To comprehend this aspect of many women's maternal journey is to appreciate that tension between mothers and their children are inevitable given the pernicious consequences of IPV. The traumatic reactions originating from being victimized are responsible for many mothers' inability to attend to the psychosocial needs of their children, as opposed to moral failings, an important aspect of mothering and IPV that should characterize service delivery and clinical work.

Excerpts from a Qualitative Interview with Janet

Ten abused mothers participated in an exploratory study and provided compelling accounts of parenting their adolescent sons while dealing with partner abuse (Aymer, 2019). Face-to-face interviews (each lasting three hours) with the women took place at a battered women's shelter. Janet was a forty-four-year-old African American woman with three children, ages three, four, and seven, and she disclosed that partner abuse was present during her adolescence, young adulthood, and adulthood. The abuse she suffered during adolescence occurred at fourteen with her first boyfriend, John, who would berate her if she disagreed with him. Delineating numerous instances when he emotionally attacked her resulted in tears during the interview. Janet questioned if she could have done anything to curb his behavior other than acquiescing to his control. In one situation, they agreed to meet at the local delicatessen to purchase lunch during the summer. When she arrived late, he attacked her in front of their peers and friends, purchased his lunch, and left the delicatessen without her. Janet noted this incident still affects her because she felt belittled and humiliated. Ending this relationship was difficult because she liked John, who was also a friend of her family. She had similar experiences with other boys but felt John's abusive behavior was more injurious.

Young adulthood ushered in a pattern of dating rife with relational violence from several men. Like her teen dating-abuse experience, many of these men degraded her by engaging in body and slut shaming. She said that she was "a bit chubby" during this period of her life, and men used her appearance to attack her during arguments and disputes. She was perceived as fat, ugly, and chubby, names that made her felt self-conscious about her body. She eventually had difficulty with sexual intimacy with many of these men, and this led to a diminishment in sex, for which she was accused of infidelity by boyfriends, who referred to her to as a whore and a slut. Though Janet understood that the experiences she had during her adolescence and young adulthood meant that she was being abused, she did note that at least these relationships did not involve physical violence. It became evident during the interview that Janet felt physical abuse was more significant than emotional abuse.

Meeting Cyril and marrying him after a six-month courtship felt comfortable for Janet, who did not encounter any abusiveness until their marriage. The initial episode of abuse happened during their wedding night, when she was unable to be sexually intimate due to fatigue and migraine headaches. Cyril exercised physical abuse to signal to Janet that her state of being on their wedding night was unacceptable to him. Shocked by his reactions, Janet conceded to his sexual desires for the following reasons: she wanted the aggression and violence to stop, and she wanted to fulfill what she referred to "as her wifely duties," remarking that she felt guilty for not being sexually responsive to his needs on their wedding night. The ensuing years with Cyril were saturated with all forms of IPV (sexual, physical, emotional, and economic). She observed his irritability during her pregnancy; he accused her of not paying attention to him, and condemned her character as a woman, mother, and partner. In particular, Cyril's abuse became frequent and more destructive over the years. He stabbed her once, raped her several times, and bludgeoned her self-esteem with a barrage of insults, innuendos, and hateful comments. Her ambivalent feelings for Cyril prevented Janet from pursuing legal action against him, and she also did not want her children to grow up without a father, which would have been like her own family life. Her parents' marital discord was marked with fights and arguments, sparking memories of the police removing her father from the family due to his violence. A bitter divorce signified the end of her parents' marriage, and the resulting impact centered on conflicts around the payment of child support and visitation issues. Holding her mother responsible for splintering the family was a recurring theme that dominated her mind until her early twenties. At the time of the interview, Janet admitted that she still felt to some extent that her mother could have sought family counseling to cope with her abuse and preserve the family.

Though Janet was reticent about seeking police intervention, she made it clear that it had become increasingly challenging to cope with Cyril's violence; his threat of homicide after a heated argument between them felt palpable, and for that reason she reported the incident to the police. Cyril was arrested, and after court proceedings Janet obtained an order of protection that led to his removal from the apartment. After several months, he violated the stipulations (the judge ordered him to stay away from Janet) when he attempted to return to the apartment and threatened to hurt Janet and the children. These actions motivated her to avail herself of shelter services. Prior to this, Janet stayed with her mother without her children for several weeks as a means of managing Cyril's violence. Believing he would not hurt the children bolstered her confidence in taking the risk of leaving them in his care so that she could feel some sense of relief from his abuse. But she reported that her decision to leave the children with her abuser left her with regrets. She was preoccupied with abandoning the children in order to sever the relationship. The thought of abandoning her children was incongruous with her conception of motherhood, and this created a great deal of conflict about what it meant to be a "mother and a wife" whose life was engulfed by maltreatment and terror by someone who claimed to love her.

Reflections of Janet's Narrative

As noted, my relationship to Janet was that of a researcher who sought to conduct an exploratory study focusing on parenting in the midst of IPV. Because the purposes and functions of a researcher are different from being a clinician, I was not allowed to employ interventions with Janet (or any of the other women). Reflections on the interview, however, are presented as a conceptual frame for deepening our view of the responsibility women deal with as they parent and maintain healthy relationships with their children while remaining safe. Therefore, in thinking of Janet's story, it makes sense to view it through multiple lenses: her exposure to violence at home as a child, her abusive relationship during adolescence, and her encounter with IPV as an adult. How familial and intimate abuse has intruded on her psychological growth offered a fuller picture of the apparent sense of vulnerability she had to undergo (and perhaps continue) throughout her life. Even with such a view, it should be understood that feelings of vulnerability are common among many abused mothers irrespective of whether they have gone through the abusive events that have been imprinted on Janet's life.

It cannot be denied that being a woman contributed to the abusive relational patterns Janet confronted. And central to this inference is that all the men in her life used emotional and physical abuse to control her actions and mind. We know that women's self-growth in the context of IPV can be diminished by psychological maladies, including depressive symptoms, heightened feelings of anxiety, and traumatic reactions (Hardest et al., 2015; Herman, 1992). Their effects impair the psychic foundation mothers need in order to instill a stable and secure base in children, who may be preoccupied with their mortality, as Janet noted. For example, leaving her children with her abusive husband was a practical strategy for her to remain alive—given the severity of the violence—and, taking a closer look at her narrative, her decision to do so may have been indicative of her desperation. The need for peace, physical safety, and security seemed to have been resonant for Janet, considering the worrying conditions she lived through. And based on this fact, mothering through pain, sadness, and regret seemed to characterize her relationship with her children, reinforcing how partner abuse charts a complex familial course for abused mothers and their children.

Excerpts from Clinical Practice

Suzanne is fifty-four-year-old white woman who sought help from a clinic to deal with issues of grief and mourning due to a tumultuous and abusive relationship with her ex-husband, Neil, who has custody of their two sons, ages twelve and thirteen. Suzanne met Neil several years ago and dated him briefly prior to marriage. They seemed to have a good relationship until one day when he became explosive when they had a disagreement over finances. Unbeknownst to Suzanne, Neil had withdrawn a significant amount of money from their joint checking account. Her query about this matter elicited an angry outburst from Neil, who yelled at her and grabbed her throat. His rationale for reacting in this way was that he felt emasculated; he did not believe Suzanne should have questioned him about their funds. To be clear, Neil felt Suzanne was "out of place" for questioning his motives and integrity even though he did not inform her about his withdrawals. Prior to this incident, she described him as low-key and quiet: he had not displayed any signs of aggression toward her. Several months subsequent to the tension regarding his withdrawal of funds from their account, she observed combativeness in their communications; he reacted defensively when she shared her observation with him, which brought about a sense of uneasiness in her. Their communications shifted radically, and tenseness and silence enveloped their marriage, causing fear and nervousness in Suzanne.

Both children were affected by the household dynamics, according to Suzanne, who believed that her husband shared negative thoughts about her with the children—a ploy that turned them against her—and strained her relationship with them. Suzanne spoke of the emotional pain she felt as the children gravitated toward their father, a clear indication that he wanted to alienate the children from her. Suzanne felt disrespected and expressed how much this behavior undermined her as a woman and a mother. In the midst of alienating the children from Suzanne, Neil continued to degrade her, calling into question her competency as a mother and a wife: he blamed her for destroying the marriage and damaging the children's mental health. Diagnosed with depression and anxiety, both children were taking medication and receiving psychotherapeutic services from a community mental health clinic. Both parents were expected to attend family sessions as an adjunct to the children's treatment regimen; however, this proved to be contraindicated based on the contentious arguments that ensued during family sessions. Such behavior made it difficult for the children to process feelings and express themselves via therapy. The therapists for the children terminated family meetings in order to protect the mental health of the boys.

Prior to their divorce, misery and fear exemplified their marriage. The divorce, however, eased the emotional and psychological hurt Suzanne felt from Neil. But she was unhappy and troubled by the outcome of a bitter custody trial, during which the court granted Neil custody of the children, following their wishes to reside with him. Not anticipating such a result, Suzanne was shocked and surprised, which further reinforced the vitriolic comments made by her husband about her competency as a parent. Depressive symptoms that affected her work performance and her social life motivated Suzanne to avail herself of psychotherapy. Her primary concern focused on her desire to have a healthy relationship with the children so that she could maximize her visitation rights. Still emotionally managing the remnants of her abusive relationship, she verbalized the likely impact of her feelings on her sons during their time together, acknowledging that she realized this could continue to weaken their relationship. Suzanne appeared extremely committed to salvaging her psychological ties with her sons, who were showing some interest in being with her despite the familial turbulence, and this was an additional incentive for Suzanne to address her personal challenges in therapy.

Clinical Assessment

Neil's abusiveness, a destabilizing force in Suzanne's life, affected her relationship with her children. The constellations of violent acts (including sexual assault, withholding funds, and physical altercations) he perpetuated affected her sense of self. She made every effort to cooperate with him, an attitude she felt was intrinsic to her role as a wife. At the same time, living with chronic abuse weakened her relationship with her children in that he tried to alienate them from her. His actions made it problematic for her to feel she could cultivate a close and loving relationship with them. Yet she had to constantly find a course of action that would preserve her physical and emotional safety while nurturing a parental course instilled with love and a sense of connection in spite of the alienation she felt on the part of the children.

A closer examination of her plight showed she had depressive symptoms: inability to sleep; chronic feelings of sadness, fear, and anxiety; constant crying; and lack of physical energy. Suzanne did not frame these reactions as depressive symptoms; instead, she spoke of them in a straightforward, unemotional fashion. Her demeanor and reaction appeared to be emblematic of how she attempted to cope with the chaos, uncertainty, and lack of safety that punctuated the marriage. Increased understanding of how all forms of Neil's abusive behavior affected her after the divorce, particularly given the emotional strain she felt during and after visitation with her sons, caused her to think about the importance of personal healing so that she could feel more psychologically connected to them. All of this seemed to be indicative of Suzanne's resilience and that she was determined not to give up on herself or her children. Such a theme also emerged throughout the previously noted qualitative study conducted by Aymer (2019): all participants demonstrated a resolute love for their children, despite the multiplicity of effects of violence on their emotional functioning.

Suzanne's Therapy

At first, therapeutic work with Suzanne focused on the reverberations of her husband's abuse on her psychological well-being. She expressed hurt and regret throughout the sessions. First, she spoke of the psychic and physical damages that lingered, pointing to a facial scar that had resulted from her husband's cruelty, and complained of having nightmares in which he was abusing her. Second, she voiced regrets about her failure to dissolve the relationship following the first episode of abuse. The intent of therapy was to provide a safe place—one that would validate and affirm the sense of hope that enabled her to survive a brutal ordeal. Survival, however, meant grasping how the negative behavior she endured from her husband pierced her cognitive schema and influenced her thoughts and actions. The literature suggests that a person's schema permits them to structure and synthesize information and experiences that can have an effect on behavior (e.g., Granvold, 2011). Many women internalize the psychological and physical abuse they endure; in turn, they can experience cognitive distortion about themselves, arousing negative affect that results in depression, a factor the seemed evident in therapy with Suzanne. Her anxiety and self-doubt were attributed to Neil's criticisms of her as a mother and a spouse. The construct of cognitive therapy specifies that the meaning clients attribute to negative messaging they receive from others tends to exacerbate their view of life. Using this approach, therapy helped Suzanne explore an array of ways Neil's behavior became the template for how she perceived herself. Feelings of inadequacy as a mother were framed for her as a cognitive distortion centering on the abusive messages she heard from Neil and even society's messages about what constitutes "good mothering," especially when IPV is present. Reframing cognitive distortions is a technique used in therapy to help a client identify the origins of their faulty thought processes and the resulting implications for socioemotional functioning. Beck (1967), one of the major researchers on cognitive therapy, indicates that cognitive distortions can have a wide-ranging impact on how people see themselves and the world around them. Distortions about self and others undermine people's mental health. For instance, Northcut et al. (2016) state that clients affected by cognitive distortions often suffer the following:

dichotomous thinking (using polarized categories such as "I am all bad or all good"); *overgeneralizing* (taking an isolated incident and assuming all events are due to the same incidents or will result in the same ending); *catastrophizing* (focusing on the worst); *personalizing* (assuming personal responsibility for events in which there is no control); and *discounting the positive* (explaining away any positive events as unimportant or suspect). (p. 237)

Two distinctive cognitive distortions present in Suzanne's formulation of herself were dichotomous thinking and personalizing. The process of reframing occurred when Suzanne and her therapist examined the triggers that tend to stimulate negative misrepresentations of herself. Northcut et al. (2016) assert that this permits the therapist to develop a contextual grasp of the client's cognitive schema in a holistic fashion. Thus, therapy reframed for Suzanne that abuse did not have to define her, emphasizing she was not only an abused, divorced mother who was estranged from her children. Instead, it helped her search for other dimensions of herself, such as the fact that she is a survivor seeking personal restoration and growth as a woman and a mother, enabling her to think of her story in more adaptive and strengths-based ways. Likewise, personalizing her situation proved to be counterproductive: she blamed herself for not terminating the marriage during the initial phases of Neil's emotional abuse and violence. Pointing to the culture of fear she claimed Neil promoted in order to manipulate and control her was another reframing approach used in therapy to facilitate self-reflection regarding the emotional stresses and strains associated with sustaining her continued existence under dire circumstances. Overall, the goal was to minimize self-blame, an emotional feature common among abused women that can foster depression and anxiety (Aymer, 2019; Walker, 1979). In order to sustain the therapeutic work, Suzanne was introduced to the notion of maintaining a diary in which she would chart her cognitive, emotional, and behavioral processes. Charting allowed her to make connections among feelings, actions, and thought process, in particular when she experienced intrusive thoughts about her history of being battered. The following therapeutic points, inspired by CBT (Beck, 1967; Corcoran, 2006), were suggested as a basis for practicing personal introspection:

- What specific feelings do you have when you think about Neil?
- What specific thoughts are present when you think of the relationship you had with Neil?
- When do you find yourself thinking or focusing on your abusive experiences?
- How long do these feelings and reactions last in your thought processes?
- What actions come to mind when you have feelings/reactions and thoughts about your children, yourself, and Neil?

The promotion of mindfulness from these questions lessened Suzanne's anxiety and depression, and her therapist's emotional support served to bolster her ego psychological functioning (i.e., helping her maintain good rationality and good judgment about herself and others). She reported feeling less overwhelmed by her feelings and thoughts and could begin to process her concerns rationally—meaning she demonstrated less of a tendency to hold herself responsible for Neil's violent behavior. A corollary to her growth was that she blamed herself less for not having a strong emotional relationship with her children after realizing that this was another tactic of Neil's emotional abuse used to control her mind (Bancroft et al., 2012).

Feeling better emotionally made it possible for Suzanne to express a maternal desire to have a few therapeutic sessions with her sons. Noting that this could only occur if the children agreed demonstrated she was not only thinking about herself but considered their needs as well. Following much processing of her emotions and intentions, it was felt that meeting with her sons would be of mutual interest to the family. The intention articulated by Suzanne was to bring out healing and peace between her and her sons. All of this corresponds with findings from Aymer's (2019) qualitative research in which mothers showed a strong interest in desiring productive and nurturing relationships with their sons who had been caught in the cross fire of partner abuse. Another important facet of this finding was that the mothers in this study felt emotionally protective of their sons even though at times they may have neglected their needs in order to survive, and consequently they wanted to forge a strong sense of attachment with them.

Six sessions were planned and executed with Suzanne and her sons. Although they were complicated, emotional, and challenging, the sessions offered an opportunity for Suzanne to hear the meaning her sons attached to violence they witnessed between their parents. Blame was assigned to both parents; the misinformation about their mother that their father conveyed blemished the young men's perceptions of their mother. Furthermore, they questioned why their mother did not try to protect them from their father's behavior. In spite of feelings of disappointment Suzanne felt in hearing her sons' views, she remained calm and nondefensive, an indication of her capacity to regulate her emotions even when triggered. Suzanne spoke of her motivation to reconnect with her sons, supporting the feelings they shared. Overall, an integrative family approach to their communications allowed the therapist to use the skill of "joining" to affirm the lived experiences of both mother and sons with the hope of facilitating psychological attunement and attachment (Van Hook, 2019). Regarding the use of this modality, Aymer (2019) postulates that

> intervening in this fashion with mothers and their sons could reduce self-blame, promoting an understanding of their shared vulnerability, denoting that the presence of violence within the family systematically weakens the psychological well-being of all members. Finally, all of this offers the opportunity to help facilitate mother-to-son healing and recovery from the trauma of battering, and reduce and/or develop empathy in young men exposed to violence in the home, making it possible for them to gain compassion for the fortitude that helped their mothers survive the insidious cycle of domestic violence. (p. 13)

Therapy with Suzanne lasted for approximately one year, during which a therapeutic holding environment provided support and allowed her to examine her feelings, thoughts, and behaviors relative to herself and her children. She gained insights into her history of abuse, embracing the realization that she has a voice that should be heard and respected in all relationships, irrespective of gender. Designed to counteract the sense of invisibility and objectification she felt, this was an important outcome of her therapy because it underlined a psychological rebuilding of her and her relationship with her sons.

Conclusion

This chapter offered some reflections on motherhood in general and examined an array of issues tied to IPV and women's maternal role. Building on existing research and writings on the topic, the chapter addressed the complexities and nuances associated with mothers' attempts to survive intimate violence while maintaining sanity and psychological steadiness for their children. Drawing from qualitative findings involving abused mothers and their sons, the chapter makes the point that the stress and anxiety mothers endure in their roles as survivors and protectors of their children cannot be ignored, but suggests that it is important for professionals to use a strength-based perspective to assess mothers' courage and fortitude when parenting in a context of IPV. Finally, the chapter presents therapeutic work with Suzanne, an abused mother whose husband alienated their children from her, underscoring how maternal perseverance can lead to healing and the restoration of a connection between a mother and her children.

Discussion Questions

1. Prior to reading this chapter, what was your understanding of IPV and mothering/motherhood?
2. What reactions do you have about mothers who leave their children with the abuser in order to remain safe or alive?
3. What stood out for you as a result of reading Janet's story?
4. What stood out for you as a result of reading Suzanne's scenario?
5. In general, how has this chapter contributed to your knowledge about mother–child relational experiences in the context of IPV?
6. In particular, what did you learn about IPV and mothering/motherhood?
7. What aspects of the chapter allowed you to grasp the plight of mothering/motherhood in the midst of IPV?
8. How could this chapter facilitate therapeutic work with abused mothers and their children in your work setting?
9. What additional questions are you reflecting on as a result of reading this chapter?

CHAPTER 6

Toxic Masculinity and Men Who Batter

Men are not a monolithic group, yet irrespective of their social identity (sexual orientation, racial identity, gender or identity expressions), the harmful effects of patriarchy continue to pierce their socioemotional existence. One of the effects of patriarchy is that it provides an emotional mask for men, shielding them from accessing feelings of vulnerability and fragility—qualities that are intrinsic to humanity. By focusing on the ideology of patriarchy and its bearing on men's way of life (i.e., the need to possess strengths and not experience vulnerabilities), this chapter explores toxic masculinity and clinical work with men who batter. Ideas from social leaning theory and an array of sociopolitical issues stemming from gender politics, race and racism, and gender hierarchies in families and society will gird the thesis of this chapter, which posits that men's desire to use power and control in intimate relationships is an embodiment of toxic masculinity. Finally, theoretical concepts from narrative therapy will be presented to increase readers' knowledge of how practitioners can engage and work with abusive men in therapy to shift their thinking away from the narrative of toxic masculinity.

Social Learning Theory

Social environment plays a key role in regulating human behavior. Bandura's (1973) seminal research on social learning underscores this point, stressing that people's actions and behaviors are highly motivated by social contexts and experiences. A central aspect of this theory is that situational factors are inextricably linked to how people comport themselves, whether functionally or dysfunctionally. Likewise, Bandura states, "it is evident from informal observation that human behavior is to a large extent socially transmitted, either deliberately or inadvertently through the behavioral examples provided by influential models" (p. 68). Society is a powerful exemplar through which the value and worth of boys and men are communicated through the perpetuation of male privilege. Still, that boys and men comprehend that they "matter" (especially white cisgender heterosexual men) in ways that may differ qualitatively from their female counterparts (this relates to all the factors specific to gender inequality in society) throughout their life course trajectory speaks to what Bandura refers to as "observational learning," which reflects societal projections of ideas about the primacy of masculinity and manhood. This type of learning unconsciously or consciously reinforces men's sense of self and underscores their sense of privilege. It also undercuts their ability to be more fully present and human (i.e., the ability to be aware of all aspects of their emotions), especially in contexts where being hypermasculine is valued.

Accordingly, Bandura's (1973) theory explains that "observational learning" culminates in modeling what he coined "imitative behavior" (p. 45). In traditional heterosexual families, for instance, the notion of having biological fathers and other paternal substitutes in a boy's socialization is often considered essential to the maturation process. In addition, within families, boys begin to form what scholars call a "masculine self," which relates to the development of identity and its implications for who they are becoming as men (Schrock & Schwalbe, 2009, p. 281). The suggestion behind such a notion is that heterosexual cisgender boys and men are more inclined to internalize and imitate the behavior of other men, and according to conventional thinking this facilitates gender identity formation (Blos, 1962). Moreover, "vicarious reinforcement," as discussed by Bandura (1973, p. 45), reminds us that this group's identity formation—whether inner (the personal and family environment) or outer (the external social environment)—is evaluated against the backdrop of experiences with other men and social forces that emphasize the values of systemic patriarchy and the devaluation of feminism. Within Bandura's (1973) framework, he discusses the function of self-efficacy in the human condition, positing that it allows people to think and process personal judgment based on their capacities. For many men, the emotional façade that patriarchy provides often erodes abusive men's self-efficacy, and plays a role in hindering their ability to examine the social contexts and experiences from which their philosophy about women and intimate relationships emanated.

Contextual Features of Toxic Gender Issues

Current discourse on gender and masculinity often uses the words *toxic masculinity* to describe behaviors and attitudes of men that are damaging to women and children. (It is interesting to note that the term was not coined by feminists but by the men's movement, which was active in the 1980s and 1990s.) Likewise, human service organizations addressing the needs of IPV clients tend to use the notion of toxic masculinity in their analyses of batterers' behaviors and use of power and control to oppress their female partners. This is not an exhaustive catalogue of settings and domains where "toxic masculinity" is used to frame the positionality of men within society, and there is no question that toxic masculine characteristics are entrenched in the ethos of men exposed to patriarchy, and many men have consciously or subconsciously held onto its corrosive standards. It is necessary to explore the idea and saliency of gender in order to contextualize toxic masculinity because we know that essentializing gender often manifests in the male/female binary. That is, gender is often linked to primary (i.e., physiological differences related to the reproductive system, in particular the testes, genitalia, and ovaries) and secondary (i.e., physiological differences, in particular the presence of facial hair on men, changes in voice tone, and the enlargement of the breasts in women, all of which stem from testosterone and estrogen) sexual characteristics that are socially accepted markers of a person's gender identity. Once it is determined that a person possesses specific sex characteristics, gendered expectations are expected to correlate to gendered activities, mores, and rules. Schrock and Schwalbe (2009) note that "based on differences in reproductive anatomy, humans are sorted into categories of 'male' and 'female,'" reflecting a belief that males and females should become different kinds of people (p. 279). What is important to consider in terms of essentializing gender is that differences in sexual characteristics are used to promote rigid assumptions about what constitutes maleness and femaleness, culturally, socially, and politically.

In addition, when a reductionist approach is used to explain social and cultural phenomena, it omits nuances and complexities, which creates an anemic epistemology. In contrast, a postmodern perspective points out that society's positioning of gender largely shapes our conceptions of what it means to be male and female, genital differences notwithstanding. Utilizing a constructivist lens to investigate phenomenological events frequently leads to critical questioning and analyses, and as such, reality is not perceived as static but instead as complex ways of knowing and interpreting social phenomena, circumstances, and behaviors. Thus, gender is presumed to be socially constructed and internalized from children's exposure to the social environment, a view consistent with Bandura's (1973) research. Historic and contemporary stories about manhood, boyhood, and masculinity are replete with specific images and words pointing to the centrality of gender behaviors based on the differentiation of roles and behavioral expressions, all of which are designed to denote differences. Designations of certain types of toys for children based on perceived gender and the differentiation of color schemes for an unborn baby once the physician has determined the gender are powerful examples of environmental influences on conventional constructions of gender. Within the scope of children's play, society tells boys that trucks and action figures like Superman, Batman, and the Hulk are earmarked for them. At the same time, girls learn that princess figures and dollhouses are earmarked for them; considering these expectations, it can be argued that play activities are linked to the use of gender-based toys, which can thwart a child's ability to express themselves independently from their genitalia and genital differences. This thinking traditionally originates from a model of gender conformity and is aligned with stories and images embedded in society intended to locate and separate maleness from femaleness.

Toward an Exploration of Toxic Masculinity

According to the *Merriam-Webster Collegiate Dictionary*, the word *toxic* is defined as "of, relating to, or caused by a poison or toxin." This same dictionary indicates that *masculinity* is used to define "a class or form of the masculine gender." The former definition encompasses negative associations such as *risk*, *hazard*, and *death*. Given this link to the notion of masculinity, it seems useful to think through what it means for heterosexual cisgender men to embrace a frame of mind where the essence of their being (as a man or a boy) is perceived as baleful. Research on toxic masculinity during the early 1990s paved the way for exploring myriad ways that it impacts men's overall health and well-being (Halder, 2016, p. 556; Oliffe & Phillips, 2008). Men's use of aggression and control are by-products of toxic masculinity, and they inhibit men from knowing their emotional lives: the internal capacity to feel and own a range of emotions. In this regard, hooks (2004) postulates, "Patriarchy demands of men that they become and remain emotional cripples" (p. 27). To feel sadness, fear, depression, anguish, or melancholy, for instance, can evoke a strong sense of weakness in many men. Avoidance and denial are ego defenses often used to mitigate against their discomfort with such feelings, reinforcing toxic masculine behaviors. It is sensible to view men's performance of toxic masculinity through the lens of their socialization (i.e., the constructivist perspective noted above). This point is validated by Orenstein (2020), who states, "Young men who most internalize masculine norms (though which, at least to some extent, do not?) are six times more likely than others both to report having sexually harassed girls and to have bullied other guys" (p. 13).

For boys, precursor behaviors to toxic masculinity are derived from the meaning they assign when observing traditional gendered relational and transactional interactions between their parents, where ostensibly there is an omission of egalitarianism, and they may witness the subjugation of their mothers. That tasks and responsibilities within the family may be distributed unevenly between parents, and this imbalance based on gender differences, which may also extend to and be experienced by siblings, may elicit feelings of privilege among boys. Amin et al. (2018) believe that "parents contribute to gender socialization through both direct and indirect communication with their children in terms of different rules and sanctions and expectations from boys and girls" (p. 2). Boys raised by a single mother may have a different familial reality (i.e., observing mothers as the primary caretaker and breadwinner) than ones raised in a two-parent household; however, media portrayals of patriarchal order in relation to family lifestyle and functioning make it impossible for these boys to escape foundational ideas about the division of labor among fathers and mothers and among men and women. Boys raised by two fathers or two mothers might be influenced by egalitarianism—or the lack thereof—depending on the degree to which their parents have subscribed to the culture of heterosexism. Hennen (2005) makes the observation that many LGBTQ+ people internalize a heterosexist view despite being part of a subculture intended to insulate them from homophobia. Hennen also remarks on the fact that although some gay men struggle with heterosexism, for some the performance of conventional masculinity can be linked to a desire to have large muscular bodies. That is, muscular bodies project strength—an attribute that can be a proxy for a type of masculine ideal among some men. All of this speaks to the notion of internalization noted in the previous chapters, an important psychological process associated with human development, which takes place within the home and the social context, and thus it is critically important to appreciate the dominance of male imagery, underlined by patriarchal standards, and their injurious effects on men's lives regardless of men's diverse social groupings, sexual orientations, and gender identities.

A focus on toxic masculinity should dispel the myth that it is a diagnosis or mental disorder. It is not in the *DSM* (*Diagnostic and Statistical Manual*), a reference book used to diagnose psychiatric disorders. Use of this gendered trope, popularity notwithstanding, should not be correlated with men's psychic functioning. To do so implies that the vast majority of men (if not all) whose masculinity is identified as toxic would be struggling with a "pathology," a clinical term specifying medical and psychological abnormalities. Toxic masculinity is not a psychiatric condition for which medication is required. The problem inherent in thinking about masculinity in this way is that it raises questions about whether men can grow by divesting themselves from the stories, images, and values associated with internalized patriarchy.

Like patriarchy, racism and white supremacy promulgate messages and behaviors that hobble the lives of black and brown people in the United States. Yet society does not pathologize racism and white supremacy by concluding that its proponents are mentally ill. Instead, we continue to promote laws to combat inequality, we engage in activism, we create workshops designed to educate and foster understanding about implicit bias, and we raise public awareness about acts of racism, all stances that recognize that racism and white supremacy are perennial problems in our society warranting ongoing interventions. Toxic masculinity can be viewed through a similar frame, and the unit of attention would be on men's appropriation of misogynistic behaviors (e.g., rape, sexual assault, IPV, and femicide) that violate the lives of women, girls, and themselves. Employing legal intervention is certainly one important way to hold men accountable for acts of misogyny. On the other hand, noncriminal responses to toxic masculine behavior can involve change processes designed to help men develop a critical consciousness about themselves. Watts et al. (1999) point out that "oppression is the principle target for critical consciousness" (p. 260).

The literature on masculinity postulates there are many ways to understand this construct—stressing the multifaceted features of its manifestations (Connell, 2000). The argument holds that masculinity is mediated and shaped by other social identities, including social class, race, religion, gender identity, sexual orientation, ethnicity, national origin, and other factors. These intersecting variables cannot be divorced from our definitions of masculinity or the notion of "real men." It is interesting that "real men" are perceived as being strong, assertive, and confident, among other strengths-based qualities. These attributes are not innate but are constructed and nurtured by social environments, and depending on the social situation, men enact these perceived qualities as they deem appropriate. Take, for example, the lounge of the men's gymnasium locker room I frequent after my workouts. At any given time, a number of men may be present in the lounge. Of these men, a third of them may be involved in conversations about sports and politics, exhibiting what I would refer to as boisterous interactions—talking over one another without any apparent self-awareness. These same men could also switch the topic to women in general (including the women they are dating or married to) by discussing issues of rape or sexual harassment though a lens of misogyny (e.g., how can a man rape his wife or his girlfriend?). This experience has prompted me to ponder the following questions: Why do some men (including me) present during such banter not participate in such exchanges? Why do other men vociferously join such exchanges? What is different about groups of men who feel comfortable performing aspects of "macho masculinity" in public spaces? What do we make of the silence among men (including me) who are not actively participating during such exchanges when misogyny and sexism are trending among other men regardless of their social identities? This anecdotal scenario encapsulates the idea that even though a culture of men exists, the performance of hypermasculinity among its members can vary, reinforcing the point that there is not a single view of masculinity. This is not to suggest that the underpinnings of patriarchy are omitted from men's dispositions and the discourse of multiple masculinities; instead, the point is that men's performance may be colored by intersectional factors such as race, social class, culture, ethnicity, sexual orientation, and gender expression.

It is common for men in such circumstances to remain silent when other men use sexist epithets to talk about women and girls and not "call out" this behavior. Thus, a conspiracy of indifference among men tends to flourish, preventing them from loosening the corrosive soil responsible for their attitudes, values, and beliefs about their social location vis-à-vis women. One important explanation for this conspiracy of indifference is the "boy code," as hypothesized by Pollack (1998), who indicates that as a metaphor it gives men a tacit approval to subscribe to the basic tenets of masculinity, and this is often associated with being strong and stoic. This makes it a challenge for men to question the sexist posturing of other men; the conspiracy of indifference tacitly supports actions about and expression of antifemaleness, regardless of the consequences. To move beyond or away from the boy code could invite skepticism from other men, a perspective noted by Wexler (2009), who writes, "Violations of any of the central precepts of the Boy code often lead to ridicule and the experience of shame" (p. 7). In my practice with abusive men in groups, invariably men inquired about my motivation for working with abusers. At times, there is considerable distrust, and the men in the group suggest that I could not possibly believe in a curriculum that essentially holds men accountable for using power and control in intimate relationships. I am aware that my commitment to working against IPV unconsciously heightens men's anxiety in group therapy because of its intrusion on the boy-code sensibility embedded in their personas. Based on these points, I argue that toxic masculinity can unearth consciously or unconsciously the following stressors in boys and men:

- The need to be strong
- The pressure to withhold affect in front of others, especially other men
- The need to be cool
- The need to use violence and aggression to solve interpersonal discord with female partners

- The need to use violence and aggression to solve interpersonal problems with other men
- The need to be right
- The need to project stereotypical images of masculinity
- The need to remain stoic and in control
- The need to conflate violent behaviors with emotional expressions
- The need to embrace anger as a default to other emotions such as vulnerability and sadness
- The need to overlook emotional difficulties such as depression and anxiety
- The pressure to take on the provider role
- The need to handle personal, social, and familial problems without asking for support or help
- The need to use sex to regulate emotions and affect
- The need to "man up"
- The pressure to feel omnipotent
- The need to define masculinity without asking for help

Therapeutic work with men can help them identify the ways their lives are affected by these stressors and help them relinquish ideas and values that cohere with inflexible definitions of manhood and masculinity. The rapper Jay-Z spoke in the *New York Times* a couple of years ago of experiencing many of these stressors, especially generalized anger and anxiety, which were connected to his upbringing; the expectation was that he had to be tough and rough to contend with the harsh reality of growing up in a hostile neighborhood riddled with violence, poverty, and uncertainties.

Toxic Masculinity and Racial Injustice

By definition, the performance of toxic masculinity results in oppressive behaviors and attitudes that impair the social and psychological functioning of women and girls and even men and boys. Furthermore, male privilege means unearned differential benefits come to men simply because of the weight assigned to them within a patriarchal system. Given these sociopolitical "truths," which are true for many sectors of society, it can seem inharmonious to attempt to ponder the nexus between race and (toxic) masculinity. Research has made it clear, however, that race matters in the United States because of the horrendous original enslavement of African people (Aymer, 2016; Butler, 2017; Coates, 2015; DiAngelo, 2018; Neal, 2006; C. M. West, 2004). Moreover, other discourses have addressed the connection among race, social class, and IPV, especially in relation to black and brown women (Aymer, 2011; hooks, 2015). Given the historic and contemporary backdrop of white supremacy in the United States, this exploration of toxic masculinity would be incomplete if racial oppression and its impact on black and brown men were omitted.

Alexander (2010) posits that enslaved black people experienced cruelty and inhumane treatment, including lynchings and other forms of degradation, designed to render them inferior to whites and make them "other." Alexander's thesis speaks to the enduring legacy of white supremacy in our society in terms of dispensing (in)justice to black and brown people, especially men, who disproportionately experience racism from the criminal justice system. This thesis has historical and contemporary relevance vis-à-vis the lived realities of black and brown men, whose psychosocial functioning can be understood through the lenses of patriarchy, racism, and social injustice (Aymer, 2011, p. 355). Race and gender have and continue to be integral to these men's existence. Ferber (2007) notes that "gender is constructed through race and race is constructed through gender, they are intersectional and mutually constitutive" (p. 15). This perspective on race and gender specific to black men is echoed by Garfield (2010), who contends, "the power of racial and gender structural relations creates its own narratives for black men's lives, regardless of what they may feel, think, and do" (p. 7). Lynchings of black male bodies were based on race and gender and the purported need to protect white women (Petersen & Ward, 2015). One notable historical example is the case of Emmett Till, a black fourteen-year-old boy who was lynched because it was alleged he had looked at a white woman. Furthermore, the Central Park jogger case of 1989 reverberated throughout New York City when it was discovered that a young white woman was brutally raped by eight young black and brown boys (referred to as "the Central Park Five"). Despite there being insufficient evidence (i.e., no DNA and no eyewitness account from the victim), they were convicted and sentenced to five to fifteen years in prison. After much controversy about the legal mismanagement of the case, grassroots organizing, and legal advocacy, they were exonerated, and the city was ordered to pay them millions of dollars for wrongful conviction. Neither Emmett Till nor the Central Park Five benefited from male privilege, illuminating the racial and gender conundrum of these men who nevertheless live in a patriarchal structure. Instead, these men were perceived as guilty given the nature of the alleged crimes.

Privilege as given to white men is never given to black and brown men; it takes on a different set of sociopolitical meanings and ramifications when applied to their bodies: societal stigma, stereotypes, and contempt often place them in dangerous situations where the appropriation of male privilege on a macro level is often nonexistent. Take, for instance, the video seen recently on social media (created in May 2020) of a male black birdwatcher who was the victim of racial profiling. Race and gender were weaponized by a white woman, who threatned to call the police on the male black birdwatcher simply because he asked her to leash her dog—a request that accorded with the rules of the park. Specifically, a verbal dispute ensued between them as the woman refused to leash her dog; the video captured her telling the birdwatcher that she would call the police to report that an African man was threatening her life. What was strikingly painful to watch was the fact that her racialized intentions and threats could have resulted in the death of this black man if police intervention had occurred. This conjecture is based on the repeated gratuitous killings of unarmed black and brown men by police, which suggest that this group's humanity is disregarded and viewed though a lens of criminality (Aymer, 2016; Butler, 2017; Coates, 2015). Thus, it is fair to conclude that gender and race expose black and brown men to racial toxins (e.g., stereotypical images of themselves, police brutality and killings, discrimination, poverty) and obscure their ability to fully understand the multiplicity of ways that patriarchal socialization has impinged on their lives. By the same token, cultural critics and academics have observed that oppressive forces in our society continue to endanger this group's survival and impede their capacity to see their roles and contribution to the patriarchal structure (Butler, 2017; hooks, 2004, 2015; Madhubuti, 1990).

These points surfaced in my group therapy practice with predominantly black and brown abusive men. Psychoeducational discussions in the group, centering on male privilege, stimulated the following ego defenses: denial, avoidance, and intellectualization. Such defenses are identified by the field of ego psychology developed by Heinz Hartmann (1939). Ego defenses surface in therapy unconsciously from an individual's resistance to maladaptive- and anxiety-inducing processes (Goldstein, 2001). Black and brown men in the group denied they have privilege because of how racism affects their lives; they avoided speaking about the connections between racism and patriarchy: this is often a new conversation requiring a shift in their worldviews and their attitudes about race and gender. Cooper (2018, p. 187) explains that "many Black men struggle to acknowledge they experience male privilege," an inference that comports with their involvement in batterers' groups. Further, driving while black, shopping while black, and living while black or Latino are profiling-inducing activities that label and "other" black and brown men, making it clear that the narrative of toxic masculinity must always consider the role of racial injustice and how it complicates these men's identity development and social location. Accordingly, as Coates (2015) reflects on the impact of systemic racism and the othering of black men, he shares the following message with his son:

> It is not necessary that you believe that the officer who choked Eric Garner set out that day to destroy a body. All you need to understand is that the officer carries the power of the American state and weight of an American legacy, and they necessitate that of the bodies destroyed every year, some wild and disproportionate number of them will be black. Here is what I would like for you to know: In America, it is traditional to destroy the black body—it is heritage. Enslavement was not merely the antiseptic borrowing of labor—it is not so easy to get a human being to commit their body against its own elemental interest. (p. 102)

Coates's postulation allows us to think about the historical underpinnings of white supremacy in America and their contemporary influences on the lives of black people, especially in the context of policing and the socialization of black men and boys.

Toxic Masculinity and IPV

Physical safety and emotional comfort are compromised when men actively engage in patriarchal thinking, a mind-set that gives rise to toxic masculinity and IPV. Regardless of the racial identity of heterosexual cisgender men, the presence and performance of toxic masculinity can be distressing for their female partners, their children, and themselves. The social dimensions of toxic masculinity are deeply rooted in the cognitive development of men and boys. Lending credence to this view is research on Bandura's (1973) social learning theory, who showed that the social environment shapes people's modes of thoughts and behaviors. The relevance of the social environment for marginalized groups, including blacks and members of the LGBTQ+ community, for instance, is well documented (Carruthers, 2018; Coates, 2015; Fanon, 1967). These writers infer that internalized racism and homophobia stem from negative societal responses and images of individuals from these groups. Through observational learning (as per Bandura) and being the recipients of unequal treatment, LGBTQ+ individuals develop marginalized feelings about themselves, which can lead to a murky sense of self-acceptance, engendering internalized homophobia. And the potency of white supremacy and its enduring presence in contemporary society generate internalized racism in black individuals, which Fanon (1967) characterized like this: "When the Negro contacts the white world, a certain sensitizing action takes place. If his psychic structure is weak, one observes a collapse of the ego. The black man stops behaving as an actional person. The goal of his behavior will be the Other (in the guise of the white man), for the Other alone gives him worth" (p. 154). My point is that the social environment penetrates the existence of people, and this should always be acknowledged in any discussion of sociocultural matters. The social environment inculcates traits and behaviors and leads to group and individual idiosyncrasies. Acknowledging this allows clinicians to fully grasp how patriarchy continues to inflict harm on cisgender heterosexual men's psychosocial development, along with shaping their conceptions of what it means to have intimate and interpersonal relationships with women.

Themes of toxic masculinity were pervasive during my eighteen years of therapeutic group work with male abusers. One psychoeducational exercise that produced responses mirroring toxic masculinity involved questions about what is manhood. Men in group therapy hastily articulated the following responses: being king, having control, being the breadwinner, winning/winner, having power, being a fighter and protector of the family and themselves, being the man of the family, being a father. There was little introspection about how such roles have affected their emotional lives. Cognitive dissonance was apparent during the creation of this list in that men often did not correlate the degree to which these roles placed them in the power position relative to their families, and how burdened they felt unconsciously about having to execute these roles. By exploring their subjective ideas about manhood in relation to the expression of rigid gender roles, they had the opportunity to become aware of the destructive facets of this type of masculinity (i.e., embracing a one-dimensional view of manhood), while allowing for reflections on other features of masculinity that can be nontoxic. I helped the men focus on elements of nontoxic masculinity, including (and this is not an exhaustive list) kindness, vulnerability, partnership, fairness and compromise, truth telling about their feelings, nonviolence, respect for women, respect for other men, gender role flexibility, power sharing, nonuse of male privilege, and the repudiation of sexual conquest over their female partners.

A poignant observation in this process was that men experienced dissonance as I engaged them on their feelings and interrupted their inflexible male identity schema. The palpability of their emotional angst was always apparent in the group, and often such cathartic moments have been used to help them think about how toxic behaviors contribute to IPV, with an emphasis on helping them develop empathy for their partners, other victims, and themselves. The clinical intent for employing this approach is twofold: first, the goal with these men was to help them refrain from physical abuse and emotional maltreatment; second, the work unpacked harmful traits of masculinity and in so doing offered alternative notions of masculinity in order to shift the socioemotional standards of what "a man is and is not."

Believability in Work with Abusive Men

"Toxic masculinity" and "men who batter" are ideas and words that provoke anxiety, anger, and fear in many practitioners, especially those who have no interest in working with this population, or those who may come to the work with preconceived notions about men's lack of openness to changing their abusive disposition. Working with men who embrace toxic masculinity can conjure up danger, fear, lack of safety, and criminality in some women who are in a therapeutic relationship with them. At the heart of such responses to men is the fact that IPV is a crime and violates and dehumanizes women. Nevertheless, men and women engaged in this type of work must be aware of their bias, recognizing that induced feelings and reactions will lead to distrust, cynicism, and doubt—feelings that are counterproductive to forming a therapeutic alliance with clients seeking services, especially male abusers, who are not always amenable to services (Cooper & Lesser, 2008). Countertransference, a phenomenon that is present in all aspects of clinical work, can account for issues of believability for the practitioner who listens to men talk about the performance of toxic masculinity and its relationship to their proclivity to exercise control over their partners. Rosenberger and Hayes (2002) discuss countertransference as an inevitable dynamic in the clinical process in which the client's problems can stimulate unresolved feelings in the therapist.

Despite all of this, I argue that it is important for practitioners to hold onto the fact that therapeutic work with men should be infused with optimism and the belief that such men can change. Consistent with narrative therapy is the fact that the problems faced by clients originate in larger discourses that affect their lives, and in order to understand the breadth and scope of the problem, it is critical to listen to the story, a concept known as *deconstruction* in narrative work (Cooper & Lesser, 2008). The issue of believability in this phase of therapy encourages practitioners to listen to men's narratives and ensure that they take responsibility for their abusive and patriarchal attitudes.

In the absence of believing men can change, clinical work with this population will remain static, blocking any semblance of growth. Basic ideas related to believability in clinical practice can include the utility of hope, the embrace of positiveness, the provision of empathy and a fundamental trust in the process of change as it relates to the human conditions, the need to bear witness to men's vulnerability, and the necessity for men to take responsibility for their violence. Such ideas fit with the premises of narrative therapy as elucidated by Nylund and Nylund (2003), who state that "by discussing the problem as the problem, rather than the person's biology or disorder as the problem, narrative therapists begin to distinguish between the person's preferred ways of being and the problem's effects on the person" (p. 389). It is unhelpful to perceive these men as bad people; we must instead help them grapple with and understand how institutionalized sexism and family of origin have underpinned their values, views, and imagination of women, thus contributing to the exercise of patriarchal dominance in intimate relationships.

Implications for Clinical Practice

In general, clinicians and counselors providing services to abusive men in nonprofit arenas often employ a group work modality, underpinned by the Duluth model, to address the violence this group has committed in their families (Pence & Paymar, 1993). That men use a plethora of abusive tactics in intimate relationships with women to control and gain power over them is an essential premise of this model, which is a widely recognized practice modality.

The basic premise of the Duluth model has informed my practice with batterers. Having a sociopolitical grasp of insidious patriarchy and its role in men's social development has, in part, strengthened my assessment of men's motivation to dominate their partners. The adoption of the term *toxic masculinity* in work with abusive men—and all men seeking therapy—has been a significant part of my clinical practice. Ideas from the Duluth model, in conjunction with framing men's relational challenges as stemming from aspects of toxic masculinity (i.e., the ways structural gendered relations produce power and control, which complicates men's identity and obstructs their potential for experiencing "healthy masculinity"), adds texture to therapeutic work with men. In my experience, some men seem to be more responsive to the phrase *toxic masculinity* than others; this may be due to its usage in the media and in conversations regarding the #MeToo movement, and anecdotally it seems to have more appeal to black and brown men who don't see themselves as possessing power and control or male privilege, especially in contrast to white men, whose privilege can be viewed either as a strength or a liability depending on the social context.

Enabling men to stop using violence in their intimate relationships is a worthwhile goal of any intervention (since the presence of IPV correlates with criminality). Clinical work should provide men the space to learn about the attributes of toxic masculinity and develop ideas for reconstructing masculinity in the context of patriarchy. Identifying the deliberate ways by which men are exposed to gender bias, inequality, and privilege, while still underscoring their culpability, can create opportunities to explore their embodiment of toxic masculinity and its effects on their lives. The postmodern modality of narrative therapy can be useful in this work because it begins with the idea that all of us possess a story that has multiple authors (Carr, 1998). The authors can include, but are not limited to, our family, society, and our affinity and reference groups. Research on this subject finds that people's lives are storied and consist of a multiplicity of meanings and nuances (Abels & Abels, 2001; Carr, 1998). Central to this supposition is that personal growth can emerge when people gain psychological awareness and insight into who they are and who they would like to become, despite their embrace of the story or stories authored by others. Relevant to this chapter, stories about manhood and masculinity are authored through lenses of the family and society and within the racial, cultural, and ethnic affinity groups of which men are a part. Clinical work begins to enable men to examine the fallacies and mythologies of these stories. For example, families embracing traditional gender norms may cast male and female siblings in stereotypical roles during childhood; this way of experiencing gender role construction can unintentionally set a model for the division of work based on gender during adulthood. This example has the potential to become part of men's narrative, leading them to believe that women should only engage in certain types of careers, despite any changes taking place in society. This corresponds with Abels and Abels's assertion that "examining with clients where these stories came from assists in exploration of the social context that puts the story in some sequence, and gives both the worker and the client knowledge of the lived life of the person" (p. 18). Based on Carr's (1998) ideas, I have helped men "externalize the problem" (p. 49) by looking through the lenses of IPV and toxic masculinity in order to help them take responsibility for their violence; by externalizing the problem therapeutically, men are invited to name and share feelings about the various messages and images they believe have shaped how they navigate relationships and react to conflicts and to understand themselves in relation to women and other men, as well as their response to gender-related situations (this could be any situation germane to gender-based violence or controversies), from the O. J. Simpson case in 1994 (a high-profile IPV case involving a black male celebrity accused of killing his white wife; he was acquitted, and the verdict created a great deal of societal tension and controversy regarding the relationship among policing, celebrity, race, wealth, the criminal justice system, and the rights of women) to the Kavanaugh hearings in 2018 (Brett Kavanaugh was confirmed as an associate justice of the Supreme Court even though sexual assault allegations during college surfaced during his confirmation hearings). White (2007) affirms, "externalizing conversations can provide an antidote to these internal understandings by objectifying the problem" (p. 11). Because this is a revelatory process, attention must be paid to men's affect because many tend to emote when they externalize what it means to hold onto and attempt to maintain personas and attitudes etched in stoicism, bravado, and guardedness. bell hooks (2004) argues,

> Patriarch[y] as a system has denied males access to full emotional well-being, which is not the same as feeling rewarded, successful, or powerful because of one's capacity to assert control over others. To truly address male pain and

male crisis we must as a nation be willing to expose the harsh reality that patriarchy has damaged men in the past and continues to damage them in the present. (p. 31)

Considering hooks's postulation, it is the therapist's job to affirm men's emotions and explore the relationship between their current feelings and their use of violence in intimate relationships. Keeping the safety of women in the forefront of one's consciousness is always of paramount importance in therapeutic work with abusive men.

In addition to externalizing the problem, White (2007) proposes another intervention known as "reauthoring," a technique used by therapists to assist clients with using their personal agency to recast and reframe their narratives. For White, to reauthor is to "invite people to continue to develop and tell stories about their lives." Therapists "help people to include some of the more neglected but potentially significant events and experiences that are 'out of phase' with their dominant storylines" (p. 61). The dominant storyline of toxic masculinity is that "a real man" abides by the dictates of patriarchy and takes part in antifeminist endeavors. Toxic masculinity entices many men to use behaviors and attitudes to conquer women (and even other men who are perceived as weak). This story omits other conditions, inhibiting men from having nontoxic experiences and nonaggressive ways of locating themselves in society. The reauthoring approach brings about "unique outcomes" and "exceptions," as per White's (p. 61) formulation.

These two angles have guided my clinical work: men learn they can liberate themselves from the traditional narratives of masculinity, and as a result they can embark on a path to change their subjectivity. An incentive to change is predicated on the therapist excavating insights into patriarchal robbery, which is associated with maintaining the storyline of masculine identities that are maladaptive. "Patriarchal limitation" means that male privilege has prevented men from experiencing well-rounded character development because predetermined gendered scripts have significantly altered their psychology. And this has affected how men, their partners, and society/the world understand their emotional life. Hurt and pain have been virtually divorced from men's emotional and cognitive schema, leaving them emotionless and prompting others to minimize or ignore any existential challenges they may be experiencing. Enabling men to be attuned to the sufferings they endure due to this limitation has the potential to lead to a self-examination of their lives that is antithetical to their patriarchal pattern of functioning. This type of radical self-reflection can motivate men to reauthor their narratives, which White believes can foster personal growth. For Nylund and Nylund (2003), growth during the reauthoring phase is possible because it "allows men to break free of essential notions of manhood and account for their daily resistance to practices of patriarchy" (p. 389). In relation to this point, the following questions could be used to guide men during the reauthoring process:

- What would an egalitarian intimate relationship mean to you?
- What impact does violence and aggression have on women and children?

- What impact does your violence and aggression have on your role as a man?
- Why do you continue to use abuse in your relationship?
- What are the benefits of ceasing violence and control in your relationship?
- What would you need to replace violence once it is omitted from your way of thinking and behaving?
- What does equality mean to you?
- What qualities within yourself comport with your current ideas of gender?
- How have traditional aspects of masculine identity affected your life?
- What are some of the benefits to changing how you see yourself as a person, as a man, and as a partner?
- What would you experience if you abandoned male privilege?
- What are the benefits of performing toxic masculinity?
- What are the emotional consequences of performing toxic masculinity?
- What attributes do you associate with the notion of "healthy masculinity"?
- What supports would you need to maintain self-growth associated with the performance of "healthy masculinity"?

Reauthoring efforts in clinical practice help men reflect on how language and words shape their perceptions and thoughts about themselves in relation to women and other men. Thus, these questions help men become more introspective as they attempt to rethink their grasp of foundational sexism. That some men view the role of a breadwinner as a virtue, for instance, ignores the pressure and anxiety associated with having the entire family solely depend on them. Such a view can lead to toxic responses from men, who prevent their partners from working in order to protect and reinforce their supremacist position. Reauthoring helps men think about the degree to which their insecurity and their tacit loyalty to patriarchy have culminated in this expectation. Men can become more aware of ways to divest themselves from expectations that are relationally destructive, and in turn to invest more in ways of being that are devoid of limitations on their social and psychological existence. hooks (2004) writes eloquently about how society must offer spaces and opportunities for men to grow and heal from the ravages of patriarchy, which has affected the soul and spirit of men. Orenstein (2020) believes parents can play a vital role in changing boys' knowledge of patriarchy, emphasizing that "mothers and fathers (and any other adults in a guy's life) need to challenge the unwritten rules of male socialization, the forging of masculinity through unexamined entitlements, aggression, and hostility toward the feminine" (p. 228).

Conclusion

This chapter explored toxic masculinity and its implications for men, especially those who are abusive to their female partners. It has argued that the social learning process men receive from the social environment and the family contributes to their view of themselves and women. The inner and outer dimensions of men's social conditioning about gender are imbued with gender politics, hierarchical gendered relational dynamics, issues of race and oppression, and other factors, all of which support unhealthy masculine identities. Although men's identities are marred by their internalizations of gendered structures that devalue women and accentuate their worth, one of the premises of this chapter is that therapy can help men unmask the injurious effects of maladaptive masculine characteristics. Narrative therapy begins with the idea that discourses privileging one group and marginalizing another affect people's lives, so the chapter addressed some theoretical aspects of this modality by exploring how men can examine alternatives to embracing and performing toxic masculinity. Externalizing and reauthoring as clinical interventions can help men examine how personal, political, and emotional factors contribute to their abuse of women. The utility of this approach builds on existing profeminist interventions as well as others (e.g., the Duluth model) used in work with abusive men. At the core of this chapter is the belief that men can be motivated to cease using violence in intimate relationships, refrain from victim blaming, and become more attuned to their false persona as manifested by the presentations of toxic masculinity that overshadow physical and emotional hurt.

Discussion Questions

1. How has this chapter increased your knowledge of toxic masculinity?
2. How has this chapter allowed for self-reflection on this topic?
3. What aspect of this chapter resonated for you?
4. How might this chapter help you work with abusive men?
5. How might this chapter help you work with nonabusive men?
6. What is your current understanding of toxic masculinity?
7. What stood out for you in the section on narrative therapy?
8. What emerged for you in the section on toxic masculinity and racial oppression?
9. What reactions did you have about intersecting issues of race, gender, social injustice, and patriarchy?

CHAPTER 7

A Self-Psychological Frame for Working with an Abused Woman

Name-calling, stalking, physical and sexual assaults, and brainwashing are among the behavioral tactics employed by male abusers to control the lives of the women intimately involved with them. These tactics of abuse adversely affect the psychological welfare of abused women, causing fear, self-doubt, and despair. This chapter highlights how these tactics create a power differential within intimate relationships, and focuses on how intimate partner violence (IPV) affects the psychosocial functioning of women. Exploring the dynamics of a case study where coercion is a hallmark of Carmen and Angel's union, the chapter stresses that practitioners should be mindful of the fact that women living in abusive relationships must often concede to subordination in order to preserve their lives. Therapeutic work with Carmen using a self-psychological framework offers the reader a perspective about this theory (self-psychology) and its relevance for understanding Carmen's early developmental history and the potential role it may have played in how she coped and dealt with the ambivalent feelings she had for her abusive husband. The chapter illustrates the importance of listening and responding to cases involving abused women who present emotional reactions consistent with trauma symptoms. For further edification, the reader is invited to reflect on a series of process questions to stimulate additional discourse about the case study.

Self-Psychological Ideas

Self-psychology is an important psychodynamic theory that can be utilized to understand what type of influence people's formative experiences may have on them and their later interactions with others. Cooper and Lesser (2008) believe that this theory is a good fit for clinical social work practice because it allows the practitioner to be attuned to how clients' unhealthy upbringing, along with complex environmental challenges, result in what they refer to as an "injury to their self-esteem through traumatic life experiences" (p. 106). That said, Kohut (1971, 1977), who constructed this theory, argued that self-development in children begins with the quality of maternal care and emotional attunement they experience during early development, and from this personal agency and self-esteem emerge. Goldstein (2001) writes that "[Kohut] called this line of development 'narcissistic' by which he meant all infants are born with normal and healthy self needs that require the responsiveness of the caretaking environment" (p. 79). Essential to this theory is that the caretaking environment is paramount to children's psychological growth, in which their sense of grandiosity is nurtured. Kohut felt that selfhood could not occur unless children were involved with important others who demonstrated love, responsiveness, and consistency throughout their early development. Kohut coined the term *self-object needs* (similar to object relations theory as noted in chapter 3, an object in self-psychology refers to an individual), making the point that children's self-development emerges from the emotional, relational, and psychical attunement between parent and children. Self-object needs are fundamental needs of children that parents must attend to. The following areas are germane to Kohut's ideas of self-object needs: *mirroring, idealization*, and *twinship*. A profound recognition of the young child's talents by caretakers/parents allows the child to feel unique, an example of a *mirroring* function that, according to Kohut (1977), addresses the child's healthy narcissism (a normative facet of the self as espoused by self-psychology), specifying that children have a primal need to be made to feel special by their parents/caretakers, who should reflect their needs. *Idealization* is predicated on the fact that children develop a strong psychic desire to merge with the admired self-object, which promotes emotional safety. And *twinship* (also known as *alter ego*) is manifested in children's desire to feel a strong sense of sameness, physically and emotionally, with the self-object, which fosters adaptive growth (Baker & Baker, 1987). In order for parents to understand the saliency of these self-object functions vis-à-vis children's development, they must be emphatically attuned, a state of being in which the emotional and physical needs of children are of primary importance in the caretaking system (Aymer, 2010a; Baker & Baker, 1987; Goldstein, 2001). All of these self-object functions are necessary in that they fortify the psychosocial development of young children (i.e., ego development, good judgment, and interpersonal skills) and, through a process Kohut (1977) calls *transmuting internalization*, self-object provision permits young children to withstand and cope with emotional distress or intended/unintended disappointment occurring during childhood. In turn, the psychic internalization of such processes enables children to cultivate a sense of identity: they are able to recognize how adult emotional needs form the model for how they will interact with themselves and their social environments. What is significant about using a self-psychological frame for appreciating the complexity of human development during early childhood is that it advances the idea that the self thrives and grows when it is emotionally attached to others who demonstrate responsiveness and empathic attunement, important self-object experiences (i.e., communicating that the child matters and that they are loved) that foster feelings of self-worth. According to Kohut, the notion of sole individuality is antithetical to the functioning of human beings; the need for emotional recognition, empathy, understanding, and affirmation (adult self-object experiences) is a lifelong pursuit innate in the human condition that arguably enriches and bolsters self-development.

Physical and Psychological Abuse

Abused women experience a range of behaviors that threaten their physical and psychological safety (Aymer, 2019; Campbell, 2004; Walker, 1979). Physical abuse may take the form of hitting, spitting, biting, stabbing, pinching, pushing, shooting, raping, and sexually abusing. Walker writes, "The violence and brutality in the sexual relationships between assaultive couples seem to escalate with time. As marital rape becomes more frequent, loving, tender sex becomes more rare. When brutality is at its height in other areas of the marriage, it seems as if more coercive techniques need to be used in order for sex to happen at all" (p. 126). Walker's research makes it clear that sexual abuse within an IPV context is intertwined with force and violence, and this is physically and emotionally dangerous for women. Women endure acts of psychological abuse, including the bullying to intimidate and torment them and the use of slurs (e.g., bitch, whore) to provoke anxiety and insecurity during arguments. Threats of homicide and physical violence are faced regularly within IPV unions (Campbell, 2004). Another abusive action common to IPV is economic abuse: the abuser may use money to manipulate the woman or make her feel she needs to depend on him. This type of financial deprivation can be manifested in the abuser's failure to pay child support and alimony; he may prevent or discourage the woman from seeking employment, promising to provide and care for her economically. Economic abuse is an insidious relational dynamic because it creates deprivation and anxiety in the woman, who must rely on the abuser for funds to take care of herself and to maintain the household. Physical violence may accompany the woman's request for funds to purchase food for the family; the abuser may perceive her request as an annoyance or showing insensitivity to his needs. These actions help the reader understand that physical and psychological assaults are ordinary activities with which many women must cope.

Discursive processes of IPV often delineate the aforementioned types of abuse in an orderly fashion, and this provides a logical way of cataloguing men's abusive behaviors. For instance, in training workshops on IPV, physical abuse is often explored and discussed separately from psychological maltreatment, yet the reality is that all types of abusive behavior violate women's bodies and psyches. It behooves practitioners to consider an integrative approach when working with abused women, so that the cruelty they are experiencing can be assessed through a trauma-informed lens. Herman's (1992) seminal work on trauma and recovery has taught mental health professionals that any life-threatening or horrific event has the potential to create psychological distress in individuals, placing their overall psychological health at risk. Pronounced feelings of vulnerability and fear are the results of traumatic occurences; people's faith in humanity may be threatened, and this has the potential to bring about existential questions about the meaning of life and safety in the context of relationships (Herman, 1992). Due to the toxicity of these relationships, abused women are forced to reflect—consciously or unconsciously—on the violence they confront from their spouses/partners. Such a process can cause women to ruminate on the precariousness of their existence—especially in situations where the abuser has exhibited homicidal tendencies. Qualitative data capturing the voices of two women in a previous study of mine is representative of the traumatic experiences that occur in partner abuse. One woman noted: "He actually took a knife, and I think it's eight inches long, and he . . . and with force he plunged it into the kitchen table, like, he said, 'I'm gonna kill you and I don't care if I go to jail for 30 years'" (Aymer, 2019, p. 7). The second woman remarked: "My safety, you know, was always on my mind. . . . I did not want to get kill[ed] by him. . . . It was not easy. I had to always focus on my safety . . . sometimes I had to think about the needs of my children as well" (Aymer, 2019, p. 9). Both quotes exemplify the horror many women in prolonged abusive relationships experience, and such experiences predispose them to a constellation of psychological problems, including anxiety, depression, self-doubt, diminishment of self-worth, and intrusive thoughts (Bancroft et al., 2012; Herman, 1992; Lavendosky et al., 2000; Peled & Gil, 2011). Herman (1992) argues that ongoing psychological problems can culminate in trauma, which can impede women's ability to function.

The psychological impact of IPV devalues women's self-worth, and this can increase their motivation to avail themselves of psychotherapeutic services (Kress et al., 2008). Their efforts to pursue therapy can intensify once there is a modicum of physical safety (assaults on the body have ceased, and the abuser has been restrained from stalking and other forms of harassment). The woman's physical safety should be of major concern to treating professionals, a point that is sometimes neglected in practice (Kress et al., 2008). Furthermore, Dienemann et al. (2002) imply that IPV places women in a state of "crisis," making it difficult for them to think about issues not related to their safety (p. 226). Safety represents a period of calm for many women because the abuser may have left the home permanently or temporarily, or the woman may have decided to relocate in order to flee the abuse. A period of calm may provide an opportunity for women to also reflect on their feelings instead of being consumed with worry about their physical survival. Women residing in a battered women's shelter indicated they were able to get in touch with the emotional hurt and pain associated with their abusive relationships once they left their abusers (Aymer, 2019). In addition, many abused women continue to think about the impact that violence has had on their lives. This is an adaptive response employed by women in service of staying alive, and should be respected by practitioners as they assess women's needs and interests in therapy.

Case Study: Carmen and Angel

Carmen, a fifty-year-old Latina woman, sought services to deal with many of the aforementioned tactics of IPV, which had plagued her relationship with Angel, to whom she has been married for several years. The couple has two sons, ages twelve and fourteen. Specifically, their relational problems were marked by heated arguments followed by threats and physical abuse. Brandishing a knife during an intense argument, Angel threatened to kill Carmen if she did not comply with his expectations; she called the police, and Angel was arrested. Although their marriage was surrounded by IPV prior to his arrest, Carmen had made several earlier attempts to contact the police but had never been able to follow through. She divulged to friends and family that Angel threatened to kill her, and even though she received support, they reminded her that in light of the ceaseless strife and fighting that characterized the marriage she needed to address the problem through the courts. Based on this feedback and her developing feeling that she wanted to end the marriage, Carmen contacted a local multiservice agency for assistance in addition to reporting Angle's homicidal ideations to the police.

Presenting Problems and Issues

It was evident from Carmen's presenting difficulties during her initial appointments that she was in crisis yet still had feelings for Angel. Carmen noted she was concerned about her living situation because Angel contributed a considerable amount of money toward the household and she was anxious about her ability to take care of herself and her children. She mentioned that financial support from her family was possible but would not be enough to maintain her household. In addition, having lingering feelings for Angel in spite of his abusive history elicited shame in Carmen. She felt her feelings for Angel contributed to her crisis and expressed interest in services to address her emotions. Since she expressed a desire to understand the ways the marriage had affected her and her children, the therapist agreed to help her, first by sorting out her living arrangement, then helping her focus on her feelings regarding her husband. This approach was designed to validate Carmen's rationale for availing herself of help.

Carmen's Relationship with Angel

Carmen and Angel moved to New York City during their adolescence, and when they met they discovered they grew up in the same part of Puerto Rico. They did not know each other as children, yet they had childhood memories and ethnic and cultural references that attracted them to each other. Their parents and extended family affirmed their relationship in light of the commonalities between them and their seeming love for each other. Both were raised in a large, close-knit family where loyalty among family members was lauded. Adored by Carmen's mother, Angel was perceived as the perfect husband for Carmen, and this message was conveyed to him. Carmen also shared this sentiment, remarking that during their courtship he was kind, understanding, and loving.

After the birth of their first son, Carmen indicated that Angel's attitude changed in terms of how he reacted to her: he became loud and boisterous whenever they had verbal exchanges. Upon further reflection, she recalled he demonstrated possessiveness, insisting she should tell him about her whereabouts, and became angry when she did not do so; he engaged in derogatory name-calling if he did not know her whereabouts. She attempted to keep him informed about her daily activities in order to curb his anger, but quarrels ensued if she inadvertently forgot to inform him. Carmen was frightened by Angel's anger—she felt unsafe and would often think that he would physically abuse her at some point. The first instance of violence between them occurred after she questioned why she needed to report her comings and goings to him. He considered this a personal affront to his role as her husband, and he grabbed her face and began to hit her.

She emphasized her love for him while noting his possessiveness and abuse, pointing out that she did not want to be abused. She noted that she initially perceived his possessiveness as a manifestation of his love for her, which was something she felt had been absent during her formative years. Her feelings for Angel, moreover, were linked to the fact that he provided for her and the children, ensuring they had food, clothing, and shelter. Carmen also noted that he was emotionally and sexually responsive to her needs, and that she had considerable romantic feelings for him—until he threatened to kill her. She felt she had overlooked the physical violence in her marriage because Angel exhibited consistent generosity to her family during their financial hardships, and this promoted a stronger overall attachment to him as well. In describing Angel, Carmen believed he was a good man who would help others who were in need before attending to his own needs. She claimed he was a good father to his two sons before the escalation of conflicts and fights between Angel and her, and she indicated he spent quality time with their children, taking them to sports events, family functions, and school activities.

Abusive Interplay between Carmen and Angel

Carmen recounted numerous times prior to involving the police when she attempted to seek help or temporarily leave the relationship. Her reaction to the initial incident of abuse was disorienting: she never thought he would hit her, even though they argued regularly. She spoke to her grandmother about her experience and indicated her desire to pursue a divorce, but her grandmother encouraged Carmen to work on her marriage, stating that Angel possessed other qualities that were good for her and the children. This advice shifted Carmen's decision to leave the marriage. Six months after this conversation with her grandmother, she was beaten again when Angel accused her of cheating on him. Seeking refuge after this assault resulted in her staying with a friend for two weeks. Angel contacted her via phone and in person to apologize for his behavior. She returned to their apartment to connect with her children, believing he was remorseful about abusing her.

In the absence of physical assaults, Angel yelled at Carmen, which made her feel insecure. Benign discussions concerning the children's school activities or their doctor's appointments often escalated into tense arguments, and concluded with Angel throwing objects at Carmen. As she defended herself, Carmen shouted at him and called him illiterate. Tension escalated between them when she brought up this aspect of his life, which was apparently a major source of embarrassment and shame for him, and her remarks may have attacked his self-esteem. Carmen also periodically criticized Angel for not being fluent in English—another example of how she attempted to defend herself when he assaulted her. These criticisms wounded him psychologically and served to heighten the pressure between them. Depending on his emotions, their arguments culminated with actual violence or with the threat thereof. To avoid this, Carmen's tendency was to remain quiet, a position that did not yield less tension between them.

She experienced sexual assault during the marriage. Carmen believed Angel had a right to take her against her will because of their marriage. That he was usually inebriated when he raped her made it difficult for Carmen to feel he was violating her. Instead, she felt his addiction to alcohol may have been a contributing factor to his overall abusive temperament, and she spoke of being fearful of him when he was intoxicated because he was unpredictable and extremely argumentative. In addition, if she was not in an amorous mood, for example, he would ridicule her by pointing out that she was fat and that other men would find her sexually unattractive. Demeaning her at the point of her protesting against his sexual advances seemed to have affected her self-esteem, and this led to the development of body issues that manifested in her gaining considerable weight. Although he called her fat, he also told her he was attracted to her body despite her weight gain. Nonetheless, he continued to engage in body shaming during arguments with Carmen, commenting on how inactive she had become due to putting on weight.

During the marriage, Carmen left her home with the children several times to obtain respite from Angel's abuse. He sought her out again and again, each time expressing regret and remorse for his controlling and abusive behavior. Acknowledging his apologies and believing him, she returned to the relationship with the hope that the abuse would stop and that she and Angel could have a loving relationship similar to their courtship. Although Carmen expressed antipathy toward Angel's abusive behavior and the hostile familial environment he created, she also spoke of still having loving feelings for him. In addition to Angel's apparent disingenuous apologies for his actions, Carmen believed her enduring romantic feelings for him kept her in the marriage; while exploring her feelings, she spoke about her fear of being alone, that she believed Angel really loved her, and that she wanted her children to grow up with a father.

Court Processes and Ancillary Human Services

After she called the police for assistance, Angel was arrested for threatening Carmen. He denied the allegations of IPV, and Carmen minimized the terror she felt when telling her story to her attorney. Central to this was that she did not want him to lose visitation rights with his children, and she stated that she felt sorry for him. The judge ordered him to enroll in a batterers' intervention program, and he was ordered to undergo a psychological evaluation to determine the appropriateness of unsupervised visits with his children. Carmen received crisis intervention services during this period to assist her with rental arrears as well as short-term counseling focusing on the immediate aftermath of Angel's homicidal threats toward her. Thus, this incident, which allowed her to seek legal and crisis-related services, also motivated her to engage in psychotherapy to deal with emotional scars from the IPV.

Carmen's Relationship with Her Children

During the intake appointment, Carmen spoke about her concern for her children and wondered to what extent they had been affected by the marital discord and IPV. Both boys experienced direct and indirect exposure to volatile arguments and physical fights between their parents. It was always Carmen's intent to protect them from observing and knowing about the fights; however, this became increasingly difficult as the violence and tension escalated. There were times when Carmen sustained visible injuries on her face from a fight; to conceal this from the children, she told them that she fell in order to deflect their attention away from the discord between her and their father. Witnessing arguments and physical abuse triggered sadness and crying in the children when they were younger, but they appeared more emotionally detached now that they were older, according to Carmen.

Carmen has a good relationship with the children, especially the younger one, who is very affectionate toward her. Her emotional attachment to them generated a sense of hope and gave her the determination to cope and survive her husband's behavior. Remaining alive in the midst of such behavior was a priority for Carmen: she wanted to see the growth of her children in spite of the dysfunction surrounding them. As a mother, she attempted to respond to their needs even in the course of her abusive situation, and she made sure they saw a counselor in order to process and talk about their feelings relative to the familial problems. Attending school activities with her husband (in spite of the IPV) in order to stay abreast of the children's academic performance was a prime concern. All this projected an unblemished image of family life that she felt would be in the best interest of the children's well-being. Taking the children to social and recreational events with her in spite of Angel's abusiveness was another way Carmen endeavored to bring some degree of normalcy to her children's lives. Though the children "acted out" in response to her setting limits to discipline them, their exposure to IPV also induced behavioral problems, and all of this generated feelings of parental insecurity. That she tolerated Angel's abuse suggested to Carmen that she was not attending to the welfare of her children. Regardless, Carmen articulated considerable love and concern for her children, and during intake appointments she said her primary goal was to take care of herself in order to parent them.

Carmen's Formative Experiences

Prior to moving to New York City, Carmen remembered having many friends in Puerto Rico and summarized her time there as "normal." Raised by her maternal grandmother, Carmen did not feel attached to her biological parents even though they lived in the same apartment in Puerto Rico. That said, Carmen moved to New York City during her early adolescence with her family (mother, father, two younger sisters, and maternal grandmother) and adjusted well to her new neighborhood, which was populated with people of Latinx descent whose primary language was Spanish. She grew up in a large extended family of many cousins, family friends, godparents, aunts, and uncles. As was the practice in Puerto Rico, her maternal grandmother continued to take care of her and her siblings. This appeared to have facilitated her acculturation process and made it possible for her to develop friendships in the community and at school. She noted that she felt emotionally disconnected from her parents, who worked long hours to meet the family's needs.

Carmen completed high school and enrolled in a local community college with the hope of becoming a nurse. Shortly after she met Angel, Carmen withdrew from college after Angel proposed to her and intimated a desire to take care of her once they were married. In the meantime, she sought employment as an office worker, a decision that led to conflict between her and her family, especially her siblings. Given the tension connected to her decision to leave college, Carmen felt it best to separate from her family, and she moved in with Angel's parents when she was twenty. The closeness she had felt with her siblings was compromised by the choices she made, including her decision to date Angel, whom her siblings felt did not deserve her due to his troubled familial background.

Carmen recalled hearing and seeing physical fights between her parents, which made her sad. Her father subjected her mother to physical assaults and psychological abuse ranging from hitting and yelling to name-calling. On several occasions, Carmen witnessed her father choking her mother, who cried out for help, but her mother discouraged Carmen from calling the police. Feeling overwhelmed by her parents' violence, Carmen discussed her feelings with her grandmother, who assuaged her feelings and told her that her parents' problems were due to stress. Carmen felt her grandmother's outlook helped her to normalize and rationalize her parents' problems. Her sisters did not talk about their parents' abusiveness, and so this also reinforced a sense of normalcy within the family dynamics. For Carmen, the lack of communication concerning parental matters also created a divide between her and her siblings, yet she maintained that her family was loving, close, and caring.

Case Conceptualization

The clinical picture revealed that Carmen faced a deluge of problems, including the emotional struggles she experienced in her family of origin and her abusive relationship with Angel. It was reasonable to surmise that Carmen's familial surroundings informed her psychosocial development and functioning. The notion that one's formative years play a significant role in adulthood is well documented by developmental and psychoanalytic theorists (Bowlby, 1988; Kohut, 1977; Winnicott, 1965). Both Winnicott and Kohut, for instance, have argued that children's development and emotional welfare are inextricably linked to the quality of caretaking they receive during childhood. Kohut centered the psychological needs of children, arguing that there is a dynamic interplay through which parents provide mirroring, idealization, and twinship, all examples of self-object needs that are essential to buttressing their psychic growth. Using Kohut's framework, clinical work with Carmen needed to explore the impact of her family of origin on her understanding of herself and others without attributing blame for being a victim of IPV.

The emotional turbulence and violence between her parents probably truncated her psychological attachment to them; this may have hindered her capacity to fully experience emotional (self-object needs) nurturance. Furthermore, Carmen's parents' abusiveness obstructed their ability to be attuned to her psychological needs. Likewise, her need for mirroring, idealization, and twinship was neglected, and this may have created challenges for her to feel special and affirmed as a child. Caretaking imbued with the noted qualities form the building blocks for self-worth in children and chart a path for them to realize their own capability in interpersonal relationships (Kohut, 1977). The development of self-soothing capacities begins to take root in adult relationships as a result of the provision of early self-object needs. In McKenzie's (2011) interpretation of Kohut's theory, he writes, "Self-objects are the emotional representations derived from human interactions that become internalized into the self. The initial nuclear self (primitive original elements of self) develops from infancy into a cohesive self (a structure of self that is fundamentally able to self-soothe) through the internalized self" (p. 8). It seems that Carmen internalized the violence and contention between her parents, and this may have been compounded by her ambivalent attachment to them, which potentially obstructed her capacity to experience what Kohut refers to as self-object needs: mirroring, idealization, and twinship, qualities that facilitate a pronounced sense of specialness in young children. This emotional void affected her self-esteem and thwarted her ability to regulate the resulting effects of witnessing the violence during childhood.

Furthermore, internalization in this sense meant that she may have felt a sense of responsibility, self-blame, or shame about her parents' strife, common responses associated with a child witnessing IPV (Aymer, 2008a). In order to alleviate these feelings and garner support and compassion, Carmen may have unconsciously gravitated to her grandmother, and her unfortunate statement that her father's violence was induced by stress may have been emotionally distressing. Carmen may have interpreted this response to mean that violence against women is attributed to male stress, and such a viewpoint may have normalized her parents' situation as well as hers. As an alternative, it would have been empowering for Carmen to receive empathy from her grandmother to facilitate self-soothing and coping behaviors during childhood and adulthood. This was evidently absent from Carmen's formative years; as a result, her understanding of herself specific to her relationship with her parents and her husband was affected.

The violence that plagued Carmen's relationship with Angel was physically and psychologically damaging. Angel employed multiple tactics of abuse to incite fear, anxiety, and self-blame in Carmen, harkening back to the experiences she felt as a child witnessing her parents' violence. Carmen struggled with the marriage for a variety of reasons: it appeared that she genuinely loved Angel, her mother's approved of him (she told him to take care of Carmen) complicated how she understood his violence, and the fact that he prohibited her from working was perceived as his way of taking care of her. The onset of Angel's abuse (i.e., verbal aggression) occurred after the birth of their first child, and this was puzzling for Carmen because he had only demonstrated consistent affection to her until this period. It was in this moment that she began to feel fearful and anxious in the context of their marriage. As noted in chapter 5, research has revealed that violence against women may escalate during pregnancy and after the birth of a child (Browne, 1993; McFarlane et al., 2002). Men's propensity for control and power may increase during this phase, placing women at risk for homicide and other violent behaviors (McFarlane et al., 2002). This supports Carmen's emotional reactions to Angel's hostile attacks because her personal safety may have been threatened, and her trust in him was shattered.

The increase of Angel's control indicated to Carmen that her marriage had shifted from a loving and caring union to one punctuated by fear, tension, and distrust. All of these factors came into focus during therapy, helping her to talk about how his domineering behaviors were just as harmful as his physical abuse of her. For instance, it appeared that she yielded to his possessiveness by informing him of her daily whereabouts in order to preserve her sanity and her life. Although she reported that he physically abused her when she questioned his need to know her whereabouts, it seemed that this action was inevitable regardless of her response. This theme was echoed in Aymer's (2019) study, in which women reported that their partners often provoked arguments in order to justify their abusive actions.

Course of Therapeutic Interventions

Carmen's physical and emotional safety was of critical importance to her therapist, who made sure her basic needs were addressed. As noted above, Carmen received crisis intervention services from the multipurpose center. Her children were in therapy to help them deal with the effects of the IPV. All of this motivated Carmen to reach out to the therapist to work on the aftermath of being abused by her partner. Her primary focus during several sessions was on Angel's abusive behaviors and how disappointed she felt about staying in the relationship. The therapist offered support and validated Carmen for surviving Angel's inhumanity, underscoring that this showed her strength and courage. This was an important intervention at the outset of treatment: it instilled hope and empathy to counteract Carmen's feelings of self-blame. Researchers suggest that the change process for women affected by IPV is correlated to the meaning they assign to their abusive narrative (Dienemann et al., 2002). Self-blame had a caustic effect on Carmen, who was also struggling with a host of other feelings, including a sense of failure for not staying in a marriage that her parents approved of. Understanding this allowed the therapist to engage Carmen on her meanings about the marriage. She compared her marriage to her parents' marriage, indicating that they are still together even though their marriage was fraught with violence. Validating this reality and exploring her feelings enabled her to talk freely about feelings of self-blame: she felt she should have sought marital therapy to address Angel's violence. In a supportive manner, the therapy focused on helping her reflect on larger contextual factors (e.g., the presence of children, social and cultural pressures, and family expectations) that underline IPV, giving her a sociopolitical lens through which she could see the complexity of abusive relationships, especially in light of how they adversely affect women's psychological well-being. The literature posits that depression and anxiety are common among abused women (Coker et al., 2002); Carmen showed symptoms of both as she blamed herself for splintering the marriage and her family.

Carmen reported she experienced the following: frequent crying, difficulty sleeping, intrusive thoughts associated with Angel's negative perceptions (i.e., body shaming and name-calling) of her, low energy, and self-doubt. These feelings are connected to trauma reactions among women who have endured IPV (Herman, 1992; Sipe & Hall, 2013). With that reality in mind, a trauma-informed approach was employed, enabling Carmen to process her feelings on all levels without judgment. Herman (1992) postulates that trauma changes people's view of the world and others around them, due to a lost sense of trust in oneself and one's community. Such a perspective meant that it was therapeutically important for the therapist (who is a man) to learn about Carmen's familial, social, and formative background. Male therapists working clinically with abused women should be mindful of the possibility of a woman to feel triggered by being in a therapeutic relationship with a man after she had been victimized by another man. Her trust in men may have been eroded, and she may struggle to develop a trusting therapeutic relationship. Moreover, seeing Carmen through the lens of a trauma-informed modality permitted the therapist to recognize that he needed to be compassionate and empathic. Carmen's relationships with Angel and her family of origin were devoid of this, and the therapeutic hope was for her to begin to feel a sense of safety in treatment. To strengthen her sense of trust and safety, the therapist actively affirmed the following: she is not to be blamed for Angel's abusive behavior; surviving his cruelty was indicative of her resilience and coping skills. These affirmations offered a larger context through which Carmen could gain insights into her narrative of abuse, and she was encouraged to share her feelings with the therapist at any time during therapy.

A point repeatedly expressed in therapy was that Carmen did not see herself as a survivor because she remained in the relationship too long. By using a self-psychological frame, the therapist was able to focus on her relationship with her parents. As per Kohut's (1977) formulation, people tend to internalize self-objects, which are "the emotional representations derived from human interactions that become internalized into the self" (McKenzie, 2011). Kohut argued that internalization has tremendous import during childhood given that psychological development is in a state of flux during this period. It was important to process with Carmen if she thought there were any connections between her experiences in her family of origin and the ways she functioned in her marriage. As stated, her grandmother raised her and took care of her instrumental needs (i.e., providing food, clothing, and emotional/physical stability), but it is questionable if Carmen felt psychologically cared for by her. Issues of financial insecurity and lack of privilege accounted for why her parents had to work to maintain the family. In addition, their relational discord and abusiveness probably contributed to their inability to fulfill Carmen's self-object functions/needs (i.e., mirroring, idealization, and twinship). In other words, their capacity to give Carmen unconditional love, care, and emotional validation may have been compromised. Kohut argues that early development is tied to the quality of the relational interactions existing between the child and his caretaker, and this overall affective process between them allows for the formation of one's individuality and identity. Carmen's caretaking system clearly provided for her concretely, but it appeared that it was lacking in the provision of emotional attunement, the overt expression of consistent love, affection, and compassion (mirroring; Baker & Baker, 1987; Kohut, 1971). A corollary to this is that children also need empathy from a parent, from which they learn that their feelings, ideas, and thoughts matter. An example of empathic failure occurred when Carmen expressed her feelings about her parents' abuse to her grandmother, who instead of being empathic told her that stress was the cause of her parents' problems (Kohut, 1977). Correspondingly, that Carmen's grandmother insinuated that she should stay in her abusive relationship with Angel because of his good qualities as a father and a spouse was another example of empathic failure. This meant that her grandmother was unable to demonstrate concern relative to the dangers that permeated her abusive relationship.

In terms of her therapy, it made sense for Carmen to reflect on two questions: First, what kind of response was she seeking from her grandmother in these two instances? Second, what impact did her grandmother's responses have on her? Understanding her familial circumstances and how they may have influenced her life—including the issue of partner abuse—enabled her to understand why she stayed in the relationship. Likewise, intergenerational transmission of violence in her family could explain her grandmother's responses, which could have suggested to Carmen, who had witnessed violence between her parents as a child, that her abusive relationship with Angel was mirroring what she observed. Like internalization, social learning theory claims that children who observe aggression and violence within their families are exposed to models that project violence as normative, and in turn they use it in interpersonal interactions with others (Bandura, 1973). In addition, therapy underscored just how fearful she was of Angel's violence and how this may have played a role in her overall process when she left the relationship. Therapeutic work allowed her to examine all the facets of the afflictions of her life.

It was helpful to examine Carmen's complex emotions for Angel. His manipulating and beguiling attitudes that pervaded their relationship endeared both Carmen and her family to him. Notwithstanding the violence, he contributed financially to the maintenance of the family, placing him in the power position, which may have led to them idealizing him. It is ironic that although Carmen wanted to be independent and did not want to be controlled by Angel, his responses made her feel special and cared for, qualities absent from her childhood. As noted earlier, she spoke of her love for him in spite of the abuse, and although this was a factor evident in the dynamics of their fraught relationship, it was helpful to explore these parts of herself as a way of validating her feelings, and alleviating her shame-based emotions for loving an abusive spouse. Treatment enabled her to talk about the negative and positive aspects of her relationship, acknowledging that she needed a great deal of empathy and emotional attunement from the therapist, a key factor that Kohut (1977) felt was necessary in the therapeutic encounter. The supposition is that the therapist should have the capacity to use him- or herself to connect with the client's sufferings and be responsive to where the client is in his or her narrative truths. The treatment process offered a safe space for Carmen to share and explore a range of feelings, including her need to be in a nonabusive relationship as well as her continuing love for Angel, despite his abusive behaviors. Carmen indicated that she would be willing to forgive him eventually because he is the father of her children and that she realized they would need to coexist for the sake of the children. Listening and supporting her feelings was an important stance employed by the therapist, who remained empathic and nonjudgmental. From a self-psychological perspective, it was helpful for the therapist to provide support and validation to Carmen in an attempt to counteract empathic failures (from her parents and grandmother) associated with her formative and adult experiences.

Therapeutic work with Carmen lasted for approximately two years. At the end of treatment, she was less symptomatic, her sleeping patterns had improved, and she reported feeling less anxious. She spoke of feeling psychologically competent to take care of herself and her children, and as an example of this she reenrolled in a nursing program at a local community college. Having minimal contact with Angel seemed to have helped her work through her fears, and filing for a divorce has helped her to feel that she can move on with her life. Carmen felt the need for more reflection on her life was warranted before dating or engaging in another long-term relationship.

Recommendations for Clinicians

This case is one example of a therapeutic process with an abused woman. The use of a self-psychological lens was effective with this client, who was amenable to long-term therapy. Long-term work might not have been possible if Carmen was faced with a crisis during therapy. That said, the therapeutic process was intersectional, which meant Carmen could talk about the abuse she endured as well as focusing on her early developmental history, all of which contextualized her lived reality as a woman. What can be learned from Carmen's therapy? Her abusive relationship needed to be understood from the vantage point of Angel's need to control and dominate her. Her familial history needed to be understood in connection to the quality (or lack thereof) of her caretaking system and her exposure to partner abuse between her parents. The case illustrates how all facets of abused women's narratives, especially those from their early development, shape their psychology, and that this can be explored in treatment in a nonblaming and nonjudgmental fashion. Healing is at the heart of any therapeutic work, and the chapter makes the point that it is possible for women to gain insights into their abusive relationships and address issues of safety. At the same time, for some abused women, introspection may lead them to think about how aspects of their development may affect their understanding about themselves in terms of how they deal with the abuse. As an example, Carmen witnessed abuse between her parents, who remained together, and the feedback she received from her grandmother regarding this shaped the meaning she ascribed to her abusive relationship with Angel. This was certainly pertinent to her healing, allowing her to be more mindful of the familial-relational dimensions of her life and in turn cease blaming herself for not leaving Angel.

Abused women enter helping systems in a variety of emotional states, requiring different types of interventions and services to address a range of physical and emotional needs. Hence, Carmen entered treatment after she received immediate, practical services geared to address housing and financial needs. It would have been challenging to engage in this type of therapy prior to addressing these issues. The ability to engage in weekly psychotherapy and deal with one's inner and outer worlds means that certain basic needs should be met. This factor in work with abused women also represents a trauma-informed response, a recognition that safety and peace of mind are psychologically important to women who have sustained traumatic injuries. In the domain of therapeutic work using a psychodynamic emphasis, the following should be considered: the therapist should be knowledgeable about the dynamics of IPV, and the use of early developmental/family-of-origin variables should be used nonjudgmentally to give greater depth to the therapeutic process.

Discussion Questions

1. What were your initial thoughts when you learned that Carmen's case would be viewed through the lens of self-psychology?
2. What type of understanding did you have about self-psychology prior to reading this chapter?
3. How have the self-psychological ideas discussed in the chapter heightened or enhanced your understanding of Carmen's attempts to cope with Angel's abuse?
4. In addition to a self-psychological approach, what other theoretical approaches might you employ to understand Carmen's formative experiences?
5. What aspects of Carmen's narrative helped you understand her resilience in the midst of Angel's abuse?
6. What did you learn about this case that contributed to your understanding of the value of working with an abused woman in a psychodynamic fashion?
7. What sociocultural questions, issues, and concerns surfaced for you as you read and process this case study?
8. What therapeutic issues and dynamics pertaining to the case could the therapist have addressed differently?
9. What is your assessment of Carmen's ambivalence as manifested in her romantic feelings for her husband?

CHAPTER 8

Men's Work
A Call to Action Concerning Violence against Women and Girls

Intimate partner violence (IPV) disproportionately affects women and children, especially girls, and because men tend to be the primary aggressors, this chapter asserts that their presence is often lacking from efforts to advance social justice. This may be due to their feelings that IPV is a woman's issue, their beliefs that men involved in this type of advocacy are recovering abusers, their perceptions that "real men" do not work on behalf of such social issues, and finally their inability to be women's allies instead of the traditional role of protector. This chapter is premised on the fact that because men are more likely to perpetuate violence in intimate relationships they should become allies in the fight against partner victimization. This requires men, whether they are abusers or nonabusers, to perceive themselves as agents of change who can work with women as a means to preserve their physical and psychic safety. Furthermore, the chapter brings into focus the #MeToo movement, which has sharply increased society's awareness of how influential men such as Harvey Weinstein, R. Kelly, Bill Cosby, Louis C. K., and Matt Lauer, for example, have used their reputation and standing to rape and assault women and girls. Given the public discourse inspired by this movement, the chapter also seeks to raise consciousness about the need for men to become involved in decentering systems of domination that marginalize and oppress women. Expanding on this idea, the chapter argues that as advocates, clinicians, counselors, and researchers, men can become allies in the fight against violence and contribute to an antiviolence and gender-based activism. Finally, the chapter raises the following questions in the context of men working on behalf of women and girls:

- How do men reflect on their social location in the world as they provide services to abused women, children, and girls?
- What is the value of men mobilizing other men to work against gender-related oppression?
- What are the gains for men who advocate for gender equality and fairness?

Reflections on a Calling to IPV Work

In theological parlance, a "calling" is a purpose that God has laid out for an individual, and the expectation is that the individual will pursue it. From a personal and professional standpoint, this resonates with me, as my involvement in the field of IPV was fortuitous. A clinical supervisory meeting designed to help me process my work with an abused woman sparked my supervisor to question my readiness to work with this client population, but instead of assigning me to a different unit (which would have been more appropriate given my lack of skills and expertise intervening in IPV cases), she arranged to have me attend an intensive weekend training seminar on IPV work with abusers and abused women. I met this suggestion with some resistance (I did not believe I needed such training because I was already a trained clinician—and I suffered from the Dunning–Kruger effect, i.e., I did not know what I did not know), but I ultimately agreed to attend the seminar. At the seminar, I made a connection with a master trainer, who offered positive responses for my interactions throughout the training. He spoke to me about becoming a group therapist for abusive men and indicated that this would be a good opportunity to work against IPV and family violence. It has been more than twenty-five years since that seminar, and I am still actively engaged in this field of practice as an academic, therapist, and researcher. IPV was not part of the plans I had made during my graduate education, but my professional trajectory led me to a path where I have maintained a strong sense of purpose and an unwavering commitment to address the needs of clients affected by IPV.

Men's Social Location and Service Delivery to Women/Girls

It is empirically impossible to know the number of men involved in IPV work, but we know that men provide a wide range of services to this population. This does not negate the fact that men occupy a social location where exposure to misogyny and patriarchy continues to have a grip on how they function in the social environment, which emphasizes the need to remain mindful of this dual consciousness. This reality is similar to that faced by white people interested in working against racism, who must grapple with how they inhabit a world that values their humanness and provides the very privileges that are foundational to the ideology of white supremacy. In her compelling book *White Fragility*, DiAngelo (2018) explains that "interrupting the forces of racism is ongoing, lifelong work because the forces conditioning us into racist frameworks are always at play; our learning will never be finished" (p. 9). This observation speaks to the notion of holding multiple truths, which is applicable not only to white allies but also applies to male allies and others. Early in my clinical practice with abusive men, I found it challenging to do this work and not feel angst as thoughts and feelings emerged about my sexism and misogyny. This meant that I had to be mindful of how sexism contributed to my views about women and my conception of the world. And in particular, such views became stronger when in the company of men who expressed sexist and patriarchal sentiments casually and professionally. Powell (2003), a cultural critic and black male feminist, captures this state of being in his essay "I Am No Hero. I Am No Saint. I Remain a Sexist Male," stressing his struggles about remaining "woke" to the negative outcome of patriarchy. Powell notes that he is "one who is now conscious of [patriarchy] and who has been waging an internal war for several years. Some days I am incredibly progressive; other days I regress. It is very lonesome to swim against the stream of American male centeredness, of Black male Bravado and nut grabbing. It is how I was molded, its what I know, and in rejecting it I often feel mad, naked, and isolated" (p. 63). Aspects of Powell's argument speak to my own personal socialization, especially his point about the loneliness men feel when they decry "American male centeredness," a feeling that is arguably universal among men regardless of their social and racial identities. Like Powell, I felt a sense of loneliness and isolation as I explored the multiple ways consciously and unconsciously misogyny affected my life and wrestled with why I was not cognizant of this fact until I became involved in the field of IPV.

During another period in clinical supervision, I was asked to think about and write down what it means to be a man working with women affected by IPV. The exercise forced me to reflect on my professional and personal selves in the context of providing services to women who have been abused by other men, and who spoke of their distrust of them. In offering support to abused women in therapy, I had to think about my social location as a man and the emotional split I felt as I developed a different consciousness as I began clinical practice with IPV clients. Circumstances related to my upbringing accounted for this emotional split, in that men mattered in my social and familiar environments, and violence against women seemed pervasive and accepted. I was fortunate to undertake clinical work with clients affected by IPV; indeed, this aroused an awakening, motivating me then—and now—to consider the potential duality that exists for me and other men who are allies in the fight against IPV. This type of reflective work can caution men not to use the field of IPV as a cover for defending their patriarchal feelings and ideas. All of this accentuates Flood's (2015) point: "Those who advocate that men should become active participants in ending violence against women often argue that, as part of this, men should engage in critical reflection of their own social locations and practices" (p. 159). Another essay of Powell (2003), "I Am a Recovering Misogynist," unearths his struggles to evolve into a black man mindful of his past misogynistic behaviors—and who is committed to his current nonpatriarchal stance. Powell's point is that men are always in the process of growing and working through issues of sexism, a necessary component for healing and transformation. That is, men should remain contemplative about what drew them to IPV work while examining how their positionality and male identity can complicate this effort. For example, what does it mean subjectively to attempt to interrupt a male abuser's commitment to male privilege once you leave the clinical situation and encounter male friends, family members, and associates who may embrace similar views? Or what does it mean when other men verbalize misogynistic ideas in your presence? These questions can help men think through their position as allies in fighting gender oppression even though their gender identity (being a man) is linked to structural forces that oppress women.

Men's Personal Ownership and Self-Awareness

In his seminal work *Pedagogy of the Oppressed*, Freire (2007) explains that the oppressor has inflicted a great deal of harm on the oppressed in order to sustain his positional authority, and as a result the humanity of the oppressed is disregarded. Freire's argument can be extended to male patriarchal behavior, which by definition devalues the humanity of women and girls. The force of oppression harms both the oppressed and the oppressor, according to Freire, who surmises that "Dehumanization, which marks not only those whose humanity has been stolen, but also (though in a different way) those who have it stolen, is a *distortion* of the vocation of becoming more fully human" (p. 44). Using this hypothesis, it can be argued that the noxious effects of sexism have disadvantaged men (i.e., they have forced men to perform an inauthentic self that restricts their ability to be whole and realize their humanity); therefore, men must own the multiplicity of ways that sexism has affected them, which is the initial step wherein men admit that personal growth is predicated on radical self-examination regarding their change efforts. Thus, men must be committed to personal work that fosters self-awareness and the development of insights concerning how gendered social and cultural conditioning has adversely affected their lives, and the people they claim to love.

Exposure to patriarchy and its consequences for men can be understood through the prism of attachment theory as espoused by Bowlby (1988), a developmental theorist who argued that attachment processes that occur during early childhood are critical to establishing self-worth and stability. Bowlby's research reveals that children experience a range of reactions, such as resistance to caretakers or emotional distress, when they do not feel securely attached. An important feature of this theory is that the attachment system between the parent and child stems from the development of what Bowlby refers to as *internal working models*, which are predicated on the pronounced emotional interactions and connections between parents and children. The development of internal working models also means that children take in the emotional and behavioral traits of their parents—which helps them to be in tune with their parents' affective rhythms—and strengthens the attachment system between and among them. This will eventually facilitate internal representations in the children, allowing them to function with themselves and others in future relationships. Although Bowlby's theory centers on the parent–child matrix, I believe it can be used in a broader sociopolitical context to understand, psychosocially and cognitively, many heterosexual cisgender men's dependence on and attachment to sexism, upon which the primacy of their existence is reinforced. The construction of men's internal working models is significantly influenced by their strong attachment and loyalty to the dictates of cultural sexism (i.e., the institutionalized discrimination and bias that affects women, and in turn benefits the lives of men and boys) that serve to shape male dominance. This observation is premised on the phenomenon of internalization (germane to cultural, social, familial, oppressive, and other factors) that powerfully affects the human condition (Fanon, 1967; Freire, 2007; Winnicott, 1965). Conceptually relating aspects of Bowlby's theory to men's socioemotional development emphasizes that their attachment to cultural sexist and patriarchal beliefs is deeply primal and resonates in all phases of their functioning. That men would critically examine themselves by exploring and taking ownership for the range of individual gender-based assaults they have perpetuated would lead to truth telling about the resulting self-harm they have also endured by holding onto patriarchal domination. The goal would be for men to experience catharsis through truth telling about constructing a masculine experience independent of power and privilege, creating a significant shift in their overall psychological state. hooks (2004) bolsters this stance by stating, "To offer men a different way of being, we must first replace the dominator model with a partnership model that sees interbeing and interdependency as the organic relationship of all living being. In the partnership model selfhood, whether one is female or male, is always at the core of one's identity" (p. 117).

The Duality of Alliances in Clinical Practice

To be an ally means to be in support of and concerned about the well-being of an oppressed group or a particular cause, and often this surfaces as a deep-seated aversion for social injustice, leading to the desire to dismantle inequity. Like white supremacy, where some white people fight racism, or like homophobia, where some heterosexuals fight heteronormativity, there are some men who consider becoming an ally of women important. Fabiano et al. (2003) stress "that it is possible to regard men as potential allies in ending violence against women by changing their personal behavior and/or intervening to confront the problematic behavior of other men" (p. 106). In addition, other researchers have inferred that there could be a decrease in patriarchal assaults as more men become allies opposing violence, and that such efforts also have the potential to motivate other men to become activists (Drury & Kaiser, 2014). The question is, at what point in a man's (or a boy's) life might he consider becoming an ally? My work in IPV has caused me to ponder this question, acknowledging that my adolescent years were without any insights into how sexism and patriarchy imprinted my development. The same point was brought up in group supervision (a monthly meeting designed to help clinicians process their feelings when working with IPV cases), where male colleagues involved in IPV work revealed the formation of their awareness regarding their relationship to patriarchy and how insights into their sexist attitudes began as they provided services to both abusers and abused women. It should be noted that men who are not human service professionals or mental health providers involved in IPV work may have a different personal direction regarding their consciousness of patriarchy and its impact on their conception of reality—an important caveat to reflect on. How might a call to men resonate for this group?

My growing role as an ally (like that of other male therapists working with IPV cases) was intertwined in my clinical practice with abused women, and this became clear after two years of assisting abused woman seeking orders of protection and psychotherapy. At that time, I was asked to present a workshop on "The Dynamics of IPV" to a community group. Confronted with pronounced victim blaming from a fraction of the audience during the presentation, I was compelled to shift from a presentation mode to an advocacy stance, speaking firmly about the need for women and children to live in violence-free relationships, and encouraging the group to become supporters of abused women and opponents of all types of gender-based violence. Being thrust into this position by the workshop enabled me to reflect on my role as a clinician, and what came to light was the fact that being an ally is an inherent part of clinical practice with abused women. It seems reasonable that this requires male clinicians to deeply examine their intentions when doing this type of work—especially given the presence of countertransference in clinical work (i.e., potential feelings of identification with male abusers based on shared social identities), which will be fully addressed in chapter 9.

An axiom of working in the field of victimology is that the clinician should ensure the physical and psychological safety of victims. Thus, facets of micro practice with women is geared to address their legal, housing, medical, psychological, and child-care needs, all of which can facilitate safety. Further, men engaged in IPV work must recognize that gender-based violence is embedded in a set of sociological and political conditions and issues that place women and girls on the margins of society, which by definition means that the work has a justice-informed lens. It is unhelpful for male practitioners to subscribe to a view within which women's victimization is assessed and primarily treated as a mental health challenge. This accords with the views of many feminist scholars, activists, and clinicians.

The duality of being a male clinician as well as an ally is complex. Supporting a woman's right to self-determination even when her abuser could compromise her safety could prompt the male clinicians to offer advice, thereby muting her voice and sense of agency. Such advice can come across as patronizing for abused women, who have already been subjected to their male partners' dismissive attitudes. To avoid this, it is necessary for male clinicians to receive clinical consultations from female colleagues, counselors, and supervisors.

On Becoming an Ally in Interrupting Gender-Based Violence

As noted, men are not a monolithic group, and the notion of multiple masculinities (as posited in the literature) allows us to consider issues of diversity among and between men. The implication is that many men—including myself and many of my male colleagues—are committed to the eradication of violence against women. An important reason for this is that men have a fundamental need to be accepted and loved by intimate partners, sisters, godmothers, aunts, and female friends and associates, who wittingly add psychological nurturance to men's lives. The affective experiences emanating from being in relationships with women can be used as an inducement to work against violence. I experienced this in my work with abusive men in groups. As noted previously, denial is a major ego defense (i.e., explicit distortion of reality) present in clinical work with this group. Many men strongly deny that they have abused their partners, in spite of the court documents confirming their culpability. Projecting ownership for their abuse onto their partners and using other rationalizations (e.g., alcoholism, racism, stress at work) to justify their behavior are common tactics that prevent men from grasping the seriousness of their abusive behaviors. I have often observed a marked shift in abusive men's dispositions once I posed the following questions: What would it mean to you if your sister was in an IPV situation? What would it mean to you if your daughter was involved with an abusive man? What would it mean to you if your mother was sexually assaulted? What would it mean to you if a friend or an associate told you her intimae partner was attending a batterer's intervention program? These questions tend to shift men's cognitive and affective processes away from their intimate relationships (albeit temporarily), opening up a wider vista for them to see that women are susceptible to male violence due to its ubiquitous presence in society. Men invariably respond to the aforementioned questions by expressing a need to protect their family member or friend from male aggression and violence, and express shame and guilt for using violence in their relationships. I have used such feedback to loosen the soil of denial in batterers' groups so that empathic understanding can take root.

This anecdotal practice technique is one approach to breaking through men's defensive mechanisms in groups, and it certainly could be used to help men in society at large who still grapple with the following: that no means no during intimacy; that rape culture is real; that IPV is not predicated on love; that some women may not feel loved unless they are abused by male partners. Among many men, opposing views on these topics are blatant and are buttressed by social and political occurrences in our culture, such as congressional hearings concerning sexual assault allegations against two male Supreme Court justice nominees (allegations of sexual abuse surfaced after both Clarence Thomas [1991] and Brett Kavanaugh [2018] were nominated), which proved to be inconsequential, because in the end these men were confirmed and are currently members of the highest court in the federal judiciary of the United States. The vilification of women by many men and segments of society pervaded these cases, translating to men and boys that the victimization of women is unimportant. In a sense, the outcomes of these gendered social phenomena can elicit indifference in men and retard their motivation to interrupt the cycle of male violence against women, in particular as they observe society's tendency to blame the accusers. Still, it is beneficial to underline for men and boys the ravages of male violence on women to induce compassion for women, and to help men develop an interest in protecting women and girls. In addition, men's culpability for maintaining patriarchy and actively participating (consciously or unconsciously) in its practices must be understood in the context of motivating them to become opponents of gender-informed oppression, which reminds us that personal growth in the human condition occurs incrementally.

Some Implications of #MeToo

The advocacy promulgated by the women's movement and the violence against the women's movement paved the way for #MeToo. Building on the work of these movements, #MeToo has ushered in a different public and private awareness of the sexual abuse faced by women involved in interpersonal relationships with privileged men, highlighting that power and dominance are propelling factors underlying systemic misogyny. Further, the celebrity victims and abusers associated with #MeToo undoubtedly pierced the public's psyche: famous men have endured notable penalties (e.g., loss of employment, convictions, incarceration, and public ridicule) for exercising unwanted and unwelcomed sexual behaviors, signaling to other men that their privilege and status are no longer protection for their misogyny. Tambe (2018) advances a similar angle in her research: "Then came the slew of powerful cis-men, largely in the U.S. media and entertainment industries, who were forced to swiftly resign after allegations of sexual misconduct. This toppling continues and has expanded beyond the media to other industries where reputations matter: politics, music, architecture, and, somewhat belatedly, higher education" (p. 198). In many ways, #MeToo offered an opportunity for celebrity victims of sexual abuse to engage in truth telling. Hearing these stories and witnessing a candidate for president of the United States bragging about his misogynistic behaviors (grabbing women's genitalia) likewise inspired women in the general population to publicize their victimization. In an essay on #MeToo, Rodino-Colocino (2018) writes,

> Approximately one year after the tape of Trump's claiming to "grab [women] by the pussy" surfaced, and in the midst of over 80 women coming forward to accuse Harvey Weinstein of sexual harassment, assault, and rape (in addition to similar accusations made against powerful men in Hollywood and Washington), actress Alyssa Milano tweeted that survivors of harassment and assault shout tweet #MeToo. (p. 98)

The confluences of this factor and Tarana Burke's #MeToo advocacy efforts (which occurred in 2007 in Alabama) that proceeded Alyssa Milano's tweet resulted in raising public consciousness about the pervasive reality of the sexual coercion of women and men's culpability in this regard (Tambe, 2018).

#MeToo and its impact on present-day cultural norms and mores continue to vex some men. Women's allegations and accusations of relational maltreatment from men have resulted in outcomes (e.g., loss of employment or public shaming) that may have additional effects. Moreover, some men feel aggrieved about having to take responsibility for alleged physical assaults, rapes, or violence that took place during earlier times in their lives (i.e., abusive behaviors that occurred during high school or college). Others feel automatically implicated once accused of any type of assault by women. This vexation among some men has led to a backlash against the #MeToo movement. #MeToo continues to reform the landscape of society, and to some degree foundational notions of patriarchy are being aggressively critiqued and interrogated by the academy, social media, and even political entities. I have heard the following reactions from other men in connection to the changing social environment: "the rules for men and women are different"; "as men we do not know how to react to women anymore"; and "the workplace is boring because of political correctness." Of course, these expressions do not characterize the attitudes of all men, though they confirm the adage that when the status quo is threatened, "pushback" and resistance against change are inevitable. Glaude's (2016) research on race in America is relevant. He reminds us that a segment of white America still uses what he refers to as "racial habits" to resist the social and economic progress of African American people (p. 58):

> Racial habits are the ways we live the belief that white people are valued more than others. They are the things we do, without thinking, that sustain the value gap. They range from the snap judgments we make about black people that rely on stereotypes to the ways we think about race that we get from living within our respective communities. Both shape how we account for the persistence of racial inequality today. (p. 55)

At the same time, patriarchy and sexism have always centered men, and developments of gendered habits (similar to racial habits) have reinforced ideas about what manhood and masculinity entail. Given this orientation, society's changing ideas about the interactions between men and women and between boys and girls (as influenced by #MeToo) have destabilized some men, causing them to feel a sense of fragility, mostly due to their inability to reflexively use privilege to dominate their partners and navigate their overall existence. This is akin to the reactions of many white people who exhibit fragility when they perceive threats to white privilege. DiAngelo (2018) sums it up: "White fragility keeps people of color in line and 'in their place.' In this way, it is a powerful form of white racial control" (p. 112). Likewise, for many men, male privilege serves to bolster their social and intellectual position, and thus any semblance of social change creates anxiety, which can result in male backlash. In his book *Boys Will Be Boys*, Miedzian (2002) asserts that the movement to eradicate sexism threatened the traditional construction of masculine identity and the systems that reinforce its existence.

Living beyond the Binary of Male Supremacy

My work with abused women and children and abusers has occurred primarily on micro and mezzo levels. Conversations with other male practitioners about macro strategies to prevent violence against women were limited due to the paucity of men who were engaged in this type of work in New York City in the early 1990s. This led me to participate in women's groups working on agency-based policies and the development of service delivery. These experiences have been fulfilling professionally, and they inspired me to embark on this discursive chapter—focusing on the need for men to use their privilege to mobilize change.

A call to men to address the abuse and victimization of women means that men should partner with other men as well as women's organizations to dislocate antifemaleness within society. The idea of a partnership means that men should make a commitment to be more than bystanders and instead invest in social justice advocacy collaborations with women. The Centers for Disease Control and Prevention (CDC), for example, has documented the prevalence of the bystander role among men, notably in relation to IPV and sexual assaults (CDC, 2010). Latané and Darley (1969) postulate a schema for understanding men as bystanders. This schema is summarized by Casey and Ohler (2012): "*noting* the troubling situation, *interpreting* it as problematic, assuming personal *responsibility* for addressing the problem, *identifying* an accessible course of action, and then *implementing* that action" (p. 64). The degree to which bystanders may react is based on a set of dynamics, including the behavior of others observing the situation (i.e., the "bystander effect"), so that inactivity or indifference on the part of observers may alter the motivation of a bystander to act. The schema has had resonance in several fields, including the physical and sexual maltreatment of children and adolescents (p. 64).

Men helping men to "man up" by breaking the silence associated with their bystander positionality is a critical component of men's work. *Man up* is a pejorative term used to advance a type of masculinity that is stoic and divorced from emotionality; however, I am reframing it in this chapter to suggest that men use their will to engage in constructive bystander behaviors. The five following areas of the aforementioned schema are reframed in order to illustrate their applicability to men's work in the field of IPV:

1. By "*noting* the troubling situation," men can begin to talk with other men socially and professionally about the pervasiveness of violence perpetrated by men in intimate and nonintimate relationships. Men can use a range of venues to have small or large conversations about the hazards of violence in the lives of women and children. Helping men understand how their aggression and abuse affects their daughters' and sons' well-being would be an important aspect of *noting* the negative outcomes of men's violence against women.
2. In "*interpreting* it as a problem," men can clarify that the perpetuation of violence by men regardless of context is intentional and serves to control women. Unpacking how men's familial socialization and exposure to patriarchy promote a sense of ownership over women's bodies can help them reflect on their internalized template of sexism and male dominance.
3. In "assuming personal *responsibility*," men begin to exercise moral leadership by helping other men find the courage to denounce a toxic conception of manhood. Raising awareness about the possibility of a better world where there is equity for women and men and where the language of maleness is not synonymous with power and conquest.
4. By "*identifying* an accessible course of action," men can co-construct strategies they can work on personally via individual or group therapy, volunteering at women's organization, taking courses in gender studies at a college or university, making amends for their use of violence against women or committing microaggressions when relating to women and girls, writing op-ed articles supporting gender equality in the workplace and home, calling out

everyday misogyny and sexism, and making a commitment to talk with male friends about the need to oppose violence. All of these actions have the potential to stimulate empathy in men, enabling them to find an alternative to what hooks (2004) refers to as "patriarchal masculinity" (p. 55).
5. By "*implementing* that action," men would embrace a feminist stance that focuses on changing the conditions and circumstances that fuel the politics of male (white) superiority. Such a stance would increase gendered awareness in men, allowing them to work collaboratively with women, and promote systemic antiviolence and antisexist behaviors among men.

Men's efforts in stopping violence against women will be ineffective unless there is a strong partnership with women's organizations and groups. Men must understand their outsider role in gender-related activism, much like allies of other causes, such as LGBTQ+ liberation or the civil rights movement. Working against a specific cause when one is an outsider requires cultural humility, the need to maintain active self-awareness of and appreciation for not being an expert on the lived reality of others. Thus, men's work requires collaboration with women's groups, and there must be genuine respect for women and their ideas about the kinds of liberatory frameworks and ideas that could impede gendered-related violence. An important way to reflect on this would be for men to place themselves in the role of students of feminist and womanist thought. Of course, men can learn a tremendous amount from women despite the implicit teaching of patriarchy that suggests they should either ignore or dismiss a woman's point of view. Listening to women (from diverse experiences) with purpose and meaning can facilitate self-awareness in men, counteracting myths about women that may have shaped their biased and sexist worldviews. This cognitive and affective approach to learning does not mean that men will automatically commit themselves to the goals of feminism, but it is an important element if they are to be agents of gender equality and social change. Moreover, collaborative work with women's groups and organizations necessitates that men advocate for and demonstrate a commitment to progressive causes aimed at gender and relational equity among girls, boys, women, and men. The following are aspirational and practical steps men can embrace in their pursuit of dismantling gender-induced violence at the familial, individual, community, workplace, and societal levels:

1. Support efforts to eradicate systemic violence (e.g., interpersonal and workplace violence and state-sanctioned reproductive coercion) against women.
2. Advocate for reproductive justice by engaging in activism at local and state levels.
3. Support efforts to address the impact of IPV on women, girls, and boys.
4. Support efforts that use #MeToo as a strategy to educate society about rape culture.
5. Support community organizing efforts on college campuses, in neighborhoods, in work environments, and at places of worship to eliminate misogyny.
6. Assist in legislative activities by testifying to how men use coercive control to subjugate women and girls.

7. Assist in the development of organizational policy statements focusing on how men's violence leads to traumatic reactions in women and girls and boys.
8. Speak out at rallies, barber shops, gymnasiums, and community forums in order to advocate for justice-informed approaches to protect the rights of women and girls and boys.
9. Engage latency-aged and adolescent males in activities that call attention to gendered-informed bullying and sexting, which are often precursors to teen dating violence and rape.
10. Advocate for meaningful intersectional analyses of interpersonal violence and communities of color in the context of policing and carceral interventions.
11. Explore the myriad ways patriarchal teachings have impacted men's psychosocial functioning.
12. Explore how patriarchal masculinity has underpinned men's emotional lives.
13. Unpack the politics of patriarchy and its impact on men's formative and adult experiences.
14. Pay attention to feminist discourses to gain insights into the many ways idealized ideas of masculinity have informed self-understanding.

Men interested in taking a stand against the cycle of maltreatment of women and girls can consider these actions. The above list is by no means exhaustive, but it does provide a beginning process by which men can reflect on the importance of changing the traditional culture of men who subject women to coercive control and violence. The call to action regarding violence against women in the title of this chapter is built on the idea that men can and should be accountability partners of other men who are interested in and are willing to advocate for gender equity. Accountability partners would make it possible for men to educate other men about the ideological context of patriarchy and sexism. By definition, this type of effort would help men take ownership for their abusiveness, help them explore alternatives to using violence in intimate and interpersonal relationships, and hopefully promote discernment and mindfulness relating to how gender-based problems such as rape, sexual harassment, and IPV ultimately impede the possibility of equitable and loving relationships between women and men. Another dimension of men's work related to this call for action is the importance of partnership with women, a process by which women's voices, needs, and concerns can be at the forefront of men's consciousness, which can hold men accountable for how they help other men own their violent/abusive behaviors, while opposing the daily violent circumstances women face.

Men Who Advocate for Gender Equality

Advocacy centering on gender fairness begins when men develop a level of tenderness in their hearts and minds, guided by values that suggest that patriarchy and sexism are anathema to their view of themselves. To lessen feelings of invulnerability and emotional indifference, it is useful for men to develop the capacity to acknowledge and feel a sense of tenderness, which will enable them to be fully attuned to their "emotional life" (hooks, 2004, p. 36). This rests on getting loose from the grip of systemic patriarchy, and by doing so, shifting their perceptions of women as individuals whose primary purpose is to satisfy men's needs. More important, men can learn how their lack of tenderness (the lack of empathy and being attuned emotionally), which is emphasized by hegemonic masculinity, accounts for the violations of the human rights of women. To feel a sense of tenderness can lead to a sense of courageous empathy, the will and desire to feel the sufferings of women in the context of patriarchy. What makes this "courageous" is that it adds complexity to men's lives because they have deviated from ideas of patriarchy by attempting to place themselves in the position of women, a stance that is foreign to the patriarchal definition of maleness and that may be met with ridicule and ostracism by other men. As an example, tweets (in the wake of the #MeToo period) by men in support of female survivors of sexual violence that held men accountable were ridiculed by other men. The amplification of these detractors is shown by Pettyjohn et al. (2018), who state that "The attack impl[ies] that 'real men' maintain control over women, and that empathizing with women's experiences of sexual violence is symbolic of relinquishment of the power men have been given by living in a patriarchal society" (p. 8). Yet we know that it is morally prudent for men to move beyond the circumscribed parameters of maleness to actively engage in alliances and partnerships with women in order to correct the wrongs stemming from gender injustice.

Implications for Psychotherapeutic Interventions

This chapter explores the role of men becoming partners and allies in antiviolence work. In particular, clinicians and counselors providing services to abusive men can explore the benefits of abusers becoming advocates for social change, an action that can occur during or after therapy. This reparative stance can have a positive impact on men's personal growth, and beyond ending their use of violence in intimate relationships, this form of activism can facilitate greater mindfulness, making it possible for men to work indefinitely to end systemic gender-based violence. Antiviolence work can motivate men to immerse themselves in workshops on gender studies and to volunteer at social agencies serving abusive men, children, and abused women, which might increase their understanding of feminism and patriarchy. hooks (2015) offers this perspective:

> Feminist consciousness raising for males is as essential to revolutionary movements as female groups. Had there been an emphasis on groups for males that taught boys and men about what sexism is and how it can be transformed, it would have been impossible for mass media to portray the movement as anti-male. It would also have preempted the formation of an anti-feminist men's movement. (p. 11)

In addition, clinicians and counselors can use bibliotherapy, a cognitive technique to expand men's thought processes about a variety of subjects, including gender dynamics, feminism, and patriarchy (Diemes et al., 2011). As a therapeutic approach, bibliotherapy involves assigning relevant books to men as homework assignments and exploring their thoughts about the content. And as a socioemotional and political endeavor, men can meet in coffee shops, at barber shops, in gyms, and in other social circles to engage (peruse books) in discussions about what it means to navigate a new sense of manhood and masculinity that considers the worth and value of women and girls.

Conclusion

This chapter distills a variety of points men can consider as they attempt to become allies in the struggle to eradicate psychological maltreatment and physical violence against women and girls. In embarking on this journey, the chapter suggests that it is important for men to engage in gender-based consciousness, which could lead to greater insights into the emotional liabilities associated with their intentional (or unintentional) consent to patriarchy, and help them understand its odious impact on their psychosocial worldview (the relationship between their emotionality and cognitive schema). It is acknowledged that although men should not be considered part of a monolith, their exposure to systemic factors that locate women and girls at the margins of society may have inevitably affected their perceptions and attitudes. As argued above, men should take personal ownership for their gendered ideas and behaviors, a step in developing self-understanding that could motivate them to work with other men and with women to defeat sexism. The development of self-understanding will enable men to recognize their deep-seated attachment to the principles of misogyny, and how this attachment has deprived them of being in touch with their humanity, and therefore undercut their ability to have empathy for women and girls.

A call to action implies that men have a moral responsibility to address intimate violence against women, to speak out against this type of violence, to hold other men accountable for their sexist and misogynistic attitude (by definition, taking a moral stance), and to make it clear that gender-based victimization is reprehensible. Moreover, justice-making efforts accompanied with care and empathy, along with a deep-rooted commitment to eradicate or minimize violence in women's and girls' lives, should be at the core of men's motivation to become allies. Implicit in this chapter is that men must repudiate all forms of violence and movements designed to impede social and political progress for women and girls. Partnering with women's groups and organizations will allow men to learn what strategies work and what would best advance gender-based equality and rights. Men helping men wrestle with their need to control and dominate women becomes one of the significant pillars of interrupting IPV, sexual harassment, catcalls, and other forms of gender-related aggression. Men's culpability in consciously or unconsciously perpetuating sexism can be acknowledged even as they participate in activities aimed at addressing this type of oppression. The work of progressive men can add to existing gender-based advocacy, but it does not change the fact that gender prejudice and bias are endemic in our culture and pose threats to women and girls.

Discussion Questions

1. What did you find useful about this chapter?
2. How did this chapter increase your knowledge of allyship work and gender-based activities?
3. How might you use this chapter in clinical practice with nonabusive men?
4. How might you use this chapter to engage abusive men?
5. What reactions and questions came up for you in the section on the "duality of alliance" in clinical practice?
6. What stood out for you in the section on the implications of #MeToo?
7. What aspect of this chapter encouraged introspection in men on a professional level?
8. What aspect of this chapter encouraged "gender-based consciousness" in men?
9. What do you think of the aspirational and practical steps men can consider in their pursuit of dismantling gender-induced violence and oppression?

CHAPTER 9

Shared Vulnerability
Countertransferential Reactions, Supervision, and Self-Care

Helping professionals must pay attention to the ways they are affected by working with people afflicted by intimate partner violence (IPV) and abuse. By assisting children exposed to violence between their parents, therapists derive gratification from attending to their emotional, psychological, practical, and concrete needs. Therapists also receive professional fulfillment for being able to create physical and psychic safety for women trapped in the lethal cycle of partner violence and maltreatment. And there are therapists working with male batterers who believe this type of work is important and perceive it as another way to address the problem of partner violence. The point is that therapeutic work in this area of practice—although challenging—can be extremely rewarding because it allows therapists to provide healing spaces for clients who have been victims or perpetrators of a crime. The challenging parts of this work, however, must also be acknowledged: intervention with clients whose narratives are replete with the effects of physical, sexual, emotional, and psychological assaults can deplete therapists' empathy quotient, a potential liability that can adversely affect the curative process of therapy. To avoid this while maintaining a sense of professional satisfaction in clinical work, organizations serving clients affected by IPV should have greater commitment to providing professional support to buffer the stress, tension, and compassion fatigue of the therapist's experience.

The premise of this chapter is that, IPV notwithstanding, countertransference in psychotherapeutic work is inevitable because clients' stories and emotionality can surface conscious or unconscious feelings in therapists. The chapter asserts that this can be heightened if therapists have had experiences as a victim of partner abuse or exercised violence and aggression in a relationship. The chapter highlights that some professionals will find themselves working in this area without a preparatory understanding (e.g., the process of thinking about how IPV work may affect one's personal and professional lives) of how their personal lives may be intertwined with clients, particularly if the therapist has unresolved histories of abuse or is currently in an abusive relationship. Supervision and self-care are proposed as viable options to fuel and sustain therapists' commitment to this work.

In particular, the chapter argues that clinical supervision is an important process for professionals working with partner abuse cases: it allows them to increase self-awareness, engage in self-reflection, and enhance knowledge and skills development. Hearing clients' stories—which are usually infused with violence and trauma—requires practitioners to have a supervisory space to examine and process their feelings of countertransference and shared vulnerability, which are often linked to a sense of feeling emotionally and physically wounded. Aligning supervision with self-care, the chapter stresses that clinicians must be attuned to how they are affected professionally and personally when working with IPV clients, in particular victims and abusers. Abbreviated case scenarios of supervisees are presented throughout the chapter, highlighting how a focus on self-care illuminates feelings of vulnerability and generalized anxiety that can encumber clinical practice. Lastly, the chapter distills Kadushin's (1992) paradigm of social work supervision, stressing that the provision of clinical supervision when paired with the clinician's personal therapy and other mindfulness-based activities can mitigate burnout and vicarious traumatization.

Supervision

Supervision conjures up a plethora of reactions in people working in human services, including social workers, counselors, advocates, case managers, and other people in the allied helping professions. The variability of perspectives on this issue indicates a couple of factors: the professional socialization of people's discipline and formal training can dictate how they understand and view supervision, and the type of practice philosophy used by programs or organizations also provides models for what constitutes supervision. Reactions from these experiences are neither right nor wrong, because there are many ways organizations and programs conceptualize the structure of supervision. For instance, programs and organizations may adhere to weekly formal supervisory sessions. Others may employ an ad hoc approach based on the tempo of the clinical process and the needs of the therapists or supervisors. In this chapter, I will consider consistent supervision to be akin to self-care, largely in the context of service delivery with IPV clients.

Research on the history of social work supervision, for instance, indicates that experienced professionals were charged with the task of helping inexperienced social workers carry out their job responsibilities (Kadushin, 1992). The location of supervision during the 1950s spoke to the fact that the oversight function of supervision was a critical component of service provision. This focus of supervision persists in many human service organizations in the twenty-first century where social work services are administered, and its supposition is based on the idea that knowledge and techniques originate from the supervisor, who in turn uses both in supervision to increase the competence of the supervisees. Although this can be helpful, research indicates that supervisees should be allowed to think through their work with clients independent of constant reliance on the expertise of their supervisors (Hess et al., 2008; Holloway & Brager, 1989; Kadushin, 1992). Supervisees can be socialized to be more self-reflective and introspective when autonomy is expected by their supervisors, giving them the opportunity to step back from the crisis-laden patterns that often accompany agency-based clinical practice and to look at what they need professionally to maintain motivation and engagement in clinical work with their clients.

Components of Supervision

Much has been written about the components of supervision. Elements of Kadushin's (1992) formulation are relevant in that they line up with the focus of this chapter as well as with this text as a whole. Kadushin enunciates the following functions of social work supervision: administrative, educational, and supportive. These functions provide structure, content, and an opportunity for supervisees to feel competent and effective when delivering services to clients. First, administrative supervision centers on macro and mezzo issues within and outside of the organization. Macro issues may relate to how funding affects service delivery based on the political party that is in power and what social issues may have traction given a particular political climate. For instance, consider a victim assistance organization that primarily serves abused women. Therapists may begin to see some cases involving adolescent victims of dating abuse at the same time but may need to refer them to other programs due to less funding for such work. Addressing such areas via administrative supervision could open up conversations about insufficient funding to carry out the objectives of the organization or inadequate staff to respond to the volume of clients seeking services. Through this mode of supervision, the staff may gain an expansive perspective about organizational processes, including politics, policies, funding, the organizational mission, and even the role of the board of directors in shaping service approaches. Kadushin (1992) believes that it is important to convey this information to staff, but also states that supervisors should help staff manage this terrain as it is fraught with bureaucratic challenges that can undermine the helping process. Making the point even more emphatically, Kadushin notes, "This administrative function of supervision is implemented by offering workers the opportunity to discuss with the supervisor their questions and doubts about the agency's philosophy, rules, and procedures. Patient, open discussion of the worker's views in an accepting atmosphere is designed to help them understand the rationale of the agency's approach" (p. 74). Irrespective of larger systemic and organizational barriers, workers (supervisees/staff) should still have an opportunity to express themselves to their supervisors, and Kadushin thinks this can generate goodwill and collaboration within and between both groups. In addition, the mezzo dimension of administrative supervision is designed to hold staff accountable for complying with agency policies and standards. Furthermore, documentation of work—completed and timely submission of work products to supervisors, community partners, and funders—is a key expectation of administrative supervision. Kadushin's amplification of tasks and responsibilities connected to this facet of the supervisory process is as follows:

1. Staff recruitment
2. Inducting and placing the worker
3. Work planning
4. Work delegation
5. Monitoring, reviewing, and evaluating work
6. Coordinating work
7. The communication functions
8. The supervisor as an advocate
9. The supervisor as administrative buffer
10. The supervisor as change agent (p. 46)

Administrative supervision at its core enables the supervisor to provide structure, context, and opportunity to competently execute work activities. Nonpunitive in its application, this form of supervision means that the supervisor acts as intermediary on behalf of the administration and the staff. Because of this duality of roles, supervisees can at times feel less supported if they are being held accountable for careless work performance.

Second, by taking on a teaching role, the supervisor imparts the requisite knowledge and skills needed for the staff to complete work-related functions, an essential part of educational supervision. The role of teacher is not often highlighted in the discussion of supervision because we frequently link it to the classroom, where the emphasis is on a didactic approach to delivering course content. Yet supervisors possess expertise that can be conveyed to supervisees in an effort to help them complete work tasks, as noted by Kadushin (1992), who remarks that the content areas of the supervision vary depending on the field of practice (e.g., substance abuse, mental health treatment) and the supervisee's level of professional preparation. Thus, the needs of a recent graduate working in IPV differ from an experienced professional who has been counseling clients with trauma for several years. Nevertheless, both supervisees require educational supervision. Kadushin tells us that it is useful for supervisors to do an educational assessment to discern differing professional needs in order to assist supervisees in accordance with their strengths and challenges. Referring to an educational assessment as an educational diagnosis, Kadushin discusses the need for supervisors to appreciate the learning and teaching conditions in relation to adult learning patterns. That is, supervisors should not begin with the idea that supervisees are blank slates, but instead supervisors should appreciate the fact that supervisees are adults whose lived experiences can enhance the learning aspect of supervision.

Hence, an educational diagnosis as presented by Kadushin is formed by the following: observing the supervisee's work with clients, reading case records, reflecting on meetings with supervisees, and engaging them in conversation about what they already know and what they are interested in knowing. An educational diagnosis regarding the supervisee includes but is not limited to the following domains:

- Learning about how to engage, assess, plan, and work with clients' problems
- Attunement to how issues of countertransference and transference affect clinical work with clients
- Professional use of self in work with clients and how this idea manifests in practice
- Learning new and different ways to understand how social issues affect clients' psychosocial functioning
- Developing comfort with ambiguity in working with clients
- Managing the power differential associated with supervisory relationships

Knowing about these areas can enhance the supervisory relationship and construct an approach for clinical learning and professional development, accentuating Kadushin's assertion that an educational diagnosis recognizes that the focus of educational supervision is related to clinical matters in social work practice, and can be understood as a method of bolstering a clinician's skills. Moreover, Kadushin (1992) declares, "Educational supervision is sometimes termed clinical supervision. It is concerned with teaching the knowledge, skills, and attitudes necessary for the performance of clinical social work tasks through the detailed analysis of the worker's interactions with the client" (p. 135). An additional declaration of the interplay between educational supervision and clinical work is made by other researchers, who maintain that clinicians need to explore and examine the dynamic factors that emerge from practice, and that this can only occur when the supervisor embraces an educative function (Hess et al., 2008). These same researchers state, "In the first place, the supervisor is an educator, instructing in cognitive, affective and performance spheres using a variety of techniques that suit both the student and his or her learning needs" (Hess et al., p. 18).

Educational supervision should be infused with trust, respect, and integrity—attributes that foster a positive relationship between the supervisor and the supervisees—and in this way professional development can be maximized. The rationale is that the supervisees should feel safe enough to take risks by exposing their practice in a nondefensive fashion. Because much of the work in supervision centers on the interactional dynamics between clients and supervisees, it makes sense for the supervisors to pay attention to their relational processes with supervisees as a means of understanding enactments that may reflect clinical situations. Kadushin (1992) refers to this as "parallel process" and proposes that it is a common phenomenon whereby "the supervisee reenacts in the supervisory conference the behaviors that the clients manifested in the casework interview" (p. 217). Avoidant behaviors related to dealing with difficult conversations (e.g., how to explore sexual issues with clients or how to respond to the needs of demanding clients who might appear difficult to engage in treatment) in supervision, for example, may offer insights into the relational spheres between the supervisee and the client. Supervisees may exhibit struggles similar to that of their clients as they attempt to talk about difficult or challenging content via supervision. Hess et al. (2008) summarize this supervisory feature:

"At times therapists consciously or unconsciously identity themselves with their clients and behave similarly to them in supervision" (p. 51). The existence of parallel process in supervision also provides an opening for both the clinician and the supervisor to focus on countertransference, which will be addressed later in this chapter.

Concerned with inter- and intrapersonal factors involving the therapeutic situation, educational supervision can unearth historical or current unresolved familial feelings in clinicians, prompting them to reflect on how such emotions may be impacting them and their cases. An outgrowth of supervision is to ensure (when warranted) that clinicians obtain therapy for themselves as an adjunct to their work. Supervision should not be used as therapy because it blurs the boundary of the professional relationships between clinicians and supervisors, changing the purpose, focus, and quality of a process designed to develop skills and knowledge in clinicians (Kadushin, 1992). Supporting the clinician's effort to engage in therapy is another form of self-care in which the resolution of personal challenges can occur and can potentially add clarity to clinicians' own psychological health.

Third, supportive supervision focuses on the emotional strain that clinicians feel in their work with clients. In particular, Kadushin (1992) submits, "supportive supervision is primarily concerned with increasing effectiveness of the worker through decreasing stress that interferes with performance and increasing motivation and intensifying commitment that enhances performance" (p. 228). Considering that therapeutic work with people faced with trauma, crises, and other problems of living can have resultant effects on service providers, this type of supervision engenders hope and optimism that can mitigate the sense of discouragement that sometimes occurs when clients' issues appear to be insurmountable. Work performance strain arises from lack of resources (i.e., insufficient shelter services for abused clients), high caseload, or the lack of access to educational supervision (Kadushin, 1992). Supportive supervision attempts to help the supervisee address organizational factors that obstruct their capacity to be productive; in the absence of supervision, supervisees can feel professionally neglected and abandoned, thereby increasing the possibility for burnout and pessimism about the field of practice or vocation they have chosen.

The provision of supportive supervision shows that the organization values the professional well-being of its staff and clients. Kadushin (1992) listed the properties of this form of supervision that resonated with supervisees who responded to a survey:

- Providing recognition and positive reinforcement about my work
- Showing sensitivity to work stresses and concern for well-being
- Being consistently available for support but making it safe for me to be independent
- Offering positive feedback, giving appreciation and recognition for good work (p. 232)

Likewise, Kadushin lists attributes consistent with supervisors who offer supportive supervision to their staff:

- The ability to relate positively, fairly, and supportively
- The importance of creating an empathic, supportive environment in which workers can comfortably discuss their clinical issues
- The importance of being empathic, respectful, caring, and providing a safe learning environment
- The ability to relate to supervisees in an empathic, direct, understanding, and nonauthoritarian manner (p. 232)

Based on the aforementioned reactions, both groups possess a keen awareness of the art of helping and caring for clients and recognize the need for having an outlet to explore and examine the psychological energy needed to work with clients while still meeting the demands and expectations of bureaucratic structures and protocols. And it is the relational qualities embedded in supportive supervision that serve to reduce work-related anxiety in the supervisee, enabling them to feel efficacious.

Organizational Challenges to Implementing Supervision

In general, it is virtually impossible for practitioners and clinicians to examine the interpersonal facets of their practice without educational and supportive supervision. That said, the preceding summary of Kadushin's (1992) model of supervision is presented as a frame for the reader that illuminates its salient features and shows the implications for cultivating clinical and professional learning/teaching opportunities. As social agencies and human service organizations become more bureaucratic, and are required to provide more services to clients with fewer resources, the clinical needs of staff have become overshadowed. Lack of organizational resources speaks to this dilemma: supervisors often do not have adequate time to offer educational supervision due to the high volume of work they are expected to accomplish within a given workweek. Moreover, supervisors may not have the requisite clinical training to develop their supervisees' clinical knowledge and techniques, something I noticed during the early years of my career as a clinical administrator and see as a growing trend within human service organizations. This has led to the offering of only administrative supervision, and though some episodic supportive functions of supervision are carried out in this approach as an attempt to validate staff overall work, it may not adequately address their needs. For this reason, the preceding summary of Kadushin's model of supervision is presented as an orientating frame that will help the reader focus on the characteristics of supervision, in particular how the educative and supportive areas can be beneficial in work with IPV cases.

Unpacking Countertransference Reactions and Feelings

Supervision in clinical practice allows the practitioner to explore the inevitable countertransferential reactions and feelings of the therapeutic alliance. Kadushin and Harkness (2002) posit that the phenomena of countertransference occurs consciously and unconsciously during the therapeutic process and is based chiefly on the therapist's reactions to the unfolding of the client's life. Goldstein's (1995) position on countertransference is that it "refers not only to the worker's unrealistic, unconsciously motivated reactions, but also to all the reality-based reactions he or she has to the client's behaviors" (p. 201). Engaging in therapy women and children whose lives have been affected—directly or indirectly—by violence can arouse a variety of emotions in many therapists coping with their own childhood history of abuse or current narrative of relational violence. Men who perpetrate violence against women in intimate relationships and are seeking therapeutic work can induce strong countertransferential reactions in therapists irrespective of whether they have had a personal history with relational or childhood abuse. Research stresses that countertransference occurs on multiple levels of the therapeutic relationship. The therapist may have a strong unconscious emotional response to the client's problems that may impede or enhance the work (Rosenberger & Hayes, 2002). The client's affect may arouse feelings of aggression in the therapist and thus prevent them from being empathic. On the other hand, clinical work could be enhanced if clients' stories unearth benevolence in therapists, and this could be manifested in a strong therapeutic alliance. In reflecting on IPV work in particular, anxiety, trepidation, and terror may reveal countertransference in many therapists; listening to stories about personal abuse, violence, and violation, and actually observing marks, bruises, and physical wounds on abused women's bodies during therapy sessions, can have a palpable impact on many therapists, igniting personal questions/feelings about their own relationships. Such observations in the therapeutic situation with abused women provoke feelings in therapists, and these feelings may be more resonant when there is a professional sense that women are in grave danger. All of these factors can compound countertransference feelings and may create a psychic urge within therapists to "rescue" women from their abusive partners, a well-intended stance that may minimize women's sense of agency.

Annie's Supervisory Process

An abbreviated case scenario concerning a supervisee demonstrates how themes of rescue and feeling sorry for a female victim of IPV pervaded her practice. After two years of postgraduate training in social work, Annie secured a clinical position in a community mental health organization that offered services to IPV clients for many years. Prior to this position, she worked in a school setting providing supportive counseling and advocacy to adolescents diagnosed with learning disabilities. Although she did not have direct experience counseling abused women, many parents of the children she treated in the school periodically reported that they were experiencing violence at home. Referring parents to an outside organization for assistance was the protocol Annie was expected to follow due to her role as a child therapist. Influenced by these experiences, Annie pursued work exclusively with IPV clients in order to expand her learning and professional development. Responsible for completing intake appointments with new clients twice per week, facilitating two trauma groups for women, and seeing individual clients during the remainder of the time meant that Annie had a full caseload consisting of women and children affected by IPV. Kadushin's (1992) three noted functions of supervision were employed by the organization. Annie usually met with her supervisor weekly for two hours; these meetings led to discussion relating to the completion of case notes, levels of services, and other pertinent administrative items. The meetings also dealt with interpersonal and clinical matters, with the aim of supporting and affirming her clinical practice.

In particular, Annie's supervisory sessions addressed questions and interventions, during which she reflected on her feelings in connection with her clients' problems. She quickly identified the struggles she faced in working on many cases, except in the case of Myra, a thirty-two-year-old, single, college-educated client who was in an abusive relationship with her boyfriend, whom she had dated for several years, and this became a point of discussion in the supervision meetings. Annie repeatedly raised questions about Myra's irrational decision to remain with her boyfriend, noting that this triggered a sense of powerlessness and helplessness in Annie. Exploratory discussions revealed that Annie was acutely aware of the role of ambivalence in the sequelae of the battered woman's situation, but in spite of this Annie had a strong wish for Myra to end her abusive relationship. Myra, however, wanted the abuse to end but wanted to remain with her partner due to her strong feelings for him. A closer look at Annie's clinical work indicated that she would become upset with Myra, and at times would cancel therapy appointments and take mental health days in order to avoid the process. Making the case that they were not a good fit as therapist and client, Annie requested to be relieved from Myra's case. It should be noted that Annie verbalized sadness and at times cried when she focused on Myra's abusive relationship, at which time the supervisor encouraged her to share her feelings in hopes that this would enable her to be more emotionally available to Myra during therapy sessions.

Educational and Clinical Supervision with Annie

An educational/clinical assessment of Annie's work showed that although her lack of experience with abused women may have contributed to the struggles she had with Myra, her countertransferential feelings were influencing their therapeutic interactions. It was reasonable for the supervisor to evaluate these features given their prominence in the supervisory dynamics, a position advanced by Kadushin (1992), who encourages supervisors to assess the professional and clinical needs of staff in order to identify and address their strengths and limitations. Embarking on an educational assessment can prevent the supervisor from embracing a moralistic attitude (i.e., the degree to which good and bad attributes are assigned to the interpersonal characteristics of the therapy) relative to the behavioral and affective performance of the supervisee. Hess et al. (2008) stress the primacy of competence in the therapeutic process, elaborating on the need for the supervisor to engage in an ongoing evaluation to hone the clinical expertise of the supervisee. Regarding Annie's newness to IPV, the supervisor explored an array of conceptual, practical, and psychosocial issues germane to battered women, namely, how ambivalence, fear of the abuser, and relational violence affect women's self-esteem. Herman (1992) writes, "The woman who becomes emotionally involved with a batterer initially interprets his possessive attention as a sign of passionate love. She may at first feel flattered and confused by his interest in every aspect of her life. As he becomes more domineering, she may minimize or excuse his behavior, not only because she fears him but also because she cares for him" (p. 82). Herman's thesis emphasizes that leaving an abusive relationship can be emotionally difficult for many women, and this is symptomatic of the terror caused by their abuser's behaviors, which can be debilitating, a subject of education/clinical supervision with Annie. Making use of the supervisor's years of practice wisdom (over twenty years working in this field) and the literature on trauma and IPV, the expectation of the supervision was that Annie would develop knowledge so that she could feel more grounded in her work.

Helping Annie reflect on potential gaps and strengths in her knowledge about IPV led to introspection about her therapeutic alliance with Myra. She admitted that hearing and processing content regarding IPV was extremely useful; nevertheless, she revealed that she had reached an impasse in therapy with Myra, which correlated to her countertransferential reactions. Here is the point: Annie only had this response to Myra and not the other abused women attached to her caseload, and as a result this became an important topic in supervision. Clinical themes in Annie's work that emerged centered on Myra's reluctance to sever her emotional ties with her boyfriend—and that she appeared more passive than other women on Annie's caseload—which caused a sense of powerlessness, leading to Annie's desire to rescue Myra from the abuser. Critical to clinical supervision was a discussion about Annie's countertransferential feelings and how she could use them to propel the therapeutic process with Myra. Discussions enabled Annie to recognize that her reactions to her client were deeply rooted in her personal narrative and view of life. The following questions guided the supervisory discussions:

- What emotional reactions can you recall during your initial appointments with Myra?
- When were you first aware of feelings of powerlessness or helplessness?
- To what extent are the personal dimensions of your life intersecting with Myra's account of her abusive relationship?
- At what point in the therapy do you feel powerless or helplessness?
- What would it mean to rescue Myra?
- What feelings, questions, and concerns come up for you when you are in a therapy session?
- What feelings, questions, and concerns surface for you after the therapy session?

- How would you describe the impact of Myra's abusive narrative on your professional and personal life?
- If you could make things better for Myra, what would that look like?
- What are some core feelings that you experience as a result of working with Myra?

This is not an exhaustive list of questions, but they can serve as a basis for helping the therapist become more attuned to the connections between his or her personal history and the client's emotional concerns. The use of these questions over several supervisory sessions stimulated feelings and beliefs about IPV, and these were connected to Annie's formative experiences and her adult life. She witnessed potent arguments between her parents, who eventually terminated their marriage, and the ensuing consequences of the divorce created an emotional gulf between her and her father. As Annie examined her reactions to her client more closely, she revealed teen dating abuse difficulties that occurred during adolescence: her fifteen-year-old boyfriend controlled her actions and would often slap her if she did not comply with his demands. As a fifteen-year-old adolescent whose parents were embroiled in marital strife, Annie chose to keep her abusive relationship from them, a decision also marked by the fear her boyfriend produced, which was due to his controlling attitude and his affiliation with a street gang. Feeling that her parents were preoccupied with their troubles and terrified that if she shared her abuse her father would attempt to hurt her boyfriend supported Annie's need to keep her abuse private.

Annie's reactions to Myra were informed by her formative years—she projected feelings of being trapped in her own abusive family and in her intimate relationship with her boyfriend onto the case. Goldstein (1995) contends that projection manifests as a defense mechanism in the human condition: "When an individual attributes to others unacceptable thoughts and feelings that he himself has but that are not conscious, he is using projection" (p. 78). Annie was not aware that her frustration with Myra was tied to feelings of powerlessness that were antecedents from her early childhood and adolescence abuse history. The reverberation of these unresolved issues echoed loudly in the therapeutic relationship and hindered Annie's ability to feel empathy for Myra. Goldstein's (1995) research emphasizes that projection is unhealthy, for it alters other people's reality and prevents those who use it from tuning into their own feelings. Further, Goldstein indicates that the defense mechanism of projection "diminishes the capacity to test reality" (p. 79). The feelings Annie experienced were projections of her emotions that had become distorted and were directly placed onto Myra. Having insight into her work with Myra helped Annie move beyond a sole interest in social justice, which was a primary motivation for working with IPV cases. Consistent with her feminist sensibility, Annie's interest in IPV work was to help women cope with men's violence and to eradicate misogyny and patriarchy. Supervision supported her sociopolitical agenda, reinforcing the need to also become more psychologically astute. This requires being present for the ways the therapist is affected by the client's narrative. If there is a lack of empathy for the client, the therapist should engage in emotional stock-taking, an effort that can surface internalized feelings and attitudes about unfinished family-of-origin factors. Awareness of these personal historical or present events permits a more deliberate use of a therapist's professional self so that they can access their emotions to support clients in the healing journey.

John's Supervisory Process

Although our clients sometimes share feelings of contentment with aspects of their lives by talking about a romantic other who brings them joy, or by describing an activity that brings them gratification, for the most part, stories replete with pain, disappointment, fear, anger, rage, sadness, revenge fantasies, and even hate frequently dominate therapeutic sessions with IPV cases (McWilliams, 1999). Hearing stories like these is foundational to the therapeutic encounter, and they have an impact on the therapist in a variety of ways. McWilliams (1999) writes that "patients [meaning clients] fill our offices with feelings; they touch us, frustrate us, demoralize us, enrage us, delight us, and surprise us" (p. 105). The implication of McWilliams's research is that the therapeutic alliance evokes a great deal of feelings in therapists, and to remain present and engaged in this process, organizations must support their work/clinical performance, a central theme in Kadushin's (1992) research, who indicates that support for workers should center on helping them manage work-related stress.

Clients' stories that are saturated with relational violence, abuse, psychological neglect, lack of kindness, trauma, anxiety about living and dying, and sexual assault can intensify feelings of stress and anxiety in many therapists. And still, therapeutic work with male abusers who perpetrate violence against women and provoke fear and anxiety in them requires the therapist to listen and hear stories of power, control, and conquest that have disempowered and victimized women; this too produces stress and unpleasant feelings of apprehension. With this frame, the supervision of John, albeit abbreviated, illustrates how elements of supportive supervision were used to enhance practice with a male abuser, Kevin. John facilitated a psychoeducation group for batterers and also provided individual therapy for many. He received clinical supervision to assist him with issues in the group and strategies to address batterers' abusive behaviors. In addition, he received individual educational/clinical supervision to address his clinical concerns relative to his individual work. Although having access to supervision was greatly appreciated, John identified with Kevin, whom he struggled with, requesting considerable support to help him in his clinical practice. That John was aware of this challenge in his practice pointed to his ability to examine his personal and professional processes with his clients. Receiving more support via supervision mitigated John's feeling emotionally overextended with Kevin's case. He could listen diligently to his story, including his abusive childhood history. John also felt his burgeoning feelings of burnout and dismay about IPV work should be explored and expressed a desire for increased support and validation regarding his practice.

Clinical and Supportive Supervision with John

The cruelty that Kevin subjected his partner to caused bodily injuries, and John reported that he felt overwhelmed when he met with Kevin. In terms of countertransference, John recognized that as much as he tried to distance himself from Kevin's abusiveness, it made him reflect on his own aggression and the role it had played in his interpersonal relationships with men and women. Research on contemporary psychotherapy posits that the therapeutic alliance between the client and therapist is co-constructed, and as such each has an influence on the other (Frank, 2002). Key to such a perspective is that therapy is predicated on the notion of a "two-person psychology," a relational process fused with mutuality, thus co-creating issues of countertransference. Supportive supervision validated this dynamic synergy between Kevin and John, stressing the gendered reality of their relationship (the implications of men working with other men in therapy) and its possible contribution to their therapeutic exchanges. Within the clinical purview of a male therapist delivering therapeutic services to other men, it is realistic for the therapist to think about what it means to have been exposed to misogyny and sexism, the same sociopolitical ills that to a large extent propel many men's violence against women. Male therapists must think about two areas in work with male perpetrators of IPV. First, to what degree do they unconsciously identify with issues of exercising power, control, and dominance vis-à-vis interpersonal relationships, because this is a traditional component of patriarchal teaching? Second, to what degree do they disassociate from abusive men as a way to make accommodation for their professional role, especially for therapists who are working directly with IPV cases? Informed by men's internalized ideas of masculinity and patriarchy, these questions can be answered through authentic conversations via supervision, with the goal of helping male therapists recognize that although they are working to eradicate IPV, they may carry remnants of male superiority that correspond with their clients' feelings. To pretend that male therapists magically shed their views of masculinity and femininity, considering that they have inculcated years of traditional corrosive values about patriarchy, is problematic at best and naïve at worst. For instance, John distanced himself from Kevin, who indicated that his use of violence was due to his wife's provocation. What was upsetting for John was that he did not challenge Kevin's rationalization for his abusive behavior, and this led to doubts about his professionalism, calling into question his competency in working with male abusers and whether he was colluding with him. In supervision, however, he discussed the shame he felt about having similar views as Kevin given his feelings about his intimate relationships. Not judging John for having these feelings, but instead helping him identify how Kevin triggered feelings in him that were common to his gender and socialization, was an integral part of clinical supportive supervision. Validating his emotions was a strategic way to mute his sense of shame and prevent him from losing hope in Kevin's capacity to change. All of this underscores Kadushin's (1992) claim that "the supervisor can validly reassure the worker that both the client and the relationship can survive a mistaken intervention, a poor interview, or a temporary lapse in professional conduct" (p. 269).

John was very aware that, emotionally, it was challenging listening to Kevin's childhood abusive narrative. The reason was that he felt Kevin used it to justify his violence, and knowing this fostered a judgmental attitude, signaling to John the need for more clinical supportive feedback via supervision. Contributing to his posture is the fact that abusive men utilize numerous defenses, including minimization and denial, to deflect responsibility for their actions, which can be counterproductive to their self-growth (Henning & Holford, 2006). Acutely aware that Kevin's defenses were geared to blaming his girlfriend and others for his violence, John found himself frustrated, angered, and annoyed, preventing him from having any real empathy for Kevin. Hearing content in therapy centering on violence and victimization arouses strong emotions in the therapist, which can affect the process (Berger & Quiros, 2014). In addition, listening to the abusive actions of men in therapy can be worrying, a viewpoint noted by Tyagi (2006), who suggests that "some of these narratives can be particularly alarming, and shock and disgust even the most experienced therapist" (p. 10). John not only heard Kevin's defenses, but he imagined the trauma and fear Kevin's partner experienced due to his abuse and the defense mechanism that blocked him from comprehending the pain he inflicted on her. Keeping the safety of the victim in mind is important in work with male abusers. Rather than allowing this to guide the work, it impeded John's capacity to be fully present for Kevin's needs.

Another contributing factor to John's lack of tolerance for Kevin's abuse history is that abusive men are perceived as criminals in light of their actions. And although this has validity, it makes it difficult at times for many therapists to see the abuser's humanity, much less their childhood victimization that may have affected their psychological functioning. Take my clinical experience as a case in point. Men shared childhood victimization experiences (being subjected to familial and community violence) in group and individual therapy sessions; however, limited support was provided for this aspect of their lives, in that batterers' intervention groups typically focus on educating men so that they will develop alternatives to abuse. Related to this philosophical underpinning, the training I received to intervene in IPV cases pointed out that many abusers use their formative abuse histories to defend their abusive actions; as such, this socialization shaped my early professional stance with this population, which meant I ignored their abuse histories. A consequence was that the scope of the work was truncated, and this inhibited having a full portrayal of their lives. It is important to note that not all abusers have been subjected to childhood abuse, and I am not positing that there is always a correlation between IPV and childhood victimization. Instead, practitioners and clinicians should be cognizant of those men who share indirect or direct exposure to violence during their early lives, keeping in mind that "traumatic events have primary effects not only on the psychological structures of the self but also on the systems of attachment and meaning that link individual and community" (Herman, 1992, p. 51). A corresponding observation is made by Wexler (2009), who indicates that abusive childhood victimizations experienced by men can adversely affect their lives in adulthood; thus, Wexler argues, they should be exposed to a therapeutic milieu that teaches them alternatives to violence and ways to identify familial traumas that may induce dysfunctional patterns affecting themselves and others.

In contrast, individual therapy with abusers can have a dialectical focus that addresses their culpability while still offering support to validate the victimization they endured as children.

> A psychodynamic approach gives clients a bird's eye view into their own history and allows them to link the past with the present. It also allows clinicians to observe victim's safety by holding men responsible for their abuse while they work on impulse control and relational skills. Combining this with psychoeducational and cognitive approaches permits men to overtly "tune into" their behaviors and attitudes, a process designed to address cognitive distortions. Finally, this approach can be beneficial for those who are motivated to examine their problems separate from their partner's expectations and/or desires to remain in the relationship. (Aymer, 2008b, p. 330)

Returning to John, unpacking anecdotal elements of the supervisor's practice provided valuable clinical support because it gave John a sense of universality, a concept espoused by Yalom (Yalom & Leszcz, 2005) in his seminal work on group psychotherapy. Yalom claims helping people understand they are not alone in their distress can ease the pronounced sense of loneliness they feel. In sharing facets of practice, the supervisor's intent was to offer John a larger framework for understanding the angst and dilemma he felt addressing Kevin's childhood abuse histories. Clinical supportive supervision acknowledged John's feelings, helping him grasp that Kevin was an abuser who was also abused as a child. Accordingly, that meant he was dealing with possible childhood trauma and may have needed empathy from John. This observation corresponds with the research of Good et al. (2005), who assert that "to the extent the therapist holds biased views of clients that label them 'perpetrator,' 'resistant,' or 'difficult,' the process of developing empathy for men's struggles will be inhibited and the likelihood of forming effective therapeutic alliances will be diminished" (p. 702). Given this assertion, what is important is that John could have provided space in the therapy to explore his childhood trauma and still help Kevin take ownership of his violence and its effects on his partner, a clinical consideration that must be thoroughly understood in work with this population.

Burnout and Vicarious Trauma

John expressed feelings of fatigue, disappointment, and a sense of helplessness in assisting his clients. Mainly, he questioned the efficacy of the help he was rendering them, a recurring thought that raised concerns about his need to change his field of practice from intervening with abusers to working in the field of substance abuse. Critical to his attitude was that therapy with abusive men stirred considerable emotions in him, leading to a great deal of personal inventory; he spoke of feeling tired and considered leaving the field of social work, an awakening that was anxiety producing given that he had personally and professionally invested so much in his career. It is important to note that irrespective of working with male abusers, the feelings John shared can emerge for many therapists whose use of self becomes the instrument that facilitates clients' self-growth and restoration. The notion of using one's self in therapy requires the therapist to be emotionally available, expending psychic energy to listen, respond, and reflect and support the psychological needs of clients. In general, this serves to contain the fragility, distress, and other challenges, leading to problem resolution and personal progress. With this in mind, it must be acknowledged that listening to and working with a clientele whose presenting problems and personal narratives are replete with advancing violence, anger, and cruelty to others, and whose emotional lives may be affected by childhood maltreatment, can have a different effect on therapists, who are acutely aware that such abusive behaviors have inflicted harm on others and that the resulting outcomes can be fatalities.

Conveying to John that his struggles were normal, the intent was to help him sort out his feelings concerning his clinical practice. He was reminded that the field of IPV is analogous to doing trauma-informed intervention, a viewpoint he was aware of but had not quite translated to working with male abusers. He did not understand that he was doing trauma-informed work with men who are perpetrators of violence in their intimate relationships. The supervision enabled him to reflect on the following: (1) men's violence produces trauma in women, (2) men's childhood abuse history is also emblematic of their trauma, and (3) therapists' psychological absorption of these conditions can be harmful to their practice and themselves. Situating John's work in this way enabled him to appreciate how he was affected and fostered discussions on the phenomenon of vicarious trauma. Berger and Quiros (2014) argue that it is important to inform supervisees about the construction of vicarious trauma so that they have a perspective about it. John and his supervisor discussed that professionals involved in trauma-related treatment are affected emotionally by the events their clients narrate in therapy (Baird & Jenkins, 2003; Pearlman & Saakvitne, 1995). Therefore, the effects of vicarious trauma can prompt professionals to rethink their personal values about the human condition, depending on how they are triggered by their clients' trauma histories. Notions about intimate or nonintimate relationships surrounded by violence or danger, for instance, may elicit in therapists questions about themselves and others. Baird and Jenkins (2003) advise that vicarious trauma can unearth helplessness, causing pessimism in therapists, who may also feel a sense of distrust in the world and in others based on the corrosive effects being induced by their clients. Further, Tarshis and Baird (2019) state, "There also may be additional changes in social behaviors (e.g., social withdrawal, feeling estranged from friends/family) and difficulties in separating professional life from personal life" (p. 92).

The focus on vicarious trauma opened up a realm in John's personal lived experience he had not shared in supervision. He used aggression and violence once in an intimate relationship when he was an adolescent. The information emerged as we explored and conceptualized his clinical work as trauma related. He divulged that his girlfriend told him she was traumatized by his actions, and his recollection of the event was such that he was afraid and felt sad and ashamed of his actions. He claimed he apologized to her and never spoke about it until that moment in supervision. When asked to think through his feelings, he noted he still felt ashamed but felt clearer as to why he was so affected by Kevin's case. The vulnerability his girlfriend felt still lingers in his psyche, and in turn this may have gotten in the way of him being more emotionally available for Kevin, whose case might have heightened his anxiety. Consciously or unconsciously, his emotional distance from Kevin and his frustrations with his case may have been an attempt by John to avoid facing his early personal abuse history. His inability to challenge Kevin stemmed from his fear of dealing directly with how his abuse affected his girlfriend and himself during his adolescence. This avoidant behavior was undoubtedly a psychological defense that insulated him from his past. Framing all of this as shared vulnerability fostered critical consciousness; that is, John developed more depth about how the co-construction of his therapeutic relationship with Kevin triggered unacceptable responses in him, and how these feelings created a divide between them. Grappling with the idea that his adolescent dating abuse background may have been similar to Kevin's adult IPV narrative heightened the defense mechanisms of avoidance and denial, which presented a rupture in his capacity to withstand the emotional triggers he felt during the therapy.

The desire to leave IPV work and potentially his career as a social worker may have been associated with vicarious trauma and burnout. Such a desire was an attempt to assuage the anxiety he felt when working with male abusers, and indeed such a transition would allow him to escape his unresolved feelings of using IPV in his younger years. That said, it is reasonable to imply that working with batterers is emotionally demanding, whether one's background or history mirrors theirs or not. But it is also reasonable to remark that, in John's case, his unexamined past aggravated his work with Kevin and unconsciously created the impetus to detach from his work life. Many variables in the client–therapist dyad, including the impact the work produces, can contribute to burnout (Tarshis & Baird, 2019). As a process, burnout occurs over a period of time, and when unaddressed it can obstruct the therapist's ability to be productive (Ben-Porat & Itzhaky, 2011). Lack of productivity for John prompted him to request more supportive supervision, a strength he possessed as a professional, and to his credit he was open, amenable, and willing to talk about and process intersectional issues regarding his personal and professional lives. The emergence of these factors in supervision was extremely edifying, for they helped John reevaluate his attitude concerning his practice with male abusers as well as his detachment from his career. Nevertheless, it appeared that he needed therapeutic support that the supervisor could not offer him, highlighting that the supportive functions of supervision have limitations, and the existence of these limitations can lead to the possibility of boundary crossing and unethical practice on the part of the supervisor when he or she permits the process to morph into therapy (see, e.g., Kadushin, 1992). To this end, John agreed to attend therapy, and his supervisor provided a list of therapists who could be potentially helpful. What can be gleaned from this supervisory scenario was that John identified personal issues that compromised his ability to stay in tune with his clients, and this removed him emotionally from those elements (e.g., maintaining empathy, objectivity, self-awareness, critical consciousness) in his practice that were in the service of therapy.

Self-Care and Rest-Care

The provision of supervision within a social work and mental health organization, as well as in private practice, is foundational to a therapist's professional development. Skills, knowledge building, and emotional intelligence derived from supervision bolster the therapist's professional self. These outcomes are critical to the practice of therapy, and yet they may not totally address feelings of burnout, fatigue, disillusionment, frustrations, cynicism, and other by-products of work-based stress in therapists who use themselves as instruments to facilitate change in their clients (i.e., pouring out psychic energy and affect to create a safe enough environment for clients to release their pain, hurt, and suffering), especially those who bring histories of violence, trauma, and emotional abuse to the therapeutic alliance. Furthermore, the process of change in the course of IPV treatment means therapists must bear witness to the perilous situations confronted by victims, who may still feel unsafe or bear witness to abusers who use blame to deflect from their abusiveness. As such, therapists absorb the emotional toxins from being psychologically present for clients, and indeed it is this consistent exposure to and experience with IPV cases that can have a cumulative impact on their personal and professional selves, for which self-care strategies are necessary.

Self-care, a recurring theme among mental health professionals serving IPV clients, speaks to the need to be mindful of how this type of work, although gratifying, can also be emotionally strenuous and draining. The literature on self-care typically offers pragmatic strategies such as the use of regular exercise, the practice of yoga, and other activities to combat or deal with burnout. Students enrolled in my violence against women class usually articulate a sense of indifference as a result of reading articles on the topic. Instead, what seemed to be more beneficial for them was a desire to talk and process their feelings, questions, and concerns about the nexus among their work and their personal and professional lives in a nonsupervisory context. Inspired by their candor, I propose the following ways to begin conversations about self-care and rest-care:

- Being kind to one's self by knowing and doing
- Healing one's self through knowing

Being Kind to One's Self by Knowing and Doing

As previously noted, IPV work is challenging—it at times elicits doubts in therapists because they have no control over the vortex of abuse and violence that couples find themselves in. A fear of lethality abounds because we know that violence tends to escalate over time and that women can endure severe physical and psychological wounds. Attending to these wounds is a common urge among therapists, yet they must contend with the limitations of their work, using what they know about the change process involving IPV clients. From the perspective of self-care, clarity about professional limitations means having expectations about clients consistent with their overall individual and relational dynamics. Self-care means appreciating that IPV work is "messy" and complex and similar to the lack of control women feel in abusive relationships—and that some therapists tend to have parallel experiences that may challenge their sense of omnipotence. After helping a client secure an order of protection, for instance, a therapist may learn in therapy that the client is still seeing the abuser—perhaps out of fear and coercion or ambivalence, or both. In this scenario, both the client and the therapist may feel a loss of control as the therapy moves on a divergent path. Self-care in this regard means recognizing that viable assistance (e.g., safety planning, court-related information) has been rendered to the client and that the therapist accepts direction of the work without feeling totally responsible for the client's decision-making process. The point is that therapists should be kind to themselves by refraining from self-critiques when they feel challenged by the work. Instead, they should remind themselves that their intent is always to do no harm to their clients, recognizing that their role is to empower and support as opposed to rescue. A key factor in understanding self-care is to understand one's motivation and interest in embarking upon this type of work. If the goal is to rescue women from their abusers, instead of helping them reflect on nonabusive life course options, develop insights into their lives, secure safe spaces to live, or advocate for their rights, then as therapists our purpose for helping may be inherently filled with pressure to safeguard our clients, which is impossible. A corollary to this point is underlined by Carruthers (2018), a black queer activist who reminds us that any type of justice-informed work (at the macro, micro, or mezzo levels) is fraught: advocates, activists, and practitioners can become tired, weary, and emotionally spent as they fight against social injustice, particularly when personal unresolved afflictions stemming from trauma and other psychosocial challenges intersect with their activism. The need to embrace both "self-care and community care" is advanced by Carruthers and other activists who promote healing justice for marginalized people (Carruthers, 2018, p. 73). The point is that activists are not omnipotent—therefore, self-care and rest-care are needed to promote health and restoration. Taking a respite, or deciding to leave activism, is one example of rest-care, which can enable individuals to critically evaluate their personal needs (i.e., mental, emotional, physical, spiritual, and social health) in the context of their politics and their commitment to effectuating social reform.

Healing One's Self through Knowing

Purpose matters in the delivery of services to clients affected by IPV. That is, therapists should always reflect on the intended objectives and outcomes of being agents of change whose aim is to interrupt relational violence and abuse in order to assist women and their children, and also create therapeutic opportunities for abusers to work on themselves. Moreover, having a purposeful view of this zone of practice means that therapists should be mindful of the unintended consequences of how IPV work penetrates the soul of the therapist. Beaumont (2012) motivates us to examine the notion of soul in the spiritual domain of psychotherapy. I argue that we cannot ignore the presence of our soul and spirit when we work with people, because the considerable personal pain, anguish, terror, and other terrible challenges released by our clients in sessions have major effects on the circumstances of our personal lives as therapists. Beaumont does not use *soul* and *spirit* in their theological or metaphysical sense; rather, he believes they are linked to people's daily lives, enabling them to synthesize and make meaning of their experiences (p. 2). In referring to the notion of soul, he writes,

> It describes a dimension of everyday experience. It refers to a kind of actual, sensory experience that almost everyone can find without difficulty. Used in this way, it is not a subject for abstract speculation. It is a domain of experiences to be observed, described, and worked with. This soul is not eternally unchanging, but rather, learning, growing, and maturing. Soul knows hurt and pain as well as joy and serenity. (p. 2)

Beaumont's amplification denotes that soul is a salient dimension of selfhood and is consistent with a body–mind–spiritual connection. The penetrating effects of undertaking trauma-related and victimization work have the potential to deplete the mental, emotional, psychological, and physical energy of therapists, a consciousness that enables them to procure pathways and rituals for renewal. The following are examples of self-care and rest-care strategies when there is a reduction of psychic energy:

- Engage in individual psychotherapy to explore and address how the work may be impacting your personal life.
- Reflect on whether you are still motivated to do this type of work.
- Reflect on whether you need a respite from working with this client population.
- Engage in peer-led support groups to garner affirmation and build personal and professional stamina.
- Attend conferences and seminars on IPV to gain new and fresh perspectives about this work.
- Attend conferences and workshops (e.g., taking a course in gardening or a foreign language) that are related to your personal interests or hobbies.
- Reflect on the cases that are emotionally demanding, and seek consultation to address your specific concerns.
- Engage in focused journaling where the emphasis is on the intersection of work and personal issues.
- Engage in hobbies and activities that are antithetical to your role as a therapist and as a provider of IPV services.
- Take your vacation, personal, lunch, and compensatory time.

- Reflect on whether you need to see fewer IPV clients or whether you need to work in a different field of practice.
- Reflect on whether your need is to empower your clients or rescue them.
- Reflect on your initial motivation for working with IPV cases (women, children, and men).
- Own aspects of your clinical work that are helpful to your clients' growth and restoration.

The notion of healing one's self through knowing focuses on the need for therapists not only to embrace the term *purpose* in their work with clients but also to recognize the purpose of remaining psychologically healthy and enlivened. Finally, the strategies noted above are conversation starters for therapists and supervisors, with the hope of advancing the discourse about self-care and its utility in the personal and professional lives of therapists who are subjected to vicarious emotional injuries due to their clinical involvement with clients faced with IPV.

Conclusion

This chapter focused on the fact that supervision is essential to the professional enhancement of therapists, emphasizing that those working in the area of IPV can experience a sense of personal vulnerability stemming from their clients' stories of abuse, violence, and cruelty. Kadushin's (1992) model of social work supervision served to set the tone of the chapter. The educative and supportive functions of this model were presented to illustrate how they were used to help two supervisees, Annie and John, who grappled with various practice concerns and dilemmas. For both supervisees, the chapter addressed how the therapist's subjectivity (e.g., countertransference; family-of-origin themes; unresolved feelings about one's own relationship to violence, abuse, and aggression in intimate relationships) complicates and informs clinical practice. Issues relating to burnout and vicarious trauma formed the other part of the chapter, making the point that trauma-informed practice can be psychologically harmful to therapists. In this spirit, I stressed the importance to therapists of self-care as a way to understand that clients' narratives are often entangled with theirs and that this results in conscious or unconscious pain and anguish affecting the body–mind–soul dimensions of the self. Finally, the chapter delineated several elements associated with personal and professional renewal that can be used as conversation starters regarding self-care and rest-care.

Discussion Questions

1. What are your initial reactions to this chapter?
2. What aspects of this chapter resonated with you as a supervisor?
3. What additional questions or concerns might you have about Annie's process with her client?

4. What observations have you made about the supervisory process with Annie?
5. What additional reactions do you have to John's process with his client Kevin?
6. What observations have you made about John's supervisory process?
7. What aspects of this chapter resonated with you as a therapist or counselor?
8. How has the chapter enhanced your knowledge of supervision in the context of clinical practice with IPV cases?
9. What thoughts surfaced in you while reading the section on burnout and vicarious trauma?
10. What type of learning emerged for you after reading the section on burnout and vicarious trauma?
11. What new learning emerged for you after reading the section on self-care?
12. What part of this chapter was most useful or germane to your practice?
13. What additional questions have surfaced for you?

APPENDIX 1

Key IPV Terms

Allyship: To be an ally means to be in support of and concerned about the well-being of an oppressed group or a particular cause, and often this can surface empathy and compassion leading to justice-informed advocacy on behalf of the respective group (Casey & Ohler, 2012).

Bibliotherapy: A therapeutic approach in which relevant books and other reading materials can be used in therapy to help clients explore their thoughts and feelings about a range of issues germane to their presenting issues.

Ego Defenses: Drawing on ego psychology, Goldstein (1995) notes that "the individual develops unconscious, internal mechanisms called defenses to protect him- or herself from painful experience of anxiety or from fear-inducing situations" (p. 65). Correspondingly, Goldstein argues that such defenses can range from denial, avoidance, intellectualization, and reaction formation to projection, introjection, undoing, splitting, projective identification, idealization, and more.

Internalization: A psychological process whereby people inculcate images, values, behaviors, messages, and norms stemming from the family and society that serve to inform identity development. Psychodynamically, therapists assess the extent to which early parental and societal influences have shaped the relational life course trajectory of their clients in order to understand the dimensions of their interior lives.

Male Privilege: Pence and Paymar (1993) argue, "Male privilege is a belief system that you as a man are entitled to certain privileges simply because you are male" (p. 151). Privileges are unearned benefits men accrue simply because of their gender; such privileges are derived from many domains of society, including the family, the workplace, and politics.

#MeToo: Beginning in 2006, #MeToo is a social movement that addresses sexual abuse and sexual harassment of women and girls. It exposes the multiplicity of ways men, especially those in power, use their positional authority to victimize women and girls.

Narrative Therapy: A therapeutic modality based on the notion that the manifestations of personal problems are rooted in people's social and cultural contexts, and that personal issues and resolutions are rooted in the meaning that people attribute to them. Still, the premise of narrative work suggests that clients' stories are authored by others, namely, parents, society, or parental others. The therapeutic process can help clients reauthor their stories based on emotional and cognitive truths.

Object Relations Theory: Although the term is mechanistic, it should not deter the reader from appreciating that it can aid practitioners in assessing how clients' early familial relationships shape their internal world and sense of self. According to Goldstein (2001), an important feature of this construct is that "the infant takes in (internalizes) the outside world, thereby acquiring basic perceptions of and attitudes toward the self and others that become structuralized within the person" (p. 7).

Patriarchy: According to hooks (2004), "patriarchy is a system that insists that males are inherently dominating, superior to everything and everyone deemed weak, especially females, and endowed with the right to dominate and rule over the weak and to maintain that dominance through forms of psychological terrorism and violence" (p. 18).

Protective Factors: Protective factors minimize risk and danger relating to personal and environmental problems. Protective factors may be linked to the existence of social support, caring family/parents, opportunities for employment, emotional intelligence, and the like.

Risk Factors: Risk factors can be rooted in ecological, biological, or familial circumstances, including food and housing insecurity, poverty, and exposure to traumatic events (Fraser & Kirby, 1997). Their presence in people's life course can truncate their ability to cope with taxing and stressful situations.

Self-Psychology: Central to this theory is that the relational matrix between the child and its caretakers is salient to the psychosocial development of the individual during adult relationships. As developed by Kohut (1977), a self-psychological framework suggests that clinicians should pay attention to the type and quality of parental care (i.e., self-object needs such as mirroring, idealization, and twinship, which reinforce self-development) or lack thereof, which may be informing a client's functioning.

APPENDIX 2

A Biopsychosocial Assessment Framework for IPV Cases Involving Cisgender Women

Definition

This process can be used by practitioners to assess and evaluate clients' lived experiences. Messer and Kaslow (2020) note that "history taking and inquiry" on the part of practitioners can unearth significant events and activities that may have considerable implications for developing a dynamic understanding of a client's presenting problem (e.g., IPV) and its corresponding issues (p. 29). Consequently, practitioners can deepen their knowledge of how to intervene and work with IPV clients.

Questions to aid practitioners in formulating a biopsychosocial assessment and evaluation are the following.

Biological Factors

1. Are there any hereditary illnesses or conditions (genetic vulnerabilities) in your family of origin?
2. Do you have knowledge of any neurological issues (cognitive/learning challenges) concerning yourself or your family?
3. As a child, did you have access to health care (including preventive, dental, and mental health)?
4. As an adult, do you have access to health care (including preventive, dental, and mental health)?
5. As a child, did you experience any illnesses (chronic or acute) that resulted in hospitalization?
6. As an adult, have you experienced any illnesses (chronic or acute) that resulted in hospitalization?
7. Are you aware of any untreated current or past health problems?
8. Did you experience dating abuse (including physical, emotional, sexual, or cyber abuse) during your adolescence (and at what age)?
9. Did you experience any sexual abuse during early childhood or adolescence?
10. Did you receive mental health services to address this problem?

Psychological Factors

1. What type of relationship did you have with your caretakers, including biological parents, grandparents, and foster and adoptive parents? Consider attachment issues and the quality of the client's relationship with caretakers.
2. What experiences relating to IPV (if any) between your caretakers during childhood contributed to your sense of self?
3. How have your internalizations of those relationships shaped current understandings of yourself and others?
4. How would you describe your ability to function in view of your abusive situation with your partner?
5. Do you still love your partner in spite of the abuse?
6. What are the risks associated with living with your abusive partner?
7. How have those risks impacted your ability to function (e.g., fear of working, difficulty in taking care of your children and yourself)?
8. What are the effects of IPV on your interactions with friends and family?
9. How have your social identities (e.g., race, immigrant status, language, nationality, sexual orientation, religious/spiritual beliefs) affected your ability to cope with or address your partner's abuse?
10. Have you had past or current use of any medications to address physical or mental health difficulties?

Social Factors

1. How has your cultural environment (e.g., place of birth, community, religious/spiritual spaces) contributed to or impeded your ability to cope with IPV?
2. To what extent does your social location (i.e., access to institutional resources and economic opportunities) impact your perspective on partner abuse?
3. Do you trust systems and institutions designed to address the problem of IPV? This considers calling or relying on the police/criminal justice system to solve IPV.
4. What role does familial support play in helping you cope with IPV? Consider a culturally determined worldview that places emphasis on community and family interventions during personal crises, instead of seeking formal assistance from public entities.
5. How do your social support systems (i.e., family, friends, and community) feel about you seeking services to deal with partner abuse?
6. What reactions would your partner have if he knew you were seeking therapeutic or other services?
7. What systems (e.g., medical, legal, social, and mental health services) are you receiving (or did you receive) services from?
8. What messages have you heard about being a girl and a woman from your family and society?

These questions can be used by practitioners to gain in-depth knowledge of women's formative experiences and their abusive histories with their partners. These questions assess the psychological health of women and inform a plan of action to provide therapeutic services to meet their needs. In an effort to assuage the psychological pain that emanates from IPV, it is essential for the questions to be framed in an empathic and supportive fashion to build on women's ego strengths.

APPENDIX 3

A Biopsychosocial Assessment Framework for IPV Cases Involving Cisgender Men

Definition

This process can be used by practitioners to assess and evaluate clients' lived experiences. Messer and Kaslow (2020) note that "history taking and inquiry" on the part of practitioners can unearth significant events and activities that may have considerable implications for developing a dynamic understanding of a client's presenting problem (e.g., IPV) and its corresponding issues (p. 29). Consequently, practitioners can deepen their knowledge of how to intervene and work with abusive men.

Questions to aid practitioners in formulating a biopsychosocial assessment and evaluation are the following.

Biological Factors

1. Are there any hereditary illnesses or conditions (genetic vulnerabilities) in your family of origin?
2. Do you have knowledge of any neurological issues (cognitive/learning challenges) concerning yourself or your family?
3. As a child, did you have access to health care (including preventive, dental, and mental health)?
4. As an adult, do you have access to health care (including preventive, dental, and mental health)?
5. As a child, did you experience any illnesses (chronic or acute) that resulted in hospitalization?
6. As an adult, have you experienced any illnesses (chronic or acute) that resulted in hospitalization?
7. Are you aware of any untreated current or past health problems?
8. Did you experience dating abuse (including physical, emotional, sexual, or cyber abuse) during your adolescence (and at what age)?
9. Did you experience any type of physical/emotional abuse during early childhood or adolescence?
10. Did you receive mental health services to address this problem?

Psychological Factors

1. What type of relationship did you have with your caretakers, including your biological parents, grandparents, and foster and adoptive parents during childhood? Consider early attachment issues and the quality of the client's relationship with caretakers.
2. What messages did you receive from family members (especially paternal figures) about being a boy and a man? Consider how such messages may have shaped conceptions of manhood and masculinity.
3. What images of manhood and masculinity (e.g., stoicism or expression of affection) were present in your family during your childhood?
4. How were arguments and conflicts addressed in your family?
5. Did you witness any acts of physical violence, coercive control, or emotional abuse growing up?
6. How have arguments or physical violence informed your perspectives on conflict management in intimate/interpersonal relationships?
7. How have your violent or abusive behaviors toward your partner affected you? Consider the presence of ego defenses such as denial, avoidance, intellectualization, and rationalization or lack thereof in exploring this question.
8. How have your violent or abusive behaviors toward your partner affected her? Consider how coercive control and physical abuse may result in harm to the woman's body and mind.
9. How have your social identities (e.g., race, immigrant status, language, nationality, sexual orientation, religious/spiritual beliefs) contributed to your abusive behaviors?
10. Have you had past or current use of medications to address physical and/or mental health difficulties?
11. Were you in any kind of therapeutic process as a child?
12. Did you experience any form of sexual abuse during childhood? This may be a difficult area for some men due to pronounced stigma and fear.
13. What would it mean if you could move beyond the use of abuse and violence in intimate relationships?

Social Factors

1. How have your communities and cultural environments shaped your views of interpersonal/intimate problems? Consider how disagreements and conflicts are dealt with between people within the client's social context.
2. To what extent does society play a role in your perceptions of yourself as a man? Consider how proscriptive gender roles may have been internalized by the client.
3. What are your feelings regarding systems and institutions intervening in your relationship with your partner?
4. What are your thoughts about men taking accountability for their abusive behaviors toward their female partners? Consider men accepting

responsibility (or not) for perpetrating violence against their female partners and being concerned about the safety of their female partners.
5. What reactions might your family have if they became aware of your involvement in therapy to deal with partner violence/abuse?
6. What reactions might your male friends have if they became aware of your involvement in therapy to deal with partner violence/abuse?
7. What systems (e.g., medical, legal, social, and mental health services) are you receiving (or did you receive) services from?
8. What messages did you hear directly or indirectly about being a boy or a man in your community and in society at large?
9. How might these messages contribute to your use of abuse and violence in intimate and interpersonal relationships?

Exploratory Process for Assessing Precursors to Violence/Abuse in Intimate Relationships

- Explore to what extent substance use or abuse (alcohol or drugs) could play a role in setting the stage for arguments and fights during the "normal" course of communication.
- Explore to what degree suppression of feelings might contribute to the client's aggression and controlling behaviors.
- Explore to what extent displacement of feelings and other ego defenses (denial, projection, intellectualization) might contribute to arguments.
- Explore the ways relational contentions are identified and discussed by the couple.
- Explore whether issues of blame and shame are present in the couple's relationship.
- Explore how a woman's assertiveness is understood by the client during an argument.
- Explore how issues of money are addressed and processed by the couple.
- Explore how sex and sexual activities are negotiated by the couple.

These questions can provide insights into abusive men's early and current relational experiences with family, their communities, and social support systems. Knowing about these aspects of their lives can lead to an assessment of their formative exposure to IPV and how their feelings about themselves have contributed to the meanings they assign to violence and abuse in intimate relationships. Moreover, the questions provide a framework for understanding the socioemotional and psychological factors that corrode men's narratives, and as such, therapeutic work can affirm alternatives to their pattern of abusive behavior, as well as validate traumatic scars from childhood abuse.

References

Abels, P., & Abels, S. L. (2001). *Understanding narrative therapy: A guide for the social worker*. Springer.

Alexander, M. (2010). *The new Jim Crow: Mass incarceration in the age of colorblindness*. New Press.

Allard, S. A. (2005). Rethinking battered women syndrome: A black feminist perspective. In N. J. Sokoloff & C. Pratt (Eds.), *Domestic violence at the margins: Readings on race, class, gender and culture* (pp. 194–205). Rutgers University Press.

Alvarez, C., & Fedrock, G. (2016). Addressing intimate partner violence with Latina women. *Journal of Trauma, Violence, & Abuse, 19*, 488–93.

Amin, A., Kagesten, A., & Chandra-Mouli, V. (2018). Addressing gender socialization and masculinity norms among adolescent boys: Policy and programmatic implications *Journal of Adolescent Health, 62*, 1–2.

Aymer, S. R. (2008a). Adolescent males' coping responses to domestic violence: A qualitative study. *Children & Youth Services Review, 30*, 654–64.

Aymer, S. R. (2008b). Beyond power and control: Clinical interventions with men engaged in partner abuse. *Clinical Social Work Journal, 36*, 323–32.

Aymer, S. R. (2010a). The case of Edward: Exploration of intraracial dynamics and internalized oppression in the context of clinical practice. *Families in Society: The Journal of Contemporary Social Services, 91*, 287–92.

Aymer, S. R. (2010b). Clinical practice with African American men: What to consider and what to do. *Smith College Studies in Social Work, 80*, 20–34.

Aymer, S. R. (2011). The case for including the "lived experience" of African American men in batterer's treatment. *Journal of African American Studies, 15*, 352–66.

Aymer, S. R. (2016). "I can't breathe": A case study—helping black men cope with race-related trauma stemming from police killing and brutality. *Journal of Human Behavior in the Social Environment, 26*, 367–76.

Aymer, S. (2018). "I can't breathe": A case study—helping black men cope with race-related trauma stemming from police killing and brutality. In S. E. Moore, A. C. Adedoyin, & M. A. Robinson (Eds.), *Police and the unarmed black male crisis: Advancing effective strategies* (pp. 183–92). Routledge.

Aymer, S. R. (2019). Mothers' ways of knowing: An exploratory study of abused mothers' perceptions of their adolescent sons' reactions to partner abuse. *Journal of Aggression, Maltreatment & Trauma, 20*, 1–16.

Baird, S., & Jenkins, S. R. (2003). Vicarious traumatization, secondary traumatic stress and burnout in sexual assault and domestic violence agency staff. *Violence & Victims, 18*, 71–86.

Baker, H. S., & Baker, M. N. (1987). Heinz Kohut's self psychology: An overview. *American Journal of Psychiatry, 144*, 1–9.

Bancroft, L., Silverman, J. G., & Ritchie, D. (2012). *The batterer as parent: Addressing the impact of domestic violence on family dynamics* (2nd ed.). Sage.

Bandura, A. (1973). *Aggression: A social learning analysis*. Prentice Hall.

Beaumont, H. (2012). *Toward a spiritual psychotherapy*. North Atlantic Books.

Beck, A. (1967). *Cognitive therapy and the emotional disorders*. International Universities Press.

Ben-Porat, A., & Itzhaky, H. (2011). The contribution of training and supervision to perceived role competence, secondary traumatization, and burnout among domestic violence therapists. *Clinical Supervisor, 30*, 95–108.

Bent-Goodley, T. B., & Fowler, D. N. (2006). Spiritual and religious: Expanding what is known about domestic violence. *Journal of Women & Social Work, 21*, 282–95.

Berger, R., & Quiros, L. (2014). Supervision for trauma-informed practice. *Traumatology, 2*, 296–302.

Blos, P. (1962). *On adolescence: A psychoanalytic interpretation*. Free Press.

Boehm, R., Golee, J., Krahm, R., & Smyth, D. (1999). *Lifelines: Culture, spirituality, and family violence*. University of Alberta Press.

Bontemps, A. (1969). *Great slave narratives*. Beacon Press for Unitarian Universalist Association.

Bowlby, J. (1988). *A secure base: Clinical applications of attachment theory*. Routledge.

Boyd-Franklin, N. (2003). *Black families in therapy: Understanding the African American experience*. Guilford Press.

Browne, A. (1993). Violence against women by male partners: Prevalence, outcomes, and policy implications. *American Psychologist, 48*, 1077–87.

Bush, D. M. (1992). Women's movement and state policy reform aimed at domestic violence against women: A comparison of the consequences in the U.S. and India. *Sociologies for Women in Society, 6*, 587–608.

Butler, P. (2017). *Chokehold: Policing black men*. New Press.

Campbell, J. C. (2004). Helping women understand their risk in situations of intimate violence. *Journal of Interpersonal Violence, 19*, 1404–77.

Campbell, J. C., García-Moreno, C., & Sharpe, P. W. (2007). Abuse during pregnancy in industrialized and developing countries. *Violence against Women, 10*, 770–89.

Carr, A. (1998). Michael White's narrative therapy. *Contemporary Family Therapy, 20*(4), 485–502.

Carruthers, C. A. (2018). *Unapologetic: A black, queer, and feminist mandate for radical movements*. Beacon Press.

Casey, E. A., & Ohler, K. (2012). Being a positive bystander: Male antiviolence allies' experiences of "stepping up." *Journal of Interpersonal Violence, 27*, 62–83.

Cashdan, S. (1989). *Object relations therapy: Using the relationship*. Norton.

Celani, D. (1994). *The illusion of love: Why the battered woman returns to her abuser*. Columbia University Press.

Centers for Disease Control and Prevention. (2010). *Preventing intimate partner and sexual violence: Program activities guide*. https://www.cdc.gov/violenceprevention/pdf/ipv-sv_program_activities_guide-a.pdf

Coates, T. (2015). *Between the world and me*. Spiegel & Grau.

Coker, A. L., Davis, K. E., Arias, I., Desal, S., Sanderson, M., Brandt, H. M., & Smith, P. H. (2002). Physical and mental effects of intimate partner violence for men and women. *American Journal of Preventive Medicine, 23*, 260–69.

Connell, R. W. (2000). *The men and the boys*. Allen & Bacon.

Cook, A., Spinnazzola, J., Ford, J., Lankree, C., Blaustein, M., Cloitre, M., DeRosa, R., Hubbard, R., Kagan, R., Liautaud, J., Mallah, K., Olafson, E., & van der Kolk, B. A. (2005). Complex trauma in children and adolescents. *Psychiatric Annals, 35*, 390–98.

Cooper, B. (2018). *Eloquent rage: A black feminist discovers her superpower*. St. Martin Press.

Cooper, M. G., & Lesser, J. G. (2008). *Clinical social work practice: An integrated approach* (3rd ed.). Pearson.

Corcoran, J. (2006). *Cognitive-behavioral methods for social workers: A workbook.* Pearson.
Crenshaw, K. W. (1995). Mapping the margins: Intersectionality, identity politics, and violence against women of color. In K. Crenshaw, N. Gotanda, G. Peller, & K. Thomas (Eds.), *Critical race theory: The key writings that formed the movement* (pp. 357–83). New Press.
Crenshaw, K., Gotanda, N., Peller, G., & Thomas, K. (Eds.) (1995). *Critical race theory: The key writings that formed the movement.* New Press.
D'Arcy, C., Turner, C., Crockett, B., & Gridley, H. (2011). Where's the feminism in motherhood. *Journal of Community Psychology, 40,* 27–43.
Davies, P. T., & Cummings, E. M. (1994). Marital conflict and child adjustment: An emotional security hypothesis. *Psychological Bulletin, 116,* 387–411.
Davis, A. Y. (1983). *Women, race and class.* Vintage.
DeGruy, J. (2005). *Post traumatic slave syndrome: America's legacy of enduring injury and healing.* Uptone Press.
Devany, C. (2009). Children's exposure to violence: Holding men accountable. *Political Quarterly, 80,* 569–74.
DiAngelo, R. (2018). *White fragility: Why it's so hard for white people to talk about racism.* Beacon Press.
Diemes, K. A., Torres-Harding, S., Reinecke, M. A., Freemen, A., & Sauer, A. (2011). Cognitive therapy. In S. B. Messer & A. S. Gurman (Eds.), *Essential psychotherapies: Theory and practice* (3rd ed., pp. 143–83). Guilford Press.
Dienemann, J., Campbell, J., Landenburger, K., & Curry, M. C. (2002). The domestic violence survivor assessment: A tool for counseling women in intimate partner violence relationships. *Patient Education & Counseling, 46,* 221–28.
Drury, B. J., & Kaiser, C. R. (2014). Allies against sexism: The role of men in confronting sexism. *Journal of Social Issues, 70,* 637–52.
Du Bois, W. E. B. (1953). *The souls of black folk.* Fawcett.
Dutton, D. (1995). *The domestic assault of women: Psychological and criminal justice perspectives.* University of British Columbia Press.
Dutton, D. G., & Golant, S. K. (1995). *The batterer: A psychological profile.* Basic Books.
Dutton, M., Oloff, L. E., & Hass, G. A. (2000). Characteristics of help-seeking behaviors, resources and service needs of battered immigrant Latinas: Legal and policy implications. *Georgetown Journal on Poverty Law and Policy, 7,* 1–53.
Ehrensaft, M. K., Cohen, P., & Brown, P. (2003). Intergenerational transmission of partner violence: A 20-year prospective study. *Journal of Counseling & Clinical Psychology, 71,* 741–53.
Eisenstein, Z. R. (1984). *Feminism and sexual equality.* Review Press.
Erikson, E. H. (1963). *Childhood and society* (2nd ed.). Norton.
Erikson, E. H. (1968). *Identity: Youth and crisis.* Norton.
Evans, S. (1979). *Personal politics: The roots of women's liberation in the civil rights movement and the left.* Alfred A. Knopf.
Fabiano, P. M., Wesley, P., Berkowitz, A., Linkerbach, J., & Starks, C. (2003). Engaging men as social justice allies in ending violence against women. *Journal of American Health, 52,* 105–12.
Fairbairn, W. R. D. (1954). *An object relations theory of personality.* Basic Books.
Fanon, F. (1967). *Black skin, white masks.* Grove Press.
Faulkner, S. L., & Mansfield, P. K. (2002). Reconciling messages: The process of sexual talk for Latinas. *Qualitative Health Research, 12,* 310–28.

Ferber, A. (2007). The construction of black masculinity: White supremacy now and then. *Journal of Sports & Social Issues, 31*, 11–24.
Flood, M. (2015). Work with men to end violence against women: A critical stocktake. *Culture, Health & Sexuality, 17*, 159–76.
Frank, K. A. (2002). The "ins and out" of enactments: A relational bridge for psychotherapy integration. *Journal of Psychotherapy Integration, 3*, 267–96.
Fraser, M. W., & Kirby, L. D. (1997) Risk and resilience in childhood. In M. W. Fraser (Ed.), *Risk and resilience in childhood: An ecological perspective* (pp. 10–33). NASW Press.
Freire, P. (2007). *Pedagogy of the oppressed*. Continuum.
Garfield, G. (2005). *Knowing what we know: African American women's experiences of violence and violation*. Rutgers University Press.
Garfield, G. (2010). *Through our eyes: African American men's experience of race, gender and violence*. Rutgers University Press.
Germain, C. B., & Gitterman, A. (1995). *The life model of social work practice: Advances in theory and practice* (2nd ed.). Columbia University Press.
Giesbrecht, N., & Sevacik, I. (2000). The process of recovery and rebuilding among abused women in the conservative subculture. *Journal of Family Violence, 15*, 229–48.
Gilligan, C. (1982). *In a different voice: Psychological theory and women's development*. Harvard University Press.
Gillum, T. L., Sullivan, C. M., & Bydee, D. I. (2006). The importance of spirituality in the lives of domestic violence survivors. *Violence against Women, 12*, 240–50.
Glaude, E. S. (2016). *Democracy in black: How race still enslaves the American soul*. Broadway Books.
Goldstein, E. (1995). *Ego psychology and social work practice* (2nd ed.). Free Press.
Goldstein, E. (2001). *Object relations theory and self-psychology in social work practice*. Free Press.
Goleman, D. (1995). *Emotional intelligence: Why it can matter more than IQ*. Bantam Books.
Good, G. E., Thomson, D. A., & Braithwaite, A. D. (2005). Men and therapy: Critical concepts, theoretical frameworks and research recommendations. *Journal of Clinical Psychology, 61*, 699–711.
Granvold, D. (2011). Cognitive-behavior therapy with adults. In J. R. Brandell (Ed.), *Theory and practice in clinical social work* (2nd ed., pp. 178–212). Sage.
Greenberg, J. R., & Mitchell, S. A. (1983). *Object relations in psychoanalytic theory*. Harvard University Press.
Halder, S. (2016). The shooting in Orlando, terrorism or toxic masculinity (or both?). *Men & Masculinity, 19*, 555–65.
Hardest, J. L., Hands, J. D., Haselschwerdt, M. L., Khnaw, L., & Grossman, K. A. (2015). The influence of divorcing on custody evaluators' assessment in their domestic violence allegations. *Journal of Child Custody, 12*, 47–70.
Hartmann, H. (1939). *Ego psychology and the problem of adaptation*. International Universities Press.
Hass, G. A., Dutton, M. A., & Orloff, L. E. (2000). Lifetime prevalence of violence against Latina immigrants: Legal and policy implications. *International Review of Victimology, 7*, 93–113.
Hennen, P. (2005). Bear bodies, bear masculinity: Recuperation, resistance, or retreat? *Gender Studies, 19*, 49–72.
Henning, K., & Holdford, R. (2006). Minimizations, denial and victim blaming by batterers. *Criminal Justice Behavior, 33*, 110–30.

Herman, J. (1992). *Trauma and recovery: The aftermath of violence from domestic abuse to political terror*. Basic Books.
Hess, A. D., Hess, K. D., & Hess, T. H. (2008). *Psychotherapy supervision: Theory, research, and practice* (2nd ed.). Wiley.
Hines, D. A., Morrison-Malley, K., & Dutton, L. A. (2021). *Family violence in the United States: Defining, understanding and combating abuse* (3rd ed.). Springer.
Holloway, S., & Brager, G. (1989). *Supervison in the human services: The politics of practice*. Free Press.
hooks, b. (1981). *Ain't I a woman: Black women and feminism*. South End Press.
hooks, b. (1989). *Talking back: Thinking feminist, thinking black*. South End Press.
hooks, b. (1992). *Black looks: Race and representation*. South End Press.
hooks, b. (2004). *The will to change: Men, masculinity, and love*. Atria Books.
hooks, b. (2015). *Feminism is for everybody: Passion and politics*. Routledge.
Hughes, M. H. (1988). *Psychological and behavioral correlates of family violence in child witness and victims*. Brunner-Routledge.
Hull, G. T., Scott, P. B., & Smith, B. (1982). *All women are white, all the blacks are men, but some of us are brave: Black women's studies*. Feminist Press at the City University of New York.
Hunter, A. C., Friend, C. A., Murphy, S. Y., Rollins, A., Wheeler, W. M., & Laughinghouse, J. (2006). Loss, survival, and redemption: African American male youths' reflections on life without fathers, manhood, and coming of age. *Youth & Society, 37*, 423–52.
Jaffe, P., Wolfe, D., & Wilson, S. (1990). *Children of battered women*. Sage.
Jaffe, P., Wolfe, D., Wilson, S., & Zak, D. (1985). Children of battered women: The relation of child behavior to family violence and maternal stress. *Journal of Consulting and Clinical Psychology, 53*(5), 657–65.
James, M. (1994). *Domestic violence as a form of child abuse: Identification and prevention*. National Child Protection Clearinghouse (Australia). https://aifs.gov.au/cfca/publications/domestic-violence-form-child-abuse-identification
Johnson, J. E. (1982). The Afro-American family: A historical overview. In B. N. Bass, G. E. Wyatt, & P. Powell (Eds.), *The Afro-American family: Assessment, treatment and research issues* (pp. 285–90). Harcourt.
Kadushin, A. (1992). *Supervision in social work* (3rd ed.). Columbia University Press.
Kadushin, A., & Harkness, D. (2002). *Supervision in social work* (4th ed.). Columbia University Press.
Karenga, M. (1983). *Introduction to black studies*. Kawaida.
Kasturirangan, A., Krishnan, S., & Riger, S. (2004). The impact of culture and minority status on women's experience of domestic violence. *Trauma, Violence, & Abuse, 5*, 318–32.
Kawash, S. (2011). New directions in motherhood studies. *Journal of Women in Culture and Society, 36*, 969–1003.
Kendall, M. (2020). *Hood feminism: Notes from the women that a movement forgot*. Viking.
Kinniburgh, K. J., Blaustein, M., & Spinazzola, J. (2005). Attachment, self-regulation, and competency. *Psychiatric Annals, 35*, 424–30.
Klein, M. (1964). *Contributions of psychoanalysis, 1921–1945*. McGraw-Hill.
Kohut, H. (1971). *The analysis of the self*. International Universities Press.
Kohut, H. (1977). *The restoration of the self*. International Universities Press.
Krane, J., & Davies, L. (2007). Mothering under difficult circumstances: Challenges to working with battered women. *Journal of Women & Social Work, 22*, 23–38.

Kress, V., Protivnak, J., & Sadlak, L. (2008). Counseling clients involved with violent intimate partners: The mental health counselor's role in promoting client safety. *Journal of Mental Health Counseling, 30*, 200–210.

Lapierre, S. (2010). More responsibility, less control: Understanding the challenges and difficulties involving mothering in the context of domestic violence. *British Journal of Social Work, 40*, 1434–51.

Latané, B., & Darley, J. (1969). Bystander "apathy." *America Scientists, 37*, 244–68.

Lavendosky, A. A., Lynch, M. L., & Grahman-Berman, S. A. (2000). Mothers' perceptions of the impact of women abuse on their parenting. *Violence Against Women, 6*, 247–71.

Lohman, B. J., & Maldonado, A. M. (2014). "He said they'd deport me": Factors influencing domestic violence help-seeking practices among Latina immigrants. *Journal of Interpersonal Violence, 29*, 593–615.

Madhubuti, H. R. (1990). *Black men, obsolete, single, dangerous? The African American family in transition; Essays in discovery, solution and hope.* Third World Press.

Maruna, S. (2001). *Making good: How ex-convicts reform and rebuild their lives.* American Psychological Association.

Mayo, J. A. (2004). Psychotherapy with African American populations: Modification of traditional approaches. *Annals of the American Psychotherapy Association, 7*, 10–13.

McFarlane, D., Campbell, J. C., Sharpe, P., & Watson, K. (2002). Abuse during pregnancy and femicide: Urgent implications for women's health. *Obstetrics & Gynecology, 100*, 27–36.

Mckay, M. M. (1994). The link between domestic violence and child abuse. *Child Abuse, 73*, 29–39.

McKenzie, F. R. (2008). *Theory and practice with adolescents: An applied approach.* Lyceum Books.

McKenzie, F. (2011) *Understanding and managing the therapeutic relationship.* Lyceum Books.

McWilliams, N. (1999). *Psychoanalytic case formulations.* Guilford Press.

Mechanic, M. B., Weaver, T. L., & Resick, P. A. (2008). Mental health consequences of intimate partner abuse. *Violence against Women, 14*, 634–54.

Messer, S. R., & Kaslow, N. J. (2020). *Essential psychotherapies: Theory and practice.* Guilford Press.

Miedzian, M. (2002). *Boys will be boys: Breaking the link between masculinity and violence.* Lantern Books.

Mills, L. G. (2003). *Insult to injury: Rethinking our responses to intimate abuse.* Princeton University Press.

Mishne, J. M. (1986). *Clinical work with adolescents.* Free Press.

Neal, M. A. (2006). *The new black man.* Routledge.

Northcut, T. B., Heller, N. R., & Kumaria, S. (2016). Utilizing cognitive behavioral interventions in psychodynamic practice. In J. Berzoff, L. M. Flanagan, & P. Hertz (Eds.), *Inside out and outside in: Psychodynamic clinical theory and psychopathology in contemporary multicultural contexts* (4th ed., pp. 220–48). Rowman & Littlefield.

Nylund, D., & Nylund, D. (2003). Narrative therapy as counter-hegemonic practice. *Men & Masculinity, 5*, 386–94.

O'Keefe, M. (1996). The differential effects of family violence on adolescent adjustment. *Child and Adolescent Social Work Journal, 13*, 51–67.

Oliffe, J. L., & Phillips, M. J. (2008). Men, depression, and masculinities: A review and recommendations. *Journal of Men's Health, 5*(3), 194–203.

Oluo, I. (2018). *So you want to talk about race.* Seal Press.

Orenstein, P. (2020). *Boys and sex: Young men on hookups, love, porn, consent, and navigating the new masculinity.* HarperCollins.
Pearlman, L. A., & Saakvitne, K. W. (1995). *Trauma and the therapist: Countertransference and vicarious traumatization in psychotherapy with incest survivors.* Norton.
Peled, E., & Gil, I. B. (2011). The mothering perceptions of women abused by their partner. *Violence against Women, 17,* 457–79.
Pence, E., & Paymar, M. (1993). *Education groups for men who batter: The Duluth model.* Springer.
Petersen, N., & Ward, R. (2015). The transmission of historical racial violence: Lynching, civil rights–era terror, and contemporary interracial homicide. *Race & Justice, 5*(2), 1–30.
Pettyjohn, M. E., Muzzey, F. K., Maas, M. E., & McCauley. (2018). #HowIWillChange: Engaging men and boys in the #MeToo movement. *Psychology of Men & Masculinity, 20,* 612–22.
Phinney, J. S. (2010). Understanding development in cultural contexts: How do we deal with complexity? *Human Development, 53,* 33–38.
Pleck, E. (1987). *Domestic tyranny: The making of social policy against family violence from colonial times to the present.* Oxford University Press.
Pollack, W. S. (1998). *Real boys: Rescuing our sons from the myths of boyhood.* Random House.
Powell, K. (2003). *Who's gonna take the weight? Manhood, race, and power in America.* Three Rivers Press.
Reina, A. S., & Lohman, B. J. (2015). Barriers preventing Latina immigrants from seeking advocacy services for domestic violence: A qualitative analysis. *Journal of Family Violence, 30,* 479–88.
Rodino-Colocino, M. (2018). Me too, #MeToo: Countering cruelty with empathy. *Cultural & Critical Studies, 15,* 96–100.
Root, P. P. (1994) Mixed race women. In L. Comas-Diaz & B. Greene (Eds.), *Women of color: Integrating ethnic and gender identities in psychotherapy* (pp. 455–78). Guilford Press.
Rosenbaum, A., & O'Leary, K. D. (1981). Children: The unintended victims of marital violence. *American Journal of Orthopsychiatry, 51,* 629–99.
Rosenberger, E. W., & Hayes, J. A. (2002). Origins, consequences and management of countertransference: A case study. *Journal of Counseling Psychology, 49,* 221–32.
Rutter, M. (1987). Psychosocial resilience and protective mechanisms. *American Journal of Orthopsychiatry, 57*(3), 316–31.
Rutter, M. (1990). Protective factors in children's response to stress and disadvantage. In M. W. Kent & J. E. Wolf (Eds.), *Primary prevention in psychopathology: Social competence in children* (pp. 49–79). University Press of New England.
Sack, E. J. (2004). Battered women and the state: The struggle for the future of domestic violence policy. *Wisconsin Law Review, 35,* 1658–1738.
Schechter, S. (1982). *Women and male violence: The visions and struggles of the battered women's movement.* South End Press.
Schrock, D., & Schwalbe, M. (2009). Men, masculinity and manhood acts. *Annual Review of Sociology, 35,* 277–85.
Scott, L. D. (2003). Cultural orientation and coping with perceived discrimination among African American youth. *Journal of Black Psychology, 29,* 235–56.
Segal, H. (1974). *Introduction to the work of Melanie Klein.* Basic Books.
Shepard, M. F., & Pence, E. L. (1999). An introduction: Developing a coordinated community response. In M. F. Shepard & E. L. Pence (Eds.), *Coordinating community*

responses to domestic violence: Lessons learned from Duluth and beyond (pp. 3–24). Sage.
Sipe, B., & Hall, E. J. (2013). *I am not your victim: Anatomy of domestic violence* (2nd ed.). Sage.
Sokoloff, N. J., & Dupont, I. (2005). Domestic violence at the intersections of race, class, and gender. *Violence against Women, 11,* 38–64.
Staples, R. (1982). *Black masculinity: The black male's role in American society.* Black Scholar Press.
Stephens, D. P., & Phillips, L. D. (2003). Freaks, gold diggers, divas and dykes: The sociohistorical development of adolescent African American women's scripts. *Sexuality & Culture, 7,* 3–49.
Tambe, S. (2018). Reckoning with silences of #MeToo. *Feminist Studies, 55,* 197–203.
Tarshis, S., & Baird, S. L. (2019). Addressing the indirect trauma of social work in intimate partner violence (IPV) field placements: A framework for supervision. *Clinical Social Work Journal, 67,* 90–102.
Taylor, K. Y. (2016). *From #BlackLivesMatter to black liberation.* Haymarket Books.
Tyagi, S. V. (2006). Female counselors and male perpetrators of violence against women. *Women & Therapy, 28,* 1–23.
Van Hook, M. P. (2019). *Social work practice with families: A resiliency-based approach* (3rd ed.). Lyceum Books.
Vatnar, S. B., & Bjorkly, S. (2010). Does it make any difference if she is a mother? *Journal of Interpersonal Violence, 25*(1), 94–110.
Walker, L. E. (1979). *The battered woman.* Harper & Row.
Watts, R. J., Griffith, D. W., & Abdul-Adil, J. (1999). Sociopolitical development as an antidote for oppression: Theory and action. *American Journal of Community Psychology, 27*(2), 255–71.
West, C. (1993). *Race matters.* Vintage.
West, C. M. (Ed.). (2002). *Violence in the lives of black women: Battered, black, and blue.* Hayworth.
West, C. M. (2004). Black women and intimate partner violence: New directions for research. *Journal of Interpersonal Violence, 19,* 1487–93.
Wexler, D. B. (2009). *Men in therapy: New approaches for effective treatment.* Norton.
White, M. (2007). *Maps of narrative practice.* Norton.
Winnicott, D. W. (1965). *The maturational processes and the facilitative environment: Studies in the theory of emotional development.* International Universities Press.
Wolf, D., & Korsch, G. (1994). Witnessing domestic violence during childhood and adolescence: Implications for pediatric practice. *Pediatrics, 94,* 594–98.
Yalom, I. D., & Leszcz, M. (2005). *Theory and practice of group psychotherapy.* Basic Books.

Index

abandonment, threat of, 70
Abels, P., 93
Abels, S. L., 93
abuse: adolescent males exposure to, of father, 69–70; anxiety caused by, 57; assessing violence and, in intimate relationship, 159; Black women and partner, 23; children and cycle of, 72; children witnessing parental, 67–68, 79; within dating, 72–73; economic, 9; emotional, 9; in family, 53, 74–75, 139; immigration status and, 25; internalization of, by women, 77; justification of, 119; marriage and, 73; in motherhood, 80; partner, 26–30, 67–68; physical, 99–100; physical *vs.* emotional, 73; in pregnancy, 66–67; psychological, 66, 99–100; racism *vs.*, 22; relational, xi, xii; in relationship, 76–77; in relationship of parent, 58; reporting, 22–23; toward women, 3. *See also specific topics*
activism, gender, 1, 123
adolescence: masculinity in, 49–52; parenting and, 50; sociodemographic variables in, 51–52
adolescent males, 49–51; clinical work with, 59–61; exposure to father's abuse, 69–70; IPV exposed to, xiv; socialization of, 52–53; social work for, 52–61
adulthood, 73, 106
African Americans, 23, 42
African people, 18–19
agency, of women, 136
aggression, 10, 19, 75; as byproduct of toxic masculinity, 84; toward the feminine, 50–51; in marriage, 41; of parent, xiv, 53; verbal, 107; violence and, 73–74
aggressive identification, 55–56, 57
alcohol addiction, 103
Alexander, M., 87–88
alienation: motherhood and, 75–76; within parent relationship, 76–77
Allard, S. A., 4
alliances, in clinical practice, 117–18
allyship, 151; gender-based violence and, 118–19; men in, 113, 122–24, 126
alter ego, 98
ambivalence, 55, 57, 71, 137; in marriage, 73–74; about motherhood, 64; of therapist, 147
American male centeredness, 115

Amin, A., 84
ancillary human services, 103–4
anger, 54
antifemaleness, xi
anti-Semitism, 9
antiviolence work, 125
anxiety, xiv, xv, 75; abuse causing, 57; anger and insecurity resulting in, 54; anticipatory, 33–34; depression and, 65–66; race-based, 21; stress and, in clinical work, 140; stress and, in family, 43; trauma causing, 144–45
attachment theory, 72, 116
autism, in children, 40
Aymer, S. R., 70, 77, 79, 107

Baird, S. L., 144
Bandura, A., 55–56, 57, 81–82, 83, 90
battered women's movement (BWM), 1, 2, 6–7, 13
batterers' intervention program, 103–4
Beaumont, H., 69–70, 71, 148
Beck, A., 77
behavior: boys influenced by parent, 84–85; coping, 106; intersectionality in, of men, 86; intimate, 82
behavior, abusive, xi, 7, 39; in childhood, 40; minimizing, denying, and blaming for, 9
believability, 91–92
Berger, R., 144
bias, 17, 22, 91; Black men and, 23; implicit, 85
bibliotherapy, 151
biological clock, 64
biophysical assessment framework: for IPV cases involving cisgender men, 157–59; for IPV cases involving cisgender women, 153–55
Black families, 69–71
Black men, xiii, 87–89; bias and, 23; feminism and, 115; policing of, 22; violence against, 26
Black women, xiii; IPV, intersectional feminism, and, 21; marginalization of, 18–19, 21; objectification of, 19; oppression of queer, 20; partner abuse and, 23; racial stereotypes of, 18–19, 30–31; violence against, 26; white supremacy impacting, 17–18
Blos, P., 55
Bowlby, J., 72, 116–17
the boy code, xv, 86
Boyd-Franklin, N., 69

169

boys: parent behavior influencing, 84–85; socialization of, 82
Boys Will Be Boys (Miedzian), 121
Brown, Chris, 32
Brown men, xiii, 26, 87–89
Brown women, xiii, 17–19, 26
Burke, Tarana, 120
burnout, in supervision, 143–46
Bush, D. M., 6, 8
BWM. *See* battered women's movement
bystander effect, 122

caretakers: children *vs.*, 33, 34–35, 72; system of, 109
Carr, A., 93
Carruthers, C. A., 20, 147
case studies: on IPV, 21–26, 38–47, 52–61, 72–80, 100–111; in supervision, 136–50
Casey, E. A., 122
Cashdan, S., 35
catastrophizing, 77–78
Catholicism, 38, 40
CBT. *See* cognitive behavioral therapy
CDC. *See* The Centers for Disease Control and Prevention
Celani, D., 36, 45
The Centers for Disease Control and Prevention (CDC), 122
the Central Park Five, 88
childhood: abusive behavior in, 40; coping behaviors in adulthood and, 106; victimization in, 142–43
children: autism in, 40; caretakers *vs.*, 33, 34–35, 72; custody of, 75–80; cycle of abuse and, 72; gender conformity in, 83; marginalization of, in family, 55; marital discord, IPV and, 104; mothering and welfare of, 67–72; parental abuse witnessed by, 67–68, 79; psychological growth of, 98; raising, 68–69; using, 9
child support, 74
child welfare, 67–72
Christianity, 26–30
Civil Rights Movement, 4–5
clinical practice, 45–46, 110–11; duality of alliances in, 117–18; implications for, 92–95; macro and micro issues in, xii; self-awareness in, 130; shared vulnerability in, 129–50
clinical work: with adolescent males, 59–61; countertransference and transference in, 118, 133; for IPV clients, 115; purpose in, 147–49; reauthoring phase in, 94–95; stress and anxiety in, 140; trauma in, 134
Coates, T., 89

coercion, 11–12, 24, 66–67, 147
cognitive behavioral therapy (CBT), 49, 56, 59; homework assignments in, 58; questions in, 78–79; schema in, 57
cognitive distortions, 77–78
community, violence in, 52–53, 54
Cooper, B., 89
Cooper, M. G., 35, 97
countertransference, 91; in clinical work, 118; reactions and feelings in, 135–46; supervision, self-care and, xvi, 129–50; transference and, in clinical work, 133; unconscious emotional responses in, 136
court processes, 103–4
COVID-19, xvi–xvii
Crenshaw, K., xiii, 17–18, 28
criminality, 88
criminal justice, xii, 8, 33, 88
custody, of children, 75–80
cycle-of-violence model, 1–2, 10–12

DAIP. *See* Domestic Abuse Intervention Project
dating, abuse within, 72–73
deconstruction, in narrative therapy, 91–92
defense mechanisms, 145
defensive identification, 55
dehumanization, 116
denial, 119, 142
deportation, 24
depression, xiv, xv, 75; anxiety and, 65–66; within marriage, 38–45; symptoms of, 76–77
DiAngelo, R., 5, 114, 121
dichotomous thinking, 77–78
Diemes, K. A., 57
Dienemann, J., 100
discounting the positive, 77–78
discrimination, xii, xiii, 2
divorce, 74, 76
Domestic Abuse Intervention Project (DAIP), 8
domestic violence, xi
double consciousness, 22
DSM (Diagnostic and Statistical Manual), 85
Du Bois, W. E. B., 22
Duluth model, xii, 1–2, 8, 92, 96
Dunning-Kruger effect, 114
Dutton, D., 7
Dutton, D. G., 54
Dutton, M., 25

ecology, of social learning, 55–56
economic dependence, 25
ego, fortification of, 42–43
ego defenses, 89, 119, 142, 151; patriarchy informing, 84

Index   171

ego support, 34
Ehrensaft, M. K., 51, 56
emotional intelligence, 146
emotionality, 126
emotional life, of men, 124–25
empathy, 109, 110, 125, 136
enactments, 133
enslavement: of African people, 18–19; othering in, 87–88
external objects, 35–36

Fabiano, P. M., 117
the facilitative environment, 33
Fairbairn, W. R. D., 35
false self, 34–35
familismo, 25
family: abuse in, 74–75, 139; Black, 69–71; exposure to IPV in, 51, 53, 57; formation of patriarchy in, 37; gender-noncomforming, 50–51; object relations theory and IPV in, 35–36; secrets within IPV and, 69–71; stress and anxiety in, 43; women exposed to IPV through, xiii–xiv, 33–47
Fanon, F., 90
father: adolescent males exposure to abuse of, 69–70; in role of violence, 73–74
feminism, 1, 124; Black, 20, 30; Black male, 115; consciousness raising for men, 125–26; devaluation of, 82; differences in mainstream, 19–20; diversity within, 16; mainstream, 15, 22, 30, 68; race, intersectionality and, xiii, 17–19, 21; racism as issue of, 21; second-wave, 6–7; social movements and, 4–5
fetishization, 19
Freire, P., 116

Garfield, G., 7, 22, 88
Garner, Eric, 89
gender: activism, 123; children and conformity of, 83; essentialism, 83; formation of, identity, 49–52, 82; identity, 65; noncomforming, 50–51; oppression, 113; prejudice based on, 17; primary and secondary differences in, 82–83; race and, 18, 39, 88; regression and, 41–42; socialization, 84; toxic issues of, 82–83; victimization based in, 126; violence based on, xi, 118–19. *See also* men; women
gendered habits, 121
gender equality, men who advocate for, 124–25
gender inequality, xi
gender-nonconforming families, 50–51
Germain, C. B., 2
Gilligan, C., 38

girlhood, 64
girls: service delivery to women and, 114–16; violence against women and, xv–xvi, 113–27
Gitterman, A., 2
Glaude, E. S., 5, 121
Golant, S. K., 54
Goldstein, E., 44–45, 98, 136, 139, 151, 152
Goleman, D., 34
Good, G. E., 143
good enough mother, 34, 42, 44
group therapy, 90–91

Harkness, D., 135–36
Hayes, J. A., 91
Hennen, P., 84–85
Herman, J., xv, 44, 66, 72, 108, 138
Hess, A. D., 133–34, 137–38
heterosexism, 84–85
heterosexuality, xv–xvi, 3–4, 82, 84, 116–17
holding environment, xiv, 34, 42–43
homicide, 101, 107
homophobia, 84, 90
homosexuality, 26–30
honeymoon, 10, *11*, 66
hooks, bell, 16, 84, 93–94, 95, 117, 152; on whiteness, 28–29
Hull, G. T., 21

"I Am a Recovering Misogynist" (Powell), 115
"I Am No Hero. I Am No Saint. I Remain a Sexist Male" (Powell), 115
idealization, 98, 106, 152
identification, 38; aggressive, 55–56; defensive, 55
identifying, 122
identity: cultural, 26–30; formation of gender, 49–52, 82; gender, 65; queer, 19–20; race and, 28; social, 85–86
immigration, 23, 26; intersectionality and, 20, 24–25; status and abuse, 25
injustices, systemic, 23
intergenerational transmission, of violence, 109
internalization, 151; of abuse, by women, 77; in male dominance, 116–17; of self-object, 108; of violence, 106
internal objects, 35
internal working models, 72, 116
interpreting, 122
intersectionality, xiii; in behavior of men, 86; differences of, in mainstream feminism, 19–20; feminism, race and, 17–20; within IPV, 15–31; spirituality, IPV and, 26–30; subordination in, 31; undocumented immigration and, 24–25

interventions, therapeutic, 56–59, 107–10, 125–26, 129; trauma-informed, 144
intimate partner violence (IPV), xi–xii; adolescent males exposed to, xiv, 49–61; biological factors of cases in, 153–54, 157; biophysical assessment framework for cases involving cisgender men, 157–59; biophysical assessment framework for cases involving cisgender women and, 153–55; calling to, 114; case studies on, 21–26, 38–47, 52–61, 72–80, 100–111, 140; clinical work for clients of, 115; criminal justice for, 8; economic dependence within, 25; exposure to, in family, xiii–xiv, 51; family in object relations theory and, 35–36; gender-based activism addressing, 1; intersectional feminism, Black women and, 21; intersectionality within, 15–31; marital discord, children and, 104; media coverage of, 13; men's work in, 122–24; mothering and motherhood in, xiv–xv, 63–80; parenting in, 74–75; PIE and, 2–3; power-and-control model of, 7–12; psychological factors of cases in, 154, 158; psychological impact of, on mothers, 65–67; secrets within family and, 69–71; social factors of cases in, 154–55, 158–59; sociocultural and intersectional factors in, xiii; spirituality, intersectionality and, 26–30; toxic masculinity and, 89–91; traditional framing of, 1–14; trauma and, xvi–xvii, 108, 138; women exposed to, in family, 33–47; work impacting therapist, 148
intimate rage, 54
intimidation, 9, 58
IPV. *See* intimate partner violence
isolation, 9

Jay-Z (rapper), 87
jealousy, in relationship, 54

Kadushin, A., 130, 131–32, 133, 135–37, 141–42, 149
Kagesten, A., 84
Karenga, M., 4–5
Kaslow, N. J., 153
Kavanaugh, Brett, 93, 119
Kawash, S., 65
Kinniburgh, K. J., 56
Kohut, H., 97–99, 105–6, 108–9, 110, 152

Latina women, 23–26, 100–111
Lesser, J. G., 35, 97
LGBTQ+ communities, 19–20, 84, 90

listening, active, 45
Lohman, B. J., 25

male abusers: believability in therapeutic work with, 91–92; toxic masculinity and, xv
male dominance, 116–17, 126
males, adolescent: development of, 49–52; IPV exposure in, 49–61
male supremacy, 121–24
manhood, within patriarchy, 7
marginalization, xiii, 90; of African Americans, 42; of Black women, 18–19, 21; of Latina women, 26; within the US, 15; of women, 16; of women and children in family, 55
marriage: abuse and, 73; aggression in, 41; ambivalence in, 73–74; children, IPV and discord in, 104; depression within, 38–45; historical overview of, 3–4; interracial, 38–45; patriarchy within, 3–4; race and, 38–45; sexual assault in, 102–3
martyrdom, 41
Maruna, S., 59
masculine self, 82
masculinity, 82, 83; in adolescence, 49–52; internalized patriarchy and, 141; social identity and, 85–86; stoicism and, 122
McKenzie, F., 106
medication, 76
men: allyship and, 113, 122–24, 126; biophysical assessment framework for IPV cases and cisgender, 157–59; Black and Brown, xiii; in bystander role in IPV and sexual assault, 122; emotional life of, 124–25; feminism and consciousness raising for, 125–26; gender equality advocated by, 124–25; heterosexuality and cisgender, 84; inauthentic self of, 116; intersectionality in behavior of, 86; patriarchy influencing, 81, 82, 92; power used by, xi, 1–2; psychological impact of violence by, xi–xii; self-awareness in, 116–17, 123; social location of, 114–16; sociodemographic variables in adolescent, 51–52; socioemotional development of, 117; toxic masculinity and, 81–96
mental health counseling, xii
Messer, S. R., 153
#MeToo movement, xv–xvi, 17, 92, 113, 123, 151; implications of, 120–21
microaggression, 31
Miedzian, M., 121
Milano, Alyssa, 120
Mills, L. G., 30
mindfulness, 78–79
minimization, 142

mirroring, 56, 98, 106, 152
misogyny, xii, 85; patriarchy and, 114–15, 139; sexism and, 86; systemic, 120
mother: positioning of women and, 63–65; psychological impact of IPV on, 65–67; son, and abuse, 70–71
mother-child relationship: in motherhood, 20; in psychoanalytical literature, 71–72
motherhood: abuse in, 80; alienation and, 75–76; ambivalence about, 64; IPV in mothering and, xiv–xv, 63–80; mother-child relationship in, 20; mothering and, 63–65; pregnancy and, 66–67; schema and, 64; social construction of, 71–72; violence in, 68–69
mothering, 34–35; children's welfare and, 67–72; IPV in motherhood and, xiv–xv, 63–80
multiracial couple, 39–45

narcissism, 98
narrative therapy, 91– 92, 96, 151–52
New York City, 101–2, 121
1970s, 6–7
noncarceral process centers, xi
Northcut, T. B., 77–78
noting, 122
Nylund, D., 92, 94

objectification, of Black women, 19
object relations theory, xii–xiv, 33–47, 152; family in IPV and, 35–36
observational learning, 81–82
Ohler, K., 122
Oluo, I., 17
oppression, 85; gender, 15, 113; of queer Black women, 20; racial, 15
Orenstein, P., 16, 84, 95
othering, 16, 28–29, 37, 90; in enslavement, 87–88
overgeneralizing, 77–78

parallel process, 133
parent-child relationship, xiv, 34–35
parenting: adolescence and, 50; in IPV, 74–75
parents: abusive relationship of, 58; aggression of, xiv, 53; boys influenced by behavior of, 84–85; children witnessing abuse of, 67–68, 79; violence of, 105
partner abuse, xi, 67–68, 107–10; emotional effects of, xii; in social work, 26–30
pathology, 85
patriarchy, xi, xii, 5, 15, 68, 85, 152; ego defenses informed by, 84; formation of, in family, 37; internalized masculinity and, 141; manhood within, 7; within marriage, 3–4; men influenced by, 81, 82, 92; misogyny and, 114–15, 139; politics of, 124; sexism and, 16, 116, 117; socialization in, 88–89; standards of, 44; systemic, 82, 125
pay equity, xii
pay inequity, 2
Paymar, M., 1–2, 8, 9
Pedagogy of the Oppressed (Freire), 116
Pence, E. L., 1–2, 8, 9
personalizing, 77–78
person-in-environment (PIE) paradigm: IPV and, 2–3; in social work, 1, 2
Pettyjohn, M. E., 125
Phillips, L. D., 18
physical abuse, 99–100
PIE. *See* person-in-environment paradigm
police: brutality of, 52; shootings of unarmed Black and Brown men, xiii; violence intervened by, 74; violence of, 26
policing, 26; of Black men, 22
political correctness, 121
politics: of patriarchy, 124; respectability, 12
Pollack, W. S., 86
positioning, of women and mothers, 63–65
Powell, K., 115
power-and-control model, 1–2, 13; of IPV, 7–12; wheel of, 8–10, *11*
pregnancy, 66–67
prejudice, gender-based, 17
primary objects, 33
privilege: male, xi, 9, 121, 151; white, 15
protective factors, 51–52, 59, 152
psychoanalysis, 105–6; mother-child relationship in, 71–72
psychodynamic theory, xiii–xiv, 46, 97–99, 111, 143
psychoeducation, 57, 89, 140, 143
psychological abuse, 99–100
psychology, xii; two-person, 141
puberty, 49–52
Puerto Rico, 104–5
purpose, in clinical work, 147–49

Quiros, L., 144

race: anxiety and, 21; feminism, intersectionality and, 17–19; gender and, 18, 39, 88; identity and, 28; marriage and, 38–45; relations in US, 17; social class and, 65; in the US, 87
racial habits, of US, 121

racial injustice, 87–89
racial profiling, 88
racial stereotypes, 18–19, 30–31
racism, xiii, 9, 85, 114; abuse *vs.*, 22; as feminist issue, 21; internalized, 90; psychological growth influenced by, 59; systemic, 37; in US, 17; whiteness and, 17
rape, 103, 113; culture, 2–3, 119
reauthoring phase, in clinical work, 94–95
recovery, from trauma, 44
regression, 41–42
Reina, A. S., 25
relational abuse, xi, xii
relationships: abuse in, 76–77; alienation within parent, 76–77; assessing violence and abuse in intimate, 159; intimidation in, 58; jealousy in, 54
residency, unstable, 25
respectability politics, 12
responsibility, personality, 122
rest-care: self-care and, 146–49; strategies of, 148–49
Rihanna, 32
risk factors, 51–52, 152
Rodino-Colocino, M., 120
Root, P. P., 28
Rosenberger, E. W., 91
Rutter, M., 52

Sack, E. J., 3–4
safety-planning strategies, 21–22, 129
schema, 45, 77, 78, 91, 94; of bystander effect, 122; in CBT, 57; emotionality related to, 126; motherhood and, 64
Schrock, D., 83
Schwalbe, M., 83
self: false, 34–35; hopeful, 45; inauthentic, of men, 116; masculine, 82; true, 34–35
self-awareness: in clinical practice, 130; in men, 116–17, 123
self-blame, 107–8
self-care: countertransference, supervision and, xvi, 129–50; rest-care and, 146–49; strategies of, 148–49
self-concept, 56–57
self-esteem, 97–98, 103, 106
selfhood, 148
self-object, 98, 106, 108, 109, 152
self-psychology, 108–9, 110, 152; for abused women, xv, 97–111; ideas of, 97–99
sexism, xi, xii, 44; misogyny and, 86; patriarchy and, 16, 116, 117
sexual assault, 67, 102–3, 113
sexual harassment, xii, xvi, 2
shelter, battered women's, 71–72

Shepard, M. F., 8
simpatia, 25
Simpson, O. J., 93
Smith, B., 21
social bond theory, 59
social class, 65
socialization: of adolescent males, 52–53; of boys, 82; gender, 84; in patriarchy, 88–89
social justice advocacy, 121–22
social learning, 68, 81–82, 90, 109; ecology of, 55–56
social location, of men, 114–16
social movements, feminism and, 4–5
social work, 130–31; for adolescent males, 52–61; ecological model of, xii–xiii; partner abuse in, 26–30; PIE paradigm in, 1, 2; spirituality within, 26–30; violence against women in, 67
sociodemographic variables, in adolescent males, 51–52
sons, 70–71
soul, selfhood and, 148
spirituality: cultural identity and, 26–30; intersectionality, IPV and, 26–30; within social work, 26–30
splitting, 35, 55
Stephens, D. P., 18
stoicism, 122
stress: anxiety and, in clinical work, 140; anxiety and, in family, 43; toxic masculinity and, 86–87
subjectivity, of therapist, 149
subordination, intersectional, 31
supervision, 130–35; case studies in, 136–50; challenges of, 135; countertransference, self-care and, xvi, 129–50; enactments in, 133; responsibilities of, 132; supportive function of, 145–46; trauma and burnout in, 143–46; well-being within, 134
supervisor: supervisee relationship to, 132–33; supportive attributes of, 134–35

Tambe, S., 120
Tarshis, S., 144
tension, 10, *11*
therapeutic alliance, 141
therapist, male: male clients working with, 141; women working with, 108, 118
therapists: ambivalence of, 147; coercion of, 147; IPV work impacting, 148; subjectivity of, 149
therapy: male abusers and believability in, 91–92; narrative, 91– 92, 96, 151–52
therapy, marriage and family, xii
Thomas, Clarence, 119

Till, Emmett, 88
toxic masculinity: exploration of, 83–87; IPV and, 89–91; male abusers and, xv; men who batter and, 81–96; racial injustice and, 87–89; stress and, 86–87
transference, 133
transmuting internalization, 98
trauma, xv, 42, 75, 111; anxiety caused by, 144–45; burnout and, in supervision, 143–46; chronic and complex, 56; in clinical work, 134; IPV and, xvi–xvii, 108, 138; recovery from, 44; self-esteem and, 97–98; unresolved, 147
Trump, Donald, 20
Tuskegee study, 23
twinship, 98, 106, 152
two-person psychology, 141
Tyagi, S. V., 142

unconscious emotional responses, in countertransference, 136
United States: marginalization within, 15; race relations in, 17, 87; racial habits of, 121

Van Hook, M. P., 27
VAWA. *See* Violence Against Women Act
vicarious reinforcement, 82
victimization: in childhood, 142–43; gender-based, 126; partner, 113; of women, 72, 119
victimology, 118
violence, xiii, *11*; aggression and, 73–74; allies against gender-based, 118–19; assessing abuse and, in intimate relationship, 159; against Black and Brown men and women, 26; in community, 52–53, 54; cycle of, 9, 10–12; exposure to, 37–38; father in role of, 73–74; gender-based, xi, xii; intergenerational transmission of, 109; internalization of, 106; justification of, 142; in motherhood, 68–69; of parents, 105; of police, 26; police intervening, 74; psychological impact of men's, xi–xii;

relational in young adulthood, 73; strategies for preventing, 121; against women, xv–xvi, 10, 67, 113–27. *See also* specific topics
Violence Against Women Act (VAWA), 7
vulnerability, shared, in clinical practice, 129–50

Walker, Lenore, 10–12
Watts, R. J., 85
Weinstein, Harvey, 120
West, C. M., 23
Wexler, D. B., 86, 142–43
White, M., 93–94
white fragility, 5, 121
White Fragility (DiAngelo), 114
whiteness: hooks on, 28–29; in queer identity, 19–20; racism and, 17
white supremacy, 5, 31, 52, 85, 87–88; Black women impacted by, 17–18; double consciousness and, 22
wife abuse, xi
Winnicott, D. W., 33, 42, 71, 105–6; on true self and false self, 34–35
womanhood, girlhood and, 64
womanism, 30
women: abuse toward, 3; aggression toward, 50–51; biophysical assessment framework for IPV cases and cisgender, 153–55; Black and Brown, xiii; of color, 20, 28; internalization of abuse by, 77; IPV exposed to, through family, xiii–xiv, 33–47; Latina, 23–26, 100–111; male therapist working with, 108, 118; marginalization of, 16, 55; positioning of mothers and, 63–65; self-psychology for abused, xv, 97–111; sense of agency in, 136; service delivery to girls and, 114–16; victimization of, 72, 119; violence against, xv–xvi, 10, 113–27
women's groups, 123, 126
women's movement, 4, 5, 6, 13, 120

Yalom, I. D., 143

Made in the USA
Las Vegas, NV
01 February 2023